Overture of Hope

Overture of *Hope*

TWO SISTERS' Daring Plan That Saved OPERA'S JEWISH STARS from the THIRD REICH

Isabel Vincent

REGNERY
HISTORY
Washington, D.C.

Regnery History™ is a trademark of Salem Communications Holding Corporation
Regnery® is a registered trademark and its colophon is a trademark of Salem Communications Holding Corporation

Cataloging-in-Publication data on file with the Library of Congress

ISBN: 978-1-68451-406-9
Library of Congress Control Number: 2022937277

First trade paperback edition published 2023

Published in the United States by
Regnery History, an Imprint of
Regnery Publishing
A Division of Salem Media Group
Washington, D.C.
www.Regnery.com

Manufactured in the United States of America

10 9 8 7 6 5 4 3 2 1

Books are available in quantity for promotional or premium use. For information on discounts and terms, please visit our website: www.RegneryHistory.com.

For Nélida Piñón.

In memory of my friend Bill Ray, and my father,
Afonso Costa Vicente.

A NOTE TO THE READER

This is a work of nonfiction. All language appearing between quotation marks is taken from original source documents—letters, telegrams, archives, interviews, newspapers, magazines, and books. Occasionally, I have placed the endnote number at the end of a long passage of dialogue for the sake of expediency.

CONTENTS

The Leaves

The stiff brown envelopes arrived on a librarian's cart, each carefully weighed by an officious attendant who wore dust gloves and used a desktop scale. It was only after the weight was carefully recorded on duplicate research slips that I was permitted to take the envelopes—one at a time—and retreat to the little area I had carved out at a communal study table at the Victoria & Albert Archives at Blythe House in London where I sat for days sifting through the ephemera of two remarkable lives, shelved long ago and largely forgotten.

I eagerly opened one envelope after another, some stuffed with elaborately illustrated 1920s Royal Opera House programs from Covent Garden with their ads for Columbia New Process Records, Steinway grand pianos, and the Cliftophone—"the world's best gramophone." Other programs for the Salzburg Festival and opera in Berlin, Munich, and Vienna were in German, and some featured large swastikas on the covers with introductory remarks by Adolf Hitler on facing pages. There were faded black-and-white promotional photographs of stars in rich velvet tunics, adorned in brocade. "With sincere good wishes," reads the autograph of the renowned American baritone Lawrence Tibbett "as Iago," on his fan photo for the Metropolitan Opera's 1937 production of Giuseppe Verdi's *Otello*. Other envelopes yielded sheaves of handwritten correspondence from Vienna, Munich, Berlin, and New York.

One letter immediately intrigued me.

Written in a rapid, flowing hand on cream-colored stationery, embossed with "Sul Monte, N.Y." at the top of the page, it contained three pressed maple leaves. They were brown with age, but otherwise perfectly preserved, even though the date on the letter was October 16, 1931.

There was something magical about finding those leaves in October 2017—eighty-six years after the letter was written, and on the first day of my research into the lives of Ida and Louise Cook, English sisters who risked their lives to bring twenty-nine Jewish refugees to safety on the eve of war.

The pressed leaves not only spoke to the romantic character of the letter writer—the great soprano Amelita Galli-Curci, who became a lifelong friend to Ida and Louise—but also to the sense of wonder and innocence of the sisters themselves.

Who were these women whose historical legacy includes pressed autumn leaves? How did they become "Two Against Hitler," among the unlikeliest heroines of the Second World War?

I knew that part of the answer lay in their passion for opera and its stars. In appearance, Ida and Louise were unthreatening and forgettable. They were plain and anonymous civil-servant typists who lived quietly with their parents in south London. But they developed intense inner lives. They were clearly infatuated with Clemens Krauss, the dashing Austrian conductor—Hitler's favorite—who along with his wife, the soprano Viorica Ursuleac, started them on their refugee work. The Cooks formed deep friendships with the performers and musicians who found themselves stuck in a real-life melodrama in

Nazi Germany and Austria, immersed in desperate scenes punctuated by burning synagogues and helmeted Nazis wielding bayonets and rounding up women and children. Inspired by their operatic heroines, the sisters naively thrust themselves into this dark overture.

Yet they could scarcely have imagined what awaited them when they began queuing outside Covent Garden for cheap seats to performances as the Nazis began their rise to power in Germany. In the 1920s and early 1930s, the sisters innocently amassed a sizable collection of photographs that Ida took of their favorite stars and collected dozens of gramophone records. Ida, the more outgoing of the two, maintained a decades-long correspondence with her beloved prima donnas. In addition to Galli-Curci, she corresponded with Elisabeth Rethberg, and later Rosa Ponselle.

It was largely through Ida's letters, most of them tightly typed on light-blue aerograms and scattered in the miscellaneous correspondence files of some of the world's most celebrated sopranos (but also baritones and tenors) that I was able to piece together the story of these extraordinary ordinary sisters.

"My dear Ida," began the letter in which Galli-Curci enclosed the leaves from Sul Monte, her lavish estate in the Catskill Mountains, where she would invite her "English girls" for visits. The sisters held on to those leaves into their old age—priceless tokens of their opera-world adventures that began after they met the Italian diva backstage at the Albert Hall in London—and naively vowed to save enough money to hear her sing at the Metropolitan Opera in New York. It would take them two years of going without lunches and walking most of the way to their secretarial jobs to manage to buy their third-class passage to sail to the city. They made the first of many trips to their beloved Manhattan in 1927 when Louise was twenty-five and Ida twenty-two.

The same pluck and determination that launched them in their passion for opera would propel them on their increasingly dangerous missions into the Third Reich. In fact, they used opera performances as a ruse to travel into Austria and Germany to meet their refugees. "We built ourselves a reputation. The men in customs used to chuckle, 'Here come those two *verruckt* (crazy) English ladies. They are only poor office workers and they spend their money to come here to listen to German opera.'"[1]

They were too obvious to be suspicious.

When they returned to London after a weekend at the opera in Munich, Vienna, or Berlin, they did so laden with the glittering jewels, Swiss watches, and furs belonging to refugees who would otherwise have had to surrender their valuables to the Nazis upon their exit from the Reich. Boldly plastered on their Woolworth dresses, the sisters gambled that the expensive jewelry would surely look fake.

Their mission, the calling for which they would risk everything, was successful. And it would succeed again and again.

When I began my research, which took me on a three-year odyssey through archives in England, Italy, Germany, Austria, the United States, and Israel, I was convinced the Cook sisters must have been spies. After all, they engaged in dangerous undercover work, meeting clandestinely with Jewish refugees under the nose of the Nazi secret police. They worked with members of the resistance in Germany, sending coded messages and meeting at safe houses in Frankfurt and Berlin. Louise, the more studious and retiring of the sisters, taught herself German at lightning speed. They rented a flat in a central London complex frequented by British wartime spies. And, most intriguingly, Louise burned all their refugee files long after the war.

But as I delved deeper into their lives and spoke to surviving friends and even an old schoolmate, I came to realize that Ida and Louise had most likely acted on their own, at first at the behest of their beloved stars, and then when word of their relief work spread and desperate letters addressed simply to "Ida and Louise" began

arriving at British consulates in the Third Reich, they were determined
to help at any cost. In England, they established a small network of
friends and strangers who came forward with offers of financial
guarantees for the refugees. Others contributed in smaller ways. One
friend walked halfway to her office every day and gave the Cooks the
saved bus fares to buy the postage necessary for their work. Another
friend cut her cigarette consumption in half and contributed the
money towards the maintenance of one of their cases.

"We were simply moved by a sense of furious revolt against the
brutality and injustice of it all and were willing to help any deserving
case brought to our notice, to the limit of our small capacity,"
explained Ida.[2]

Maybe it was as simple as that.

There are few remaining photographs of Ida and Louise. Of those
carefully filed in the stiff envelopes at the Victoria & Albert Archives,
I could clearly see the evolution of the sisters. In their twenties, they
appear gawky and stiff, their posture tense in the homemade opera
frocks that Ida fashioned from patterns she cut out of a popular
women's magazine on the eve of their first trip to America. In the
posed studio portrait from 1926, Ida, thin and angular, wears a
slinky, satin gown, while Louise, big-boned and handsome, sports a
silk cloak trimmed with white fur at the collar, an oversized velvet
bow pinned to her left hip. Another photo, taken after their wartime
heroics, shows them as middle-aged women in comfortable shoes,
gazing confidently into the camera, by then seasoned travelers
standing on an airport tarmac after disembarking from a Trans World
Airlines flight.

By the time this last photograph was taken, the two women had
achieved some notoriety for their wartime exploits. Ida was also
known to millions as Mary Burchell, a successful writer of light
romance, who had also written *We Followed Our Stars*, a memoir
about their opera-world adventures and their relief work.

In fact, I first stumbled on the Cook sisters' story after reading Ida's memoir, which had been reissued in 2008 as *Safe Passage*. More than sixty years after the end of the Second World War, there was suddenly renewed interest in Ida and Louise and a handful of other Britons who had helped save Jews from the Holocaust. Their stories were used as part of a campaign by the Holocaust Educational Trust, a British non-profit organization, to lobby for official government recognition of these largely forgotten heroes. The British Hero of the Holocaust Award was established by parliamentary decree, and in March 2010 the silver medallions inscribed with the words "In the Service of Humanity" were presented posthumously to the families of twenty-five individuals at a special ceremony at 10 Downing Street. Among the recipients were the families of Ida, Louise, and Major Frank Foley, a passport control officer for the British Embassy in Berlin who helped thousands of Jews escape after Kristallnacht.

For me, Ida's book was frustratingly elliptical, glossing over opera-world scandals involving their beloved "stars" and the hardships faced by their refugees. What became of the musicians, scholars, and students whom the sisters risked their own lives to save, many of whom became lifelong friends? And what happened to the opera stars who defied the Nazis to save their Jewish colleagues? In Ida's account, the sisters are modest and self-effacing, and their bravery is simply referred to in passing. But what had the Cooks really done, and how? And what happened to them after the war?

Ida, the writer, had clearly tried to capitalize on the sisters' exploits. After their appearance on *This is Your Life*, a popular BBC television program that reunited them with some of their refugees more than a decade after the war, Ida tried her hand at a Hollywood script, encouraged by the enthusiasm of her friend Laurence Olivier (the famous actor) and producer Joshua Logan.

I found Ida's long-forgotten film treatment at the Library of Congress in Washington, tucked into Logan's correspondence, filed under C among letters to Truman Capote and Joan Crawford. Typed on carbon, it was difficult to read, and I often had to squint to make sense of the type, as shadows of sentences from previous pages crowded the lines of text.

Ida's first line was characteristically self-defeating: "This is the story of two squares." But in the hands of a good PR agent, those "two squares" were transformed into "Two Against Hitler," the title of a series of lectures Ida delivered across Britain in the 1960s. The promotional flyer for those lectures tumbled out of an envelope at the Blythe House reading room. It featured a black-and-white photograph of a middle-aged Ida—stolid and matronly with a prominent wide nose and permed hair combed back in a conservative coif. Her skin was pale and free of makeup, her mouth slightly open in a pursed smile.

The sisters were eventually honored by Israel's Yad Vashem Holocaust memorial, among the first women to receive the honor in the early 1960s, along with Swedish diplomat Raoul Wallenberg and German industrialist Oskar Schindler.

But while these two men had become household names with documentaries and feature films commemorating their exploits, few remember the quiet heroism of the two English sisters. Perhaps they were too quiet, forgotten for the very reasons that made them successful: they were unglamorous, largely anonymous. Their greatest weapon was perhaps also their greatest impediment: they went under-cover as themselves.

"We are scarcely James Bond ladies," Ida told two American reporters.[3] Risk averse and frugal, they were by Ida's own admission, "a couple of nervous British spinsters" who wore Marks & Spencer dresses and Woolworth's beads. At home, they were eminently prac-tical. They saved slivers of soap and once told the American reporters that their only extravagance was custom-blended tea.[4] But those plain, practical exteriors hid romantic souls—real-life heroines in the twentieth century's darkest opera. Their faith in goodness—an unwavering belief—saw them rise beyond their mundane lives to accomplish something priceless.

Perhaps it was Rosa Ponselle who put it best in her telegram congratulating Ida on a triumphant television appearance: "Your life has been like a fairy tale, only we know it's true."

To which Ida quickly responded: "Honestly, Rosa, it was enchanting—and petrifying—like being in a book."[5]

Cherish romance! Any fool can be a realist!

—Nancy Spain, quoted by Ida Cook at a meeting of
the Romance Novelists' Association

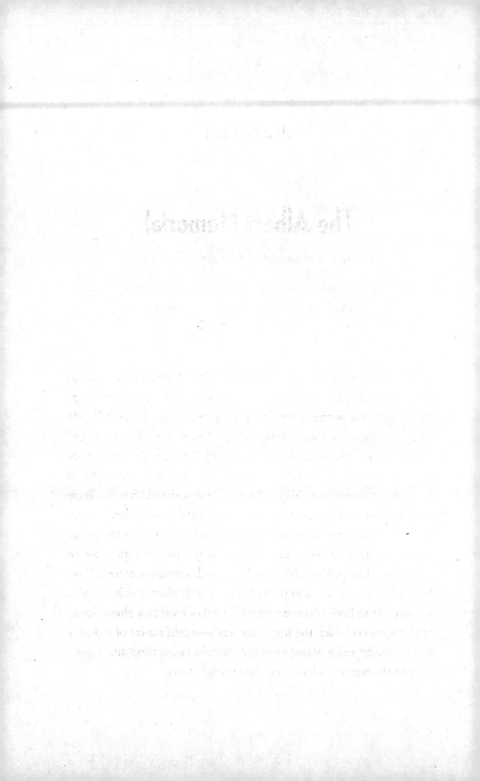

CHAPTER 1

The Albert Memorial

Ida and Louise would walk round the Albert Memorial in London thousands of times. "How I loved it," declared Ida, recalling the trips the family took to the memorial in the years before the First World War.[1] In those days, the memorial was the "limit of world wandering" for the Cooks, who in 1906 had temporarily settled in Barnes, a leafy suburb in south-west London on the River Thames. Commissioned by Queen Victoria as a shrine to her beloved husband after his death from typhoid fever in 1861, the towering Gothic Revival temple that shelters a seated-and-shiny gilt-covered bronze sculpture of the prince was to be the most elaborate public memorial that Britain had ever seen. It was Queen Victoria's own Taj Mahal, a monument to her love for her Prince Consort and father of her nine children. But it was also a testament to Britain's own romantic ideal of itself as a global force, "the empire on which the sun never sets"—a celebration of industry and ingenuity and a potent symbol of Britain's leadership and superiority in the final decades of the nineteenth century.

The memorial was mocked by architecture and art critics for its sheer excess after its unveiling in 1872. But never by John Cook, a tax inspector, and his wife Mary Brown, proud subjects of the British Crown, who must have felt it was important to show their daughters the magnificence of their heritage, even if by then the Victorian era was already in the past. By the time Ida and Louise took in the statues and carvings, Victoria and Albert's eldest son, Edward VII, had already been king for several years.

For Ida and Louise, the Albert Memorial was an important marker in their lives, largely because it embodied the "standard of personal integrity"[2] set by their "incomparable" parents. "Without [their] loving and commonsense upbringing," Ida believed, "we should never have been capable of doing the things" for which they would become known.[3] Mary Cook embraced her role as a wife and mother. Their whole lives the girls never saw their mother cry, and on her deathbed Mary Cook told them that she never had anything to cry about. "I had a good husband…and good children. A good home and good health. No one must ask for anything else. Anything else is a bonus."[4]

The dedication inscribed on the canopy surrounding the Albert Memorial was surely never lost on the sisters: "Queen Victoria and Her People" dedicated the memorial to Prince Albert "As a Tribute of Their Gratitude For a Life Devoted to Public Service." But while it was dedicated to the greater good, the memorial was also a monument to love, romance, and adventure—elements that figured prominently throughout Ida and Louise's childhoods in London and the north of England.

"I am a born romantic," Ida boasted, "and I am sure I will never change."[5]

■   ■   ■

Mary Louise was born on June 19, 1901, in Dorking, an hour south of London. Ida Cook, Mary and John Cook's second child,

Ida Cook. *Yad Vashem Archives*   Louise Cook. *Yad Vashem Archives*

was born on August 24, 1904, in Sunderland, a historic ship-
building town in northern England. The Cooks lived a quiet life
at 37 Croft Avenue in the old port town. Then, when Louise was
five and Ida was two years old, the family packed up and moved
to Barnes, on the outskirts of London where their father had been
assigned. Their brother Bill was born there in 1910. "I don't think
I was quite so nice about being the displaced baby," wrote Ida,[6]
who attended the Convent of the Sacred Heart school in the village
along with Louise.

At school the Cook sisters hated Bible class, with Louise nearly
traumatized for life after hearing the story of Adam and Eve and
their expulsion from the Garden of Eden. "I couldn't believe that
God had written it," she thought. "It seemed so mean. I hated the
picture of an angel with a sword forcing poor Adam and Eve out of
the garden. They were all naked. I kept thinking how chilly they
must have been."[7]

While they were in Barnes, they discovered that their house was haunted. A murder had supposedly taken place there, and the victim had been stuffed into a nearby well. "I only saw the ghost once," said Ida, whose belief in the paranormal and the spirit world would continue throughout her adult life. "He always appeared on the stairs, and one night when I was on my way to bed, I saw moonlight glinting off silver buttons on a man's cutaway coat."[8] The six-year-old Ida stopped at the bottom of the stairs and considered running to her father in the sitting room. But she managed to calm down long enough to walk slowly up the stairs and then quickly dive under the covers once she got to her bedroom.

The next day, when the sisters told their mother about the ghost, Mary Cook admitted rather matter-of-factly that she often spoke to the resident phantom. She had once stopped him on the stairs and said, "Poor man, I can understand that your spirit is still upset—because you met such a sudden and violent death, but after all it happened two centuries ago—why don't you go to rest?"

The ghost's reply seemed perfectly logical to her: "You don't understand. You've got it all wrong. I'm not the victim—I'm the murderer."[9]

By the summer of 1912, the family had moved again—this time back to the rugged landscape of Northumberland where they settled in Alnwick, a medieval market town on the River Aln, some thirty miles from the Scottish border. With its rough landscape, stone ruins, and winding cobblestone streets, Alnwick was a world away from London and the south of England. Not only was the barren terrain markedly unfamiliar, but northerners in general were wary and clannish, "a product...of the AngloScottish frontier, where their lives, wives and property had been since the Conquest at almost constant risk from Scottish raids."[10]

Louise and Ida were enrolled at the all-girls Duchess's School, which was founded by Frances Julia Burrell Percy (the second wife of Hugh Percy, the second Duke of Northumberland) for the daughters of their staff in 1809, when the first class numbered twenty girls. According to early records, the focus was on discipline and religion: "The Mistress was to teach the children to spell, read, knit and sew, hear them say two lessons in the morning and two in the afternoon, and teach them to repeat the creed, the Lord's Prayer, the Ten Commandments."[11] The rules were little changed the year the Cook sisters started at the school, although it was no longer just the refuge of impoverished girls and was a semi-private state institution. Free places were still available, but they were only offered to girls who passed a rigorous entrance examination. The Cooks' enrollment records do not show any exemptions from tuition fees.

Shortly after the outbreak of the Great War in the summer of 1914, the town of Alnwick was transformed into an impromptu military camp, with mansions and public buildings requisitioned for the war effort. At the Duchess's School, students were also asked to help with the war effort. In the *Duchess's School Magazine* in the summer of 1915, there are articles about a Zeppelin drill and how women could contribute to the war effort: "Every woman can help by encouraging her friends and relatives to enlist and by giving them a hearty send-off."[12]

Other than the disruptions and the steady stream of wounded soldiers who arrived at the makeshift hospital as the war progressed, the Cooks led a fairly uneventful, comfortable, middle-class life that revolved around school and family. A month after war was declared, their youngest brother Jim was born. "For Louise and me, these years in Alnwick were extremely happy ones," recalled Ida.[13]

Both sisters had been good students, although Louise, a shy and anxious girl, failed her senior arithmetic exams and never managed to get a Cambridge Certificate in her final year of high school. In the early part of the twentieth century, the vast majority of girls in Britain were finished with their schooling by the age of fourteen. Louise's crippling timidity also got in the way of a music exam, and even though she failed the test "through nervousness," she was by far the best candidate, a school administrator noted in her file. "All others passed."[14] Still, she managed to brave a "pianoforte duet" with another student, according to the school's magazine in 1917. Ida, outgoing and gregarious, was a stellar pupil and a talented violinist. In her academic bulletin, an administrator noted that she took her Cambridge Senior exam in July 1919, a month before her fifteenth birthday, although these exams were usually reserved for pupils who were seventeen or eighteen.[15]

In addition to the sisters' musical abilities, Ida showed a talent for writing, and she submitted a three-page story about a young Italian aristocrat and her doomed love to the school's magazine in 1919. No doubt influenced by her historic surroundings in Alnwick, it was entitled "A Romance of the 14th Century," in which the heroine poisons her lover, thinking he's about to marry another, but realizes too late that she is mistaken.[16] The story displayed a precocious penmanship and talent for crafting a gripping narrative (even if some sentences still betrayed a schoolgirl's clunky phrasing). With its emphasis on melodrama and a surprise ending, the story clearly showed where Ida's fascination for opera might have originated.

Louise graduated from school on July 26, 1918, a month after her seventeenth birthday, and Ida left school a year later when the family moved back to London. Louise then scored highly in Latin in her civil service exams, and Ida followed in her sister's path. The girls and their family returned to London just as a Spanish flu epidemic gripped Alnwick, forcing the closure of schools for extended periods. "Louise and Ida Cook have gone to London, and are taking up Civil Service work," read a bulletin under the "News of Old Girls" section of the *Duchess's School Magazine* in 1920.[17] A year later, the magazine announced that Ida was first out of 1500 candidates in a civil service examination and was appointed as a clerk to a local art school. "My salary was a modest £2 6s.... a week... and very pleased with it I was," Ida enthused.[18]

The salary wasn't quite enough to allow her to leave the family home, but neither Ida nor Louise felt the need to move away from 24 Morella Road and were content to live with their parents and brothers.

While it was not necessarily a given that the sisters would automatically live together, they had become adults in an era of "surplus women" when single women outnumbered single men. More than 700,000 British men had been killed in the Great War, creating a gender imbalance that had started during the Industrial Revolution. The 1851 census showed that 30 percent of British women between the ages of twenty and forty were unmarried. Following the war, there were 1,209 single women between the ages of twenty-five and twenty-nine for every 1,000 men in the same age group, according to the 1921 census. As a result, thousands of young women were forced to give up on an expectation of marriage. [19]

Women of this generation had started turning to each other to satisfy their needs for companionship, and even sex. As the controversial writer and eugenicist Sybil Neville-Rolfe noted in the mid-1930s: "The war left behind it a generation of Eves in an Adamless Eden.... Starving for love, deprived of homes and denied the joys of motherhood, many women found in friendship, one with another, some sort of substitute for these normal but lost relationships."[20] Unlike male homosexuality, lesbianism was not illegal in Britain, although legislators did try to introduce the Criminal Law Amendment Bill in

Parliament in 1921. The bill was rejected by the House of Commons and the House of Lords because of a fear of drawing too much attention to female homosexuality.

Neither sister wrote or spoke about this, although at some point both sisters made the decision that neither marriage nor intimacy with other women was for them. "There was something schoolgirlish about them that they never lost," recalled one of their friends. But Ida was always the dominant one. "Louise was like an echo," said the friend. "She was always listening benignly and nodding her head in agreement, and occasionally she would say something, and when she did it was worth listening to and you would realize that she was a thinker and had a hidden strength."[21]

As they settled into adulthood, the sisters were clearly happiest in each other's company, so much so that Ida never mentioned male suitors nor any pressure from their parents to marry or have children. "Many women of our generation made the choice of dignified spinsterhood rather than marry someone uncongenial. Perhaps Louise and I felt a bit regretful, but I don't remember that we suffered."[22] Unencumbered by the strict dictates of married life or the responsibility of raising young children, both sisters were free to direct their passion and energy to other pursuits.

According to Ida, the sisters' fascination with opera began in 1923 when Louise happened to wander into a lecture on music at the Board of Education where she worked as a "copying typist" or clerical assistant. The lecture was delivered by Sir Walford Davies, a composer and educator who would later go on to become master of the prestigious King's Music from 1934 to 1941. Davies made a series of recordings about music for the His Master's Voice label and later worked for the BBC, hosting a series of programs entitled "Music and the Ordinary Listener," which proved very popular and continued to be broadcast until the beginning of the Second World War in 1939.

After that lecture, during which Davies illustrated his points by playing gramophone records, Louise "arrived home slightly dazed and announced to an astonished family, 'I must have a gramophone,'" recalled Ida.[23] Almost immediately, Louise put a deposit on an HMV gramophone for £23 and also bought ten records. "The buying of one new record meant much consultation, much planning and, frequently, going without a few lunches—which is, I still think, the way one *should* come to one's pleasures," explained Ida, adding that she and Louise were particularly moved by the voice of Italian soprano Amelita Galli-Curci singing "Un bel dì vedremo," the famous aria from *Madama Butterfly*.[24]

"We listened to those records during all our spare time and at the end of the month our tastes and our lives were changed," said Ida.[25]

According to Ida, Louise had yet again "wandered" into the gallery of Covent Garden, where the cheapest seats were to be found, to hear the aria from *Madama Butterfly* and was so enchanted that the sisters pooled their savings to attend three other operas that season: *Tosca*, *La Traviata*, and *Rigoletto*. "Soon we were spending all the money we could squeeze from living expenses for opera and concert tickets."[26]

Galli-Curci soon became a favorite singer of the Cooks. The petite soprano had made her debut in 1906 as Gilda in *Rigoletto* in Italy. She then toured throughout Europe, Russia, and Latin America, famously singing opposite opera great Enrico Caruso in Buenos Aires in *Lucia di Lammermoor* in 1916. By the early 1920s, the prima donna was a global sensation, performing concerts featuring arias and a series of songs that showed off her impressive vocal range. But despite her years of touring abroad, Galli-Curci had never performed in front of a British audience.

Then, in the spring of 1924, it was announced she was to make her British debut at the Royal Albert Hall before embarking on a twenty-city tour. The news created a sensation. Ads in newspapers throughout the United Kingdom trumpeted "Galli-Curci—The Vocal Sensation of the World." "Galli-Curci at any price!" screamed the placards outside concert halls where she was scheduled to perform. "First appearance in this country of world famous prima donna." Over one hundred thousand tickets were sold in a matter of two weeks for her countrywide tour, while her four performances at the Royal Albert Hall, between October 12 and October 19, quickly sold out.[27]

Ida and Louise were among the frenzied ticket buyers. Not content with seeing her only once, they bought tickets to all her London performances, including one presentation at the Alexandra Palace in the northern part of the city. "By now, she was very much our favorite gramophone star, and her appearance—in London, in the flesh—was of monumental importance to us," said Ida.[28]

On October 12, 1924, Ida and Louise entered the Royal Albert Hall for the first time. Although they were already on their way to becoming habituées of opera at the Royal Opera House, Covent Garden, there was something magical about stepping into that grand concert hall, directly across the street from the Albert Memorial where Ida and Louise had spent so many happy hours as children.

In many ways, the Royal Albert Hall was the practical extension of the Albert Memorial. The concert venue had been a pet project of Prince Albert, who had envisioned it during the Great Exhibition as part of a permanent series of theaters, museums, and other venues devoted to public enlightenment. After his death, Queen Victoria set about completing her husband's vision. Sir Henry Cole, a civil servant and inventor who had collaborated with Albert on the design of the hall, said that he was inspired by his trips to Italy and the ruined Roman amphitheaters he saw there. Work began on the concert venue (which could accommodate more than eight thousand people) in the spring of 1867, and the Royal Albert Hall of Arts and Sciences was opened on March 29, 1871. At the lavish opening ceremony, which featured representatives from across Great Britain as well as foreign dignitaries, Queen Victoria, who would spend the rest of her life mourning her beloved husband, was "plainly attired in black silk dress and mantle, with a narrow trimming of satin floss, and a black bonnet." Overcome with emotion, she managed only a few words—"I cannot but express my great admiration for this beautiful building, and my earnest wishes for its complete success"—before turning over the rest of the welcome speech to her son, the Prince of Wales.[29]

In fact, the acoustics of the hall were initially criticized, and in its early days the Royal Albert Hall became a more popular venue for sporting events, political meetings, balls, and fundraisers for the First World War. Among the most important musical events was the Grand Wagner Festival in May 1877, which featured the German composer Richard Wagner himself conducting the first half of the concerts that made up the festival.

For opera aficionados, Galli-Curci's debut was of the same monumental importance as Wagner conducting his own compositions. "Initially, it was disappointing to discover that in the cruel acres of the Albert Hall, the voice sounded much smaller than on the gramophone," said Ida after the concert. "But inexperienced though we were, it did not take us long to separate the natural nervousness of the first half hour and the unsuitability of the hall from the matchless vocal accomplishment."[30]

Music critics were suitably overwhelmed. The following day, newspaper headlines blared "Famous Soprano Takes London by Storm," and "Queen of Song Wins All Hearts." A critic for the *Courier and Argus* noted the "furious" applause, the "generous clamors of her 10,000 hearers," as well as the numerous encores after her performance of eighteen songs. Of the "mad scene" from *Lucia di Lammermoor* the newspaper noted that "the coloratura passage at the end during which it was difficult to distinguish between the prima donna's voice and the accompanying notes of the flautist Manuel Berenguer—brought half the house to its feet and the last was seen of this remarkable personality waving...and throwing kisses to the excited audience as she stood amid a stage full of flowers and bouquets."[31]

For Ida, the highlight of the evening was the diva's rendition of "Home Sweet Home," by Sir Henry Rowley Bishop: "To me, the most beautiful thing about the sound was the faint touch of melancholy—often found in the very best voices—which gave to certain phrases and notes a quality of nostalgia that went straight to one's heart."[32] The sisters were so moved after the performance that they wrote a fan letter to Galli-Curci. "We were still only silly young girls—and we told her we admired her," recalled Ida.[33]

Ida also seemed to have found time in between Galli-Curci's London performances to embroider a handkerchief for the diva. "Many thanks indeed for your very kind thoughtful letter and the beautifully embroidered handkerchief," wrote Galli-Curci in a note to Ida. "I used it at Alexandra Palace...I wonder if you saw it! I hope sometime to see you backstage after the concert so that I can thank you personally."[34]

This communication was the stuff of their dreams, and all the encouragement the sisters needed. Astonished, they wrote back, immediately accepting her invitation to meet after her final London performance, and "while we were writing the letter, we suddenly decided we would save our money and go to New York to hear her sing opera," reasoned Ida. "So we told her about this project too."[35]

That evening, "there was an immense crowd" around Galli-Curci, who was signing autographs and handing bouquets of flowers to an assistant.[36] Louise was so shocked to be in the presence of her idol that she was transfixed and unable to speak. Straining to be heard

above the crowd, Ida just managed to blurt out that they would come
to see her in New York City, although it might take them a while to
save up for the trip.

"I shall remember you," said Galli-Curci to her newest fans. "Just
drop me a line and I'll keep you the seats."[37]

It would take two years for Ida and Louise to save enough for
their trip to America. Having calculated that they would need £100
each to pay for their voyage to New York, they put away a pound at
the beginning of each week and managed to save £50 each by the end
of the first year. Although they had barely traveled outside London
following their school years in Alnwick, they were undaunted about
making an Atlantic journey. To their parents, a trip to the Metropolitan
Opera seemed a strange way to spend their savings.

"After we had paid our very modest contribution at home, our
season tickets to town and our insurance, we usually had about ten
shillings a week each. From this pittance came our daily lunches,"
wrote Ida.[38] They "bought a Rand McNally guide to New York City,"
and, as Ida recalled, "when we felt hungry, we used to study this and
feel better."[39] A little more than two years after their fateful backstage
meeting with their idol, Ida and Louise boarded the RMS *Berengaria*,
the Cunard Line's flagship. "We had left England," wrote Ida. "Sailing
for New York and adventure."[40]

CHAPTER 2

The Photograph

On January 4, 1927, Ida and Louise arrived in New York City, disembarking on the West Side Pier, which was shrouded in an early morning mist. The fog and winter drizzle provided "a typically English reception in the way of weather" and hid the fabled Manhattan skyline from view, noted a reporter for the *New York Times* who had been assigned to write about the sisters' unusual journey to America.[1]

According to Ida, the newspaper had been alerted to their arrival by one of the passengers aboard their ship. They traveled in steerage both ways, and Ida later described the crossing as pleasant and uneventful. During the days, the "weather [was] so warm that sometimes we sat on deck without rugs, which was quite phenomenal for an Atlantic crossing in January." In the evenings, the sisters went for rapid walks around the deck before turning in and watching "the moonlight on the great tumbling, white-crested waves."[2]

On their last night at sea, Ida and Louise had caused "a terrific sensation" among fellow passengers when they recounted their incredible story of meeting Galli-Curci backstage at the Royal

Albert Hall in October 1924 and their determination to travel to New York to hear her sing opera.[3] Ida described how their "ruthless" penny-pinching over two years had allowed them to save enough money to make the trip.

Shortly after their arrival in the city, a reporter for the *New York Times* called them in their room at the Hotel Holley in Washington Square. "Louise picked up the phone, and I heard 'Yes—yes, yes,' at intervals, and then, in a much sterner voice: 'Well, that depends on what you want to say about us.'" When Ida interrupted to find out who was on the line, Louise replied that it was a reporter at the newspaper and that he wanted to know what they looked like. "We gazed at each other and burst out laughing," said Ida, who grabbed the receiver and told the editor, "We're just a couple of English blondes."[4]

And so their hair color was immortalized in the newspaper: "Two years ago, Louise and Ida Cook, sisters, blond, and members of the English working girl class, spent five successive evenings listening to Galli-Curci sing from the concert platform in her London debut." The article went on to describe how the sisters returned home each evening after opera "delighted to the point of exaltation" and then began to save their money to make the trip.[5]

When the reporter asked Louise what she thought of the New York City skyline, she became so tongue-tied that "she couldn't say much."

"We had never seen a skyscraper before," wrote Ida. "At that time, I think no London building was allowed to rise above twelve storeys. And some of those early skyscrapers were truly beautiful."[6] They were also amazed by another of the city's modern conveniences: "One thing in New York ... impressed both sisters," wrote the *Times* reporter. "That was the great profusion of 'lifts' or elevators as they were told to call them while here." They told the reporter they had obtained a five-week leave of absence from their "English government office" to travel to America but confessed that they were a little worried that Galli-Curci might have forgotten all about them.[7]

Following the publication of the story, the sisters became minor celebrities. As Ida described it, they grew used to the attention of "persistent men and gushing women—with or without cameras—and giving our opinion on such absorbing topics as bobbed hair, the Prince of Wales, skyscrapers, opera in England, [conductor] Sir Thomas Beecham (about whom I dared not say what I really thought)."[8]

Eager to begin their opera adventure as soon as they had finished the interview, the sisters skipped lunch and embarked on a more than thirty-block trek—"not daring to get on anything for fear of what it might cost," wrote Ida[9]—to the offices of Evans & Salter, Galli-Curci's agents near the Metropolitan Opera at Broadway and 39th Street. "We walked up Fifth Avenue, scarcely able to believe that we were actually in that famous thoroughfare at last," said Ida.[10]

When they reached the building, Ida and Louise "regarded it timidly for a few seconds" and then summoned up the courage to head to the firm's offices on the third floor. But when they got into the elevator and pronounced "Evans and Salter" in their proper British accents, the gum-chewing elevator operator decided to take them on a ride. As the elevator lumbered past the third floor, Ida and Louise grew frantic, repeating, "Evans and Salter! Evans and Salter!" until they were practically screaming out the name. "He took us right to the top of the building and then brought us all the way down again to the right floor," recalled Ida. "I suppose he guessed from our voices that we were English, and thought he would 'take a rise out of us.'"

"Somewhat shaken" from the experience, once they finally reached the right office Ida nervously approached the receptionist. "Can you give me Madame Galli-Curci's telephone number? We have just come over from England, and..."

To the Cooks' great delight, Galli-Curci's husband and accompa-
nist, Homer Samuels, greeted them like old friends and presented the
sisters with orchestra seat tickets for all his wife's performances. Ida
was so relieved to see a familiar face that she had to stop herself from
embracing him: "I restrained such an unmaidenly impulse, and the
next moment we were both being welcomed so kindly and warmly
that all our homesickness and nervousness vanished."[11]

Tall and handsome, the Wisconsin-born Samuels, then thirty-seven,
instantly captivated the sisters with his Midwestern charm. In addition
to accompanying his prima donna wife on piano, Samuels, who had
studied music in Berlin, composed some of the songs she sang on her
concert tours. Samuels married Galli-Curci at his parents' home in
1921, after her somewhat messy divorce the previous year from her
first husband—an old Italian nobleman, whom she accused of misap-
propriating her opera earnings. In 1922 she successfully petitioned the
Pope to annul her marriage to Marchese Luigi Curci, although she
kept his noble name.

It's not clear what the Cook sisters knew about Galli-Curci's
difficult past, although her bitter 1920 divorce from Curci was
well-documented, at least in the United States where the drama
played out in state supreme court in Chicago. In court papers,
Galli-Curci charged Curci, a painter, with numerous infidelities. He
responded that she was already involved with Samuels and that they
conspired to get rid of him after a decade of marriage. But in an age
in which newspaper accounts tended towards the chaste and feminine
when describing female stars, sordid personal details were not considered newsworthy, or were played down. Instead the focus was on
their fairytale lives—their beautiful clothes and marriages to debo-
nair aristocrats.

Galli-Curci was a case in point, a beloved prima donna and
clearly a master of self-promotion. Born in Milan into a musical

family, she initially studied piano but was encouraged to sing opera by the composer Pietro Mascagni, a family friend who was dazzled by her voice. The soprano studied for two years in her hometown before taking on operatic roles in Europe and Central and South America. In 1915 the director of the Chicago Opera Company heard her sing in Havana and immediately invited her to sing in two *Rigoletto* performances in Chicago. She made her triumphant American debut there on November 18, 1916, her thirty-fourth birthday. Her performance was so incredible that newspapers in the city held the presses so that critics could report on her debut without having to leave the theater early to file their stories. Following what the *New York Times* called her "sensational conquest" of the Midwest, Galli-Curci was signed to the Metropolitan Opera in New York where she first appeared as Violetta in Verdi's *La Traviata*. Nymph-like and graceful, she was also possessed of a steely determination and once sang from a wheelchair on stage in Madrid while she was recovering from a bout of typhoid fever.

With her cosmopolitan Italian accent, Galli-Curci contributed to her own otherworldly myth in many of the interviews she gave to the press during the early part of her career: "I am like a bird, which, sitting upon the branch of a tree, warbles from delight of living, warbles because it is part of its nature to give vent to the music within its heart. I sing with the same joy at the piano in my home, with my intimates at my side; I sing with my whole heart to the last and the first member of my audience."[12] She also took pains to describe to her fans how she lived a rather simple life, albeit one that included staying at the Ritz when she traveled. "Mme Galli-Curci lives the life of a well-cared-for girl of 12," one observer told the *New York Times*. "She has no dissipations; she never goes out to dinners. She takes neither wine, tea nor coffee—only sometimes a tablespoonful of coffee in a glass of milk. She devotes herself entirely to her work."[13]

The Cook sisters basked in Galli-Curci's simple glamor and the romance of the opera and its stars. They were thrilled to be in New York and told the *Times* that they planned to attend opera "voraciously" and were upset that two weeks of their five-week sojourn would be spent in transit at sea.[14]

On their second night in the city, they attended *La Traviata* to see Galli-Curci playing her most famous role, Violetta, at "the magic Met—which has resounded to the voices of every great singer known to us through gramophone records." The old Met (which opened in 1883) with its gold auditorium inscribed with the names of some of the world's most famous composers—Mozart, Verdi, and Wagner—dazzled the already star-struck sisters. According to Ida, they were "in a state of excitement quite impossible to describe" as they took their seats at the opera house.[15] Having secured their tickets to all of Galli-Curci's performances for their three-week stay in the city, they showed up at the Met in their homemade finery to watch the diva play the tragic courtesan—"the fallen woman"—who agrees to distance herself from Alfredo, the nobleman she truly loves, only to be reunited with him in the hours before she dies of consumption.

For the occasion, Louise wore a rather stiff brocade dress with a large ribbon pinned to her left hip. Ida was equally elegant in a silver frock accessorized with a fur stole. Both young women would later tell friends and family how they felt as they took their seats close to the stage. They were awestruck by the theater, with its gold damask curtain and elaborate "diamond horseshoe" boxes where New York's celebrated families—the Rockefellers and the Vanderbilts—came to watch legendary singers in opera's heyday. The sisters' luxuriant evening clothes, complete with opera cloaks, were sewn by Ida from patterns in *Mabs Fashions*, a popular weekly women's magazine with Jazz Age illustrated covers of lanky flappers in frocks that readers could make themselves. "We were two of the best-dressed people in the Opera House!!!" Ida reveled. "People quite goggled at our cloaks…other people had diamonds and bare backs and all that sort of thing, but, with all due modesty, our get-ups looked so pretty and young and colorful—besides, they had the *Mab's* touch!!"[16]

Following the performance, Galli-Curci picked the sisters out of the audience at the Met and waved to them and her husband, who was standing beside them. "She waved to us and kissed her hand, and we replied with what aplomb we could muster," gushed Ida. "It made me feel rather like royalty to have the whole audience of the Metropolitan gaping interestedly while we exchanged greetings with Galli-Curci across the footlights!" At that point Evans, the diva's agent, rushed up to Ida and Louise in the audience and said, "How did you enjoy yourselves? I want your first impressions for the morning papers." And then the sisters were taken off backstage to meet his business partner—Salter—who also wanted their opinions about the differences between opera in London and New York. "I expect we were in considerable danger of having our heads badly turned that evening," said Ida.[17]

An evening or two later, the prima donna invited the Cook sisters to her Fifth Avenue apartment for dinner and sent a chauffeur-driven car to pick them up at their hotel, complete with a fur rug to keep them warm in the back seat. "And away we bowled up Fifth Avenue to that part known as 'Millionaires' Row,'" recalled Ida. They were ushered into the diva's "marvellous" duplex apartment by the butler who left them alone in the drawing room, informing them that madame would be with them in five minutes. "I must own that my heart was fluttering," said Ida. Moments later, Galli-Curci came running down the stairs to embrace the sisters.

"At last!" they all shouted in unison, clasping hands and laughing. And then Ida and Louise made themselves right at home. They curled up on the couch in the living room, on either side of their opera idol, as Samuels demonstrated his new radio set. Later, Galli-Curci took them on a tour of the apartment. She and Samuels had just moved in a few months earlier, and she was clearly house-proud. When they reached her bedroom, she sat down and wrote a letter to Mary Cook, "so that she will know that you are in a good house tonight." The Cooks added their own messages to their mother.

Ida gushed about the "wonderful evening" they spent with the couple. By the end of the night, Galli-Curci was insisting that they call her Lita. As Ida later recalled, "That was the beginning of quite one of the most beautiful holidays that any lucky couple ever had. I could dance with excitement now when I look back on it all."

During their sojourn in New York, the Cooks were invited to other performances and saw their new friend as Rosina in *Il Barbiere di Siviglia* and as Gilda in *Rigoletto*. They heard an astounding one hundred hours of opera, including performances of *Turandot*, *Romeo and Juliet*, *Falstaff*, *Tosca*, and *La Bohème*. They also had the good fortune to secure tickets, through Samuels, to a concert by Arturo Toscanini at Carnegie Hall. The legendary Italian conductor was making his triumphant return to New York, and a few months later the New York Philharmonic Society would announce with great fanfare that it had signed him to a five-year contract.[18]

The Cooks' trip to New York broadened their horizons and gave them a different perspective on Americans. "There is a slight tendency in England to imagine that most of the virtues reside permanently this side of the Atlantic, while a good many vices stay in America," said Ida. "I would not be anything but English for all the world, but I should like to be able to think that I have some of the qualities that we found among our American friends."[19]

As they said goodbye to Galli-Curci and Samuels, the sisters' new friends invited them to Sul Monte, their sprawling country estate in the Catskill Mountains in upstate New York. The Cooks were ecstatic but warned their friend that it would take them another two years to save the money to make the transatlantic trip again. "Time and distance don't matter," said Galli-Curci before the Cooks boarded the Cunard Steamship Company's *Aquitania*, bound for Southampton in early February, "if you are really fond of someone."[20]

For these young, rather unsophisticated, Northumberland-bred sisters, the voyage across the world to meet one of the most beloved opera stars of the day had been an incredible accomplishment—a testament to their extraordinary strength of will. They were returning to London with a new sense of adventure. In many ways, that first trip to America would prove a harbinger of what was to come: together and determined, nothing would stop them.

They arrived back home a week later and considered the trip of such great significance that Ida immediately wrote to the *Duchess's School Magazine* to make sure they included a mention of their journey in their "News of Old Girls" section in the 1927 edition. "Louise and Ida Cook have been to New York to hear Galli-Curci sing in opera," the notice read, nestled among the more prosaic news of their former schoolmates, who announced new positions as teachers or nurses and their academic accomplishments.[21]

While Galli-Curci relaxed at her perfectly decorated summer retreat in the Catskill Mountains or toured the world in style, the Cooks immersed themselves in work and more opera. Searching for a way to make extra money so that they could begin saving for their next trip to New York, Ida approached the *Daily Mail* to write about their voyage to America. After the article was accepted, she wrote a piece for her favorite magazine, *Mabs Fashions*, about how she had sewed their opera ensembles. But her journalistic career was, for the time being, short-lived as Ida's time was taken up studying for an exam that would allow her to increase her salary in the law courts. Ida passed the "short-hand typist" exam and was promoted in the

Official Solicitor's Department of the Law Courts, where her salary was increased to £3 per week.[22]

While the sisters continued to count every shilling, they also became what Ida called "gallery-ites" at the Royal Opera House at a time when there was mass adulation for opera stars. For two months in the spring when the international opera season took place, Ida and Louise queued on Floral Street next to the opera house with other fanatics for the cheap seats in the gallery. Surrounded by market stalls selling fruits and vegetables, they arrived early in the morning in order to have first dibs on the gallery seats. In those days the only way to obtain these cheap seats was to queue. "Under the masterly direction of...our two 'stool men,' we hired camp stools, which marked our places whenever we had to leave for such unimportant matters as earning our living," explained Ida.[23] Like the other opera fans they came to know, the Cooks often spent their lunch hours munching sandwiches on the stools, watching for every opera star who came in and out of the stage door in order to get their autograph or, even better, a photograph. During the opera season, the biggest disadvantage for the sisters was lack of sleep. They rose at the crack of dawn to secure their place in the gallery queue before hurrying to their office jobs, then stayed out late each night at the performances, often catching the last train from Victoria Station at 12:40 a.m. "I was dreadfully weary sometimes," said Ida. "But I remember that my heart was high those early summer mornings."[24]

As the Cook sisters schooled themselves in opera, Galli-Curci and Ida continued to correspond regularly, with the opera singer writing long letters about her international opera tours and driving to the beach in New Jersey. "In July, we will drive to Atlantic City to have a good swim," she wrote, addressing a letter to "My dear girls" on June 13, 1927.[25] A year later, Galli-Curci enumerated her successes on tour and described her idyllic garden at Sul Monte in Highmount,

New York. "We are enjoying our mountains. We have so many birds this year right near the house…the flowers are beautiful—the lilies of the valley are just coming now—how happy we are up here! That's why we will keep young—no old age in the mountains—all serene and calm…and safe! Girls, I hope you can see our mountains some time." She ended her letter with the news that she and Samuels were expecting "a very interesting visitor, a man from India. He is a very dear person. We enjoy him so much."[26] The visit was from their friend and guru Paramahansa Yogananda, an Indian monk, who taught the couple yoga.

By the spring of 1929, Ida and Louise had finally saved enough money to buy their transatlantic tickets and were looking forward to sailing again on the *Berengaria* for another three-week visit to New York. "Bring warm clothes because it's chilly," wrote Galli-Curci, noting that she and her husband were expecting the sisters between September 15 and September 21 at Sul Monte. "The weather is wonderful—cool and bright, mountains are clear and the air is perfumed with flowers and woods. We will see that we have flowers in September when you come."[27]

But before the end of that season in London there was another landmark opera at Covent Garden where another prima donna, the great Rosa Ponselle, was to make her London debut in three performances of *Norma*. On May 28, 1929, Ponselle took to the stage at the Royal Opera House in a performance that had such a lasting impression on Ida and Louise that they would commemorate it for the rest of their lives.

Rosa Ponselle was born in Connecticut and had had no formal training in opera. She began singing when she was eight years old, and by the time she was eleven she was singing songs in between the reels at a silent film theater. Later, she moved to New York to join her older sister Carmela who sang on Broadway and in vaudeville. The operatic tenor Enrico Caruso discovered Ponselle when he attended one of the sisters' Broadway performances in 1918. He was so overwhelmed by the beauty of her voice that he immediately arranged for her to audition with Giulio Gatti-Casazza, the manager of the Metropolitan Opera. Ponselle, then twenty-one, made her professional operatic debut as Leonora in Giuseppe Verdi's *La Forza del Destino* with Caruso when the opera opened at the Met in November.

Six years after that stunning performance, Ponselle's opera coach took her to meet Giacomo Puccini in the summer of 1924, a few months before the composer's death. Puccini asked Ponselle to sing for him, and she obliged with "Vissi d'Arte"—an aria from *Tosca*, the opera he wrote in 1899. Although she had never sung it before on the stage, Puccini was completely moved. "At last I hear my 'Tosca,' but alas, too late," he said.[28]

A decade later, Ponselle was at the height of her fame. After she sang the "Casta Diva" prayer in *Norma* at Covent Garden, the famously reserved London audience, including Ida and Louise, went wild with excitement. As a critic for the *New York Times* noted:

> The occasion was a great triumph for this American-born, American-trained prima donna. Miss Ponselle sang her "Casta Diva" and in response to the loveliness of her voice a London audience forgot a tradition of the ancient theater and applauded...There were other great moments scattered through the four acts in which the crowd that filled every seat in the house threw caution overboard to yield themselves without restraint to the spell of the glorious voice and show their appreciation without warning.[29]

Another newspaper described in pugilistic terms the small, nightly battles waged between audience members who applauded at the wrong time and those who would "hiss them until they subsided again into silence" during Ponselle's arias. The newspaper described a "bout" between a section of the audience that became "frantically enthusiastic" and began to clap after Ponselle sang. One woman implored her seatmate to remain silent until the end of the act. "I don't care," said her neighbor. "I will clap. She is the best since Melba," invoking the immortal Nellie Melba, an Australian-born soprano, considered one of the finest opera singers of the nineteenth century.[30]

Ida and Louise, in the first row of the gallery seats, were enraptured: "At the end of the memorable evening of Ponselle's Covent Garden debut, it was no wonder that even the orchestra stood and joined in the storm of applause that broke in wave after wave through Covent Garden."[31] Despite their allegiance to Galli-Curci, Ponselle would eventually become their favorite performer of all time—"the greatest singer I ever heard," said Ida.[32]

With their love for the operatic stage reinforced in that spectacular London season, the sisters sailed again on the *Berengaria*, arriving in New York on September 13, 1929. After a day of rest, they headed to Grand Central Station to take a train to Rhinecliff, New York, where Samuels waited for them.

They drove along the Hudson River, stopping halfway to eat corn soup, fried chicken, and Boston cream pie. When they finally turned up "a rough woodland path," they arrived at Sul Monte, "the rambling stone house" built on a plateau "with thickly wooded slopes rolling away on either side."

"Homer tooted the horn as we drove up and Lita came running out, crying, '*Here* are the girls!' and there was such a kissing and greeting and talking as you never saw."

As Ida noted, "You can see sixty miles or more back and front of the house and, on a clear day, right away to the faint purple outline of the Adirondacks." The grand home was equipped with a swimming pool, dance hall, and even a cinema.[33]

For the next week, Ida and Louise enjoyed the vacation of a lifetime. They spent time in the diva's studio listening to her practice, whiled away afternoons discussing opera and politics in the library, and took the couple's pet sheepdog, Fagin, for long walks in the countryside. When they drove out to neighboring estates for a party, they were always presented as "Galli-Curci's English girls."

When their New York idyll finally came to a close in early October, Ida and Louise sailed back to Southampton on the White Star Dominion Line's *Homeric*. The name of the boat would prove rather fateful for Ida, who launched a career in writing almost as soon as they arrived in London. Not only would she continue to produce short travel articles about their adventures in America for *Mabs Fashions*, but she was also approached by the magazine's editor, Florence Taft, to become a regular writer.

Following her success with the articles, Taft offered Ida a permanent position as an editor on the magazine, a job that Ida deliberated about taking, since it would mean giving up her safe civil service job with its promise of a pension. Emboldened by a Beethoven symphony she heard for the first time in her life, Ida decided to take the plunge and began work at the magazine. She earned £4. 4s a week, which was £1. 4s more than she was earning as a government shorthand typist. "My first days at Fleetway House were some of the strangest I ever spent," she recalled. She was surrounded by women who were "terribly quick and amusing, and who spent their days talking about fashion. At first I thought, 'Oh dear, these girls will get into terrible trouble wasting all their time discussing clothes when they ought to be working.' But it gradually began to dawn on me that they *were* working."[34]

Still, Ida may have been right to worry. A month after they returned from America, the U.S. stock market collapse of October 29,

1929, ushered in the greatest economic downturn in history, which quickly spread beyond American shores. As they commuted to their jobs in central London from their comfortable family home in Wandsworth, Ida and Louise passed the long queues snaking outside soup kitchens, which were suddenly ubiquitous as unemployment rose to more than 10 percent in London.

If the effects of the Depression were bad in England, they were markedly worse in Europe where Galli-Curci witnessed firsthand the rise of a new, ugly form of nationalism. In a letter to the Cook sisters written on March 6, 1930, from the Hotel Imperial Wien in Vienna while she was on a concert tour, Galli-Curci, who had announced her retirement from opera although she continued to perform in concerts, focused on the hate that seemed to be sweeping the Continent.

> My poor Europe! How full of hatred and jealousy! I sang the first concert in Prague, gave 14 encores! Press terrible! Then I catch an awful laryngitis going to Bucharest. I cancel the concert there and get to Budapest after five days' rest. I sing *Traviata*.... The press terrible. They were lamenting that I would take away so much money from the country and that they had wonderful Hungarian artists, and why bring foreigners here, etc.[35]

By the time she arrived in Vienna, Galli-Curci was again a target of the xenophobic press accusing the wealthy opera singer of taking huge amounts of money out of Austria. Suffering from a cold and furious over her harsh treatment—one headline blared "Galli-Curci's Scandal in Vienna!"—the diva canceled the rest of her European tour. As she told the Cooks, "I never saw such hatred.... It has become an anti-American campaign. They are all mad with jealousy. We came here in good faith, happy to bring music." Although she had decided to be done with Europe, Galli-Curci still had a great deal of respect for the British. "Thanks to the Lord the Anglo Saxons with their fairness and sense of good sport are existing," she continued in the same letter.[36] And later that year the diva traveled to Britain for a series of concerts.

The friends were reunited at the Royal Albert Hall for Galli-Curci's concert in November 1930. "After the program, the audience, numbering thousands, stamped and shouted its applause, recalling the singer again and again to bow her thanks," wrote a correspondent for the *New York Times*, noting that the diva "received one of the greatest ovations of her career."[37]

Their correspondence continued after Galli-Curci returned to Sul Monte. In the autumn of 1931, Galli-Curci enclosed the pressed autumn leaves in a letter to Ida, who had already converted her friend into a fan of *Mabs Fashions*, where she was happily working full-time. "I received the two magazines and I really loved them," wrote Galli-Curci. "I am going to get industrious and cut out those patterns. By the way, could I subscribe for a year?"[38] Knowing her penchant for linens, Ida managed to find the time to embroider handkerchiefs for Galli-Curci, who praised her skills in an undated letter: "Ida you are a marvelous sewer and you surely can embroider. And now your writings were published. Good for you! We are glad and happy for you."[39]

Galli-Curci's English girls would return for another visit to the United States in January 1932, sailing on the *Samaria* from Southampton. Although the sisters were still traveling tourist class, Ida's job description had changed from "government typist" in 1927 and "government service clerk" in 1929 to "sub-editress" in 1932. Before taking the job, she had negotiated a month's leave in order to travel to America.

It was a very different New York City that greeted them when they arrived: "In those early weeks of 1932, America was still suffering badly from the depression and the atmosphere was very different from the gorgeous prosperity of our first visit, five years previous." Adding to their gloomy mood was the short time they were able to spend with their friends. "We arrived some weeks later than originally planned," noted Ida. "Because of the financial upheaval, sailings had been altered and postponed." As a result, they only saw Galli-Curci and her husband for one day in New York City, as the couple were leaving on a South African concert tour shortly after the Cooks' arrival. Despite the economic downturn all around them, the sisters still existed on the edges of the glamorous world of opera, "and so far as our own future was concerned Louise and I saw things in pretty bright colors," recalled Ida.[40]

When they returned to London, among their biggest disappointments was that Ponselle was not returning for another season at Covent Garden. So when Ida discovered that she would be appearing in *La Vestale* in Florence on May 4, 1933, she was determined to go, even though Louise could not get leave from her job to accompany her. And so their consummate fandom continued.

So obsessed were they with the glamorous goings-on in the world of opera that both Ida and Louise remained blithely unaware of the dark clouds that were forming in Europe in the early 1930s. Italy was in the fascist grip of Benito Mussolini when Ida made her first trip to the country by herself. While Ida took her seat at the Politeama in Florence at the first of Ponselle's performances in *La Vestale*, Adolf Hitler and his Reich Minister of Propaganda Joseph Goebbels were preparing a campaign to burn "unGerman" books in huge bonfires at universities across the country. But for Ida, the world came to a standstill only when Ponselle took to the stage in Florence: "The vast audience...seemed literally to hold its breath, and except for that silken thread of perfectly supported sound, there was the deadest silence I have ever experienced. According to an austere note in the program, encores were strictly forbidden, but the clapping and cheering went on and on. So did the opera but no one could hear a thing."[41]

After the Florence trip, both sisters returned to Italy, bolstered by an infusion of cash from Ida's short romance stories, which she had managed to place in *Mabs Fashions*. They attended the summer opera festival in Verona, where they were reunited with another opera-world friend they had first met in the Covent Garden queue. The "operatic charmer" Ezio Pinza was the first star that Ida ever "snapped" after she saw him walking past the queue with his five-year-old daughter Claudia during the 1930 opera season at the Royal Opera House. "I never photographed an artist without asking permission first, so I started by asking Pinza if I might photograph Claudia one morning as he came from rehearsal," recalled Ida. "Not only was permission given, but Pinza insisted on being in the photograph as well, and made me take two pictures to make sure."[42]

When Ida and Louise met Pinza he was considered one of the world's greatest bassos, and his rise from crushing poverty in Rome and Ravenna to conquer the stages of the Metropolitan Opera in New York could easily have been its own opera. Born in Rome in 1892, Ezio Fortunato Pinza was his parents' seventh child, but only the first to survive infancy. It was Pinza's father who first noticed the beauty of his voice and encouraged him to study opera, but Pinza had other plans and became a professional cyclist at eighteen. Although he won no distinction in the sport and quit after two years, he credited biking for developing his prodigious lung capacity, allowing audiences "to hear my voice even in the top row of the peanut gallery."[43]

But his operatic studies were fraught with their own challenges, not the least of which was his initial rejection by a teacher at the Rossini Conservatory who said he had no voice and the sudden death of a second. He returned to the teacher who had formerly rejected him, and this time he was able to secure a small scholarship that he supplemented by working as a handyman. He made his singing debut with a small opera company outside Milan in 1914, and when war broke out he enlisted in the Italian Army. After the war, he tried to resume his fledgling opera career, and his lucky break came when he entered the company at Milan's La Scala, then under the baton of Toscanini. After three years with the famous company, Pinza was discovered by the Met's Gatti-Casazza and made his debut there in November 1926. A critic hailed Pinza as "a majestic figure on the stage [and] a basso of superb sonority."[44]

For the Cooks he was also a lively figure of fun, who managed to sneak them into a dress rehearsal of *Les Huguenots* on their memorable trip to Verona. Pinza not only convinced a security guard at the back entrance to the opera house to allow them in, "he triumphantly installed us in the best seats in the place," gushed Ida. "What fun it was! The purple night sky of Verona overhead, pierced by a thousand golden stars, the gorgeous voices of Raisa and Lauri-Volpi to enchant our ears, and the gratification of having…Ezio Pinza, for company."[45]

The following year—1934—began in the same dreamy fashion for the Cooks with Galli-Curci and Samuels returning to England for an extended tour. The sisters attended many of their performances, but by February they were again seeing them off at Waterloo Station for what would be a very long time.

In the spring, as the sisters queued up for the annual Covent Garden opera season, they continued to ignore the menacing events that were taking place on the Continent. In Germany, Hitler consolidated his grip on power by jailing political enemies, purging dissidents in the Nazi Party, and forcing an economic crackdown on the country's Jews. "We had no idea—how could we?—that 1934, an epoch-making year for so many, would close a chapter for Louise and me too," recalled Ida. "And open another that would be written in much more dramatic language. When I look back, it seems to me that 1934 was the year the bright lines from the past and the dark lines of the future met."[46]

One day, as she took her regular seat on her camp stool on Floral Street, Ida suddenly stiffened and took notice when a tall, elegantly dressed man in a beige trench coat and felt hat rushed a voluptuous, beautifully dressed blonde woman past the stools. This had to be Clemens Krauss, the Austrian conductor who was scheduled to conduct Richard Strauss's *Arabella* in its London premiere for which they were queuing that evening.

When the Cooks first met Krauss, he was a rising star in the Third Reich. At forty-one, he had already perfected the role of the cosmopolitan and darkly charismatic conductor. Since 1926, he had been asked to conduct operas at Salzburg and was a veteran of the Vienna State Opera and the director of the Vienna Philharmonic. Nakedly ambitious, he saw his chance to rise through the highly political ranks of German and Austrian opera when the Nazis came to power in Germany. Krauss's career was marked by his willingness to take over positions from conductors who resigned in opposition to Nazi ideology. Krauss had never actually joined the National Socialist Party nor, wisely, did he hold an overt political philosophy. His lack of any stated scruples appealed directly to high-ranking members of the Nazi Party, including Adolf Hitler, himself an avid opera enthusiast, in an arrangement that suited everyone.

Krauss's rise through the ranks in this way continued the history of displacement that had shaped his life. Clemens Heinrich Krauss had always been on the fringes. He was born on March 31, 1893, in

Clemens Krauss conducting the Bavarian State Orchestra in 1936. *Süddeutsche Zeitung Photo*

Vienna, the illegitimate child of Clementine Krauss, a fifteen-year-old dancer in the Vienna Imperial Opera, and a forty-one-year-old Viennese cavalry officer, Hector Baltazzi. Krauss's father was descended from a prominent Greek banking family, but the aristocrat Baltazzi refused to acknowledge Krauss as his son, and the maestro never met his father. But Krauss was embraced by his mother's family, so much so that his young mother, who would go on to be an actress and opera singer of some renown, named him after herself: the male equivalent of Clementine. As a boy, Krauss, a musical prodigy, was a chorister in the Vienna Boys' Choir and attended the Vienna Conservatory, graduating in 1912 at the age of nineteen. Later, he became a choirmaster in Berlin before taking up positions at the Vienna State Opera. Richard Strauss was among the first to spot brilliance in Krauss. The composer took on a barely thirty-year-old

Krauss, who became an assistant to conductor Franz Schalk at the Vienna State Opera in 1922. Both Schalk and Strauss shared conducting duties at the opera house between 1919 and 1924. By 1929, Krauss was put in charge of the Vienna State Opera. Krauss worshipped Strauss, especially after attending a performance of Strauss's *Salome* in Graz.

While he may have been a talented conductor, Krauss was also arrogant and a showman. In 1929 he made guest appearances conducting orchestras in Philadelphia and New York, where "Mr. Krauss postured and cavorted on the stand" in what one music critic called "a singularly uneven" concert at Carnegie Hall. "He crouched low or bent sideways, tossed his hair, threatened the skies."[47]

That regal bearing, by turns supremely confident and brusque, both fascinated and frightened Ida and Louise. Impatient and intense, he seemed particularly contemptuous of autograph seekers. "I was unaware then that Krauss did not take very kindly to these frivolous trimmings of his job," recalled Ida. "Indeed, it is recorded that, on one occasion when he was pestered by autograph-hunters after a performance of *Carmen*, he gravely wrote 'Georges Bizet!' on several programs, and then passed on, leaving astounded speculation in his wake."[48] In order not to waste her own precious camera film, the ever practical Ida dispatched one of the regulars from the queue to ask the handsome stranger for his autograph—just to make sure he was indeed Krauss. Looking over the conductor's shoulder, Ida watched as he signed "Clemens Krauss" with "a variety of turns and twists." "Oh, it *is* Clemens Krauss!" she exclaimed, "rather too audibly."[49]

By the time she photographed Krauss and his wife, Ida had already amassed an impressive collection of what she called her opera "snaps" that she took with her trusty Brownie. Sometimes, she would make extra prints and bestow them on the delighted tenors and sopranos of whom she was particularly enamored. Her friendship with Pinza began after she handed him the snap of him and his daughter. She would give her opera stars a copy of the photo and then ask them to sign others for her and Louise.

But this brooding, handsome man seemed to cast his own spell over her.

She was "so overcome by his somewhat impatient manner that, for the first time in my snapping career, I fumbled and jerked the camera as I clicked the shutter." Although she got his companion, whom the sisters knew immediately as the soprano Viorica Ursuleac, in a jaunty hat and two-toned shoes, Krauss, his hands in the pocket of his trench coat, was captured out of focus. "I had blurred Krauss badly, to my great chagrin," recalled Ida.[50]

Undaunted, she decided to try again, and waited outside the stage door at another lunchtime for her opportunity to snap the great man: "Even now, I can't imagine how I dared to hang on. But—I lay claim to only one premonition in all this story—as I sat there, fuming, on my camp stool, I *knew* suddenly that I would be sorry all my life if I went away now."

When she finally saw the couple passing by the queue, Ida rushed up to Ursuleac to show her the picture and asked them if she could snap them again. Puffing on a cigar, and amused by this curious English turn of phrase, Krauss encouraged her to snap away. "Snap me again, snap me again," he ordered goodhumoredly.[51] And gratefully she did. The best of these photos would become the most important in their collection of opera snaps, and one of Ida's most treasured possessions. Years later, Ida wrote in pencil on the back: "Krauss and Ursuleac outside Covent Garden."[52]

It would be the photograph that would change many lives.

CHAPTER 3

The Romance Writer

In the summer of 1934, Ida and Louise excitedly packed for their first trip to Austria. They were off to the Salzburg Festival, thrilled at the prospect of meeting up with Pinza, and especially Krauss and Ursuleac, who would be among the star attractions at the month-long summer musical event. Emboldened by their growing familiarity with opera and its biggest stars, they planned to track down the famous couple to present them with the new photographs that Ida had taken—this time in sharp focus.

But on July 25, three days before performers in the grand "Salt City" were preparing to receive hundreds of opera fanatics from around the world, a group of Nazis stormed the federal chancellery 150 miles away in central Vienna. They fired two shots at Austrian Chancellor Engelbert Dollfuss that hit him at close range—the first bullet paralyzed him below the waist while the second caused bleeding around the throat. The coup leaders refused to allow a doctor to attend to the wounds or a priest to administer last rites, and the dictator, who had previously angered Hitler by cracking down on the Nazi Party, died a very slow, agonizing death. As Dollfuss lay bleeding on the floor of his office, Austrian forces mobilized to put down the attempted coup, which was communicated in bold, black, capital letters across newspaper front pages around the world as many worried that Europe could again be on the brink of war. After all, the First World War had begun with the assassination of an Austrian leader in 1914.

For the Cooks, the Dollfuss assassination would prove a jolt of sorts to their happy lives, "the first international event whose repercussions deeply affected our private affairs," recalled Ida. "I blush now to think how ignorant we were of the significance of this event."[1]

They weren't the only ones to downplay the importance of the attempted coup. British war secretary Viscount Hailsham dismissed concerns that Europe could soon find itself again at war, although he condemned the assassination: "Today, the whole civilized world is united in condemning the dastardly outrage of the Nazis and no nation would have the temerity to challenge the opinion of the civilized world."[2] But just in case the Nazis did have the temerity, and were planning to invade Austria after all, Italy—then an enemy of the Nazis—sent warplanes and ships as hundreds of Italian soldiers massed at the Austrian border. Dozens of suspected Nazi coup plotters were rounded up in Austria. In Vienna, authorities declared martial law and closed the country's borders.

In London, Ida and Louise fretted—not so much about geopolitics as about how they could make their way to the festival if the Austrian border were closed. Krauss was conducting six operas at the summer festival—most of them starring Ursuleac in leading roles—including *Der Rosenkavalier* and the gala opening night's *Fidelio*, while Ezio Pinza was going to be playing the lead role in a much-anticipated *Don Giovanni* in the original Italian. The thought of missing the festival, which was scheduled to open on July 28, filled Ida and Louise with dread. "Apart from being vaguely shocked by the way foreigners behaved toward each other, we were concerned with only one aspect of the [Dollfuss] murder: Would it put a stop to our holiday in Salzburg?"[3]

Despite the political turmoil—sporadic fighting even spilled over into the Salzburg suburbs—the music festival was only postponed by a day to accommodate Dollfuss's state funeral, although, sadly, the first night's performance of *Fidelio* had to be canceled.

Austria's borders, which had closed for a few frantic days after the assassination, reopened. Nonetheless, the turmoil kept many foreign visitors away from the festival. But it never occurred to the Cooks to cancel their journey. They traveled to Salzburg third class, by overnight train, "sitting upright," ignoring the advice of a German family in their compartment who warned that there was no possibility that the sisters would be able to cross the border into Austria after so much political unrest.

"Only in Germany, where the National Socialists are putting everything on a good orderly footing, is it safe," they said.

"But I thought this Hitler was a National Socialist," said Ida.

"Yes, yes indeed! The man who will save the country, the greatest man of the age!"[4]

As Ida later noted about this exchange, the sisters thought it "a bit steep to nominate anyone but a Britisher of this title, but... foreigners must have their own illusions."[5]

As for not being able to cross the border into Austria, Ida and Louise were nonplussed. They had booked their trip as they always did—through Thomas Cook, the venerable British travel agency. "We were completely unmoved, merely reiterating that 'the man at Cooks' had said it would be all right, so it *would* be all right," insisted Ida. "For this was how we thought in those days....The British knew best and that was that."[6] In this case, the British knew little, but the show did indeed go on. The sisters completed their journey in peace and found Salzburg "looking divine and apparently peaceful."[7]

The Salzburg Festival opened on Sunday, July 29, the same day that Kurt Schuschnigg, a former minister of justice and education in the Dollfuss regime, was installed as the new chancellor in Vienna. Krauss began the festival on a somber note, conducting Beethoven's only opera, *Fidelio*, in an 11:00 a.m. performance. In a nod to the assassination, Krauss preceded the opera, in which a Spanish noblewoman disguises herself as an errand boy in order to free her husband from prison, with the funeral march from Beethoven's Third Symphony *Eroica*. It was a memorable and eerie performance, especially as armed Austrian police patrolled the theater and were stationed at the upper galleries, according to Ida who reported on the "extraordinary and significant scene." In most stagings of the opera, singers acting as guards in period costume patrol the prison yard, but "on this occasion...the line of guards (this time in modern uniform) continued round the arc of the auditorium." The symbolism wasn't lost on Ida, who recalled the chilling scene years later—a moment when "the melodrama of the operatic world was duplicated in the modern world."[8]

While the Nazis could do little more for now to disrupt the country under another dictator, Hitler turned his attention to the Salzburg Festival. Despite German assurances that relations were back to normal between the two countries after the Dollfuss assassination, behind the scenes Hitler engaged in his own music-world sabotage. Germans caught traveling to Austria suffered heavy fines of up to one thousand Reichsmarks, and at the last minute the German tenor Hans Grahl was yanked from the festival's production of *Tristan und Isolde* because he was "peremptorily barred" by Germany from crossing the border. Grahl lingered near the frontier for weeks in hopes of obtaining a visa to Austria that was never granted.

Moreover, Hitler pressured Richard Strauss not to travel to Salzburg even though festival officials had planned a birthday tribute to the German composer—a cycle of Strauss operas to be conducted by the maestro himself. Strauss had celebrated his seventieth birthday a month earlier in June 1934 and was to have conducted two performances of *Fidelio*, a role that was hastily passed on to his Austrian protégé Clemens Krauss. Strauss was also to have conducted his own operas, *Rosenkavalier* and *Die Frau Ohne Schatten* (*The Woman without a Shadow*) but was also replaced at the last minute by Krauss. *Die Frau Ohne Schatten* was canceled due "to technical reasons," according to the festival program.

In retaliation, the Vienna State Opera, which had been in negotiations to produce Strauss's *The Taciturn Woman* for its upcoming season, decided to scrap the production altogether, threatening a total ban on works by the German composer. Strauss feared a sudden and perhaps massive loss of income and royalties because of the political crisis in which he was now a minor player. He was under a great deal of pressure both from the Nazis and the Austrian government even as he tried to remain as far away from politics as possible. Strauss never joined the Nazi Party, although he was in a privileged position with Hitler, who admired his work (even as Nazi Joseph Goebbels considered him rather tiresome).

Strauss probably thought the Nazis were a fleeting phenomenon. In any event, he was determined not to allow them to interfere with what he considered a higher calling, and at the beginning of the Nazi regime Strauss believed he could use his prestige to institute reforms for musicians. And, in open defiance of growing anti-Semitism, he continued to work with his longtime collaborator the Austrian Jewish writer Stefan Zweig until Zweig was forced to flee Vienna. Strauss also fiercely protected his Jewish daughter-in-law Alice and his two grandchildren from the Nazis. "I made music under the Kaiser, and under Ebert," Strauss said to his family, referring to former German leaders. "I'll survive this lot, as well."[9]

Shocked by Strauss's sudden cancelation, Krauss and Ursuleac tried to figure out what was really going on behind the scenes. They called Hermann Goering from the switchboard at the Bristol Hotel—a call that was wiretapped by Austrian authorities.[10] Before the Reichstag president confirmed the ban, Krauss had already sent a telegram to Strauss, urging him to come to Salzburg for the August performance of his *Elektra* that Krauss himself was conducting, and on August 17 Krauss brought his mentor on stage to deafening applause following the performance. "Even though Herr Strauss was noisily acclaimed this evening by an audience consisting principally of foreign tourists who had only a superficial knowledge of or interest in the political aspects of his recent behavior, there was considerable outspoken indignation among Austrian musicians today at his sudden about face," noted the *New York Times*.[11]

Ida and Louise were among those foreign tourists who had no idea what was going on behind the scenes. On the banks of the Salzach River, the Cooks and the King and Queen of Siam were among a large international crowd of music lovers rapturously enjoying the festival where Toscanini would also make his Salzburg debut—even as around them the politics grew ominous.

A paper bomb exploded at the festival on July 30 but did little damage: it was "used merely as a reminder that there still are Nazis in Salzburg and that they are not going to be satisfied unless they get their way," wrote Frederick Birchall, an American correspondent who attended the festival. "Herr Hitler could end all this without any special Ambassador if he would. That he does not do so is regarded here as ample proof that German intentions toward Austria have not changed in the least, despite public protestations."[12] But, largely, the dangers of the situation were secondary. Even the public show trials and hangings of the coup plotters miles away in Vienna couldn't dampen the festivities.

"I rather gather that the English newspapers are still being very alarming, but it's all my eye really," wrote Ida in a letter home to her parents. "Occasionally about twenty-five soldiers stroll along in the sun grinning a bit sheepishly and not keeping very good time, but that is the sum total of the military manoeuvres here!"[13] Beyond that, they gave the Germans little thought. When they weren't attending opera, the sisters prowled the streets of the old fortress-city hoping to catch a glimpse of Krauss. "He's the most perfect poseur I've ever seen and gets away with it so marvellously that you can only gasp with amused admiration."[14]

■   ■   ■

In spite of their best intentions to find the conductor with the movie-star good looks, the sisters were ultimately unsuccessful. Disappointed, they lingered at Café Tomaselli, the oldest café in Salzburg where fierce-looking *kuchendamen* (cake ladies) patrolled the restaurant with platters groaning with slabs of Linzer torte and apple and plum strudels dusted with icing sugar. It was at a table at the coffee house, founded in 1700, that theater director Max Reinhardt and dramatist Hugo von Hofmannsthal came up with the idea of holding a summer festival in the city and drew up plans to stage von Hofmannsthal's play *Jedermann*, which was performed in the square in front of Salzburg Cathedral, launching the festival in 1920.

Despite the Nazi threats and the prospect of bombs, Salzburg felt relatively peaceful, with families strolling along the promenade by the Salzach River and the coffee houses filled with opera aficionados. Occasionally, the Cooks came across "angry-looking people at street corners distributing leaflets and then suddenly fading away as police came on the scene."[15] The sisters innocently accepted one of the leaflets which they used to wrap up one of their hairbrushes and unwittingly transported it through German territory, blithely unaware that the possession of such dangerous propaganda could have landed them in a great deal of trouble—it accused the Germans of inspiring the murder of Dollfuss.

It was during one of their long evening walks along the river promenade near the Festspielhaus that the Cooks happened upon Krauss's wife. Viorica Ursuleac, then forty, was Richard Strauss's favorite soprano—an artist he called "the most faithful of all faithful" for whom he would create several operatic roles. For Ida and Louise, she would come to be "one of the finest artists who ever walked the operatic stage." When the Cooks had met her two months earlier in London, she was a rising star and had already appeared in the lead of Strauss's *Arabella* at its premiere in Dresden in 1933. Known as "the Balkan tigress" in music circles in Germany, "she had the bluest eyes I ever saw and the most wonderful smile," said Ida. "We fell for her, hook, line and sinker, the first time we heard her. And in an awe-stricken way, we carried a torch for Krauss, too. Theirs was probably the most romantic love-story of the operatic world."[16]

Born into a Romanian musical family in Czernowitz in the Ukraine, where her father was a Greek Orthodox archdeacon, Ursuleac studied opera in Vienna, although her debut was in Zagreb in 1922, where she sang mostly in the Serbo-Croatian language. Later, when her first marriage fell apart, she returned to her home in Czernowitz with a young daughter in tow. By 1924 she had moved back to Vienna to sing at the Volksoper. When she heard that Clemens Krauss was to become the director at the Frankfurt Opera and was searching for a lead soprano, she tried to set up an audition. But the conductor initially refused to hear her sing due to a long-held prejudice against Balkan singers. Undaunted, she auditioned under a fictitious name. Krauss hired her even as he became aware of her duplicity, and the two began a historic collaboration and a torrid affair. In 1930, when Ursuleac moved to Vienna to accompany Krauss at the State Opera, a fierce rivalry developed between her and the German soprano Lotte Lehmann, who also made her mark singing the roles of Strauss heroines. As her career advanced, Ursuleac became a favorite of opera-mad Goering, who had recently conferred upon her—a Romanian—the title of "Prussian Kammersänger."

In Salzburg, Ursuleac remembered the Cook sisters right away and in her broken, German-accented English she recalled that they wanted her husband to autograph their picture. "I know! You want Mr. Krauss to write!" she said. The sisters were received "smilingly but a trifle absently" by the soprano. As Ida noted years later, the sisters could tell even then that she had her problems "in a troubled and unstable world." Nevertheless Ida produced the photograph that she carried in her handbag and gave it to Ursuleac who promised to get his signature. She told them to collect the photograph in a few days' time at the festival box office.[17]

In the meantime, the sisters enjoyed "a glorious feast of music," including the performance by Pinza in the title role of Mozart's *Don Giovanni*. Louise was desperately in love with Pinza, and friends recalled that she blushed whenever anyone mentioned his name in her presence. If she was timid at the best of times, she was positively tongue-tied in the company of the suave Italian with his slicked-back dark, curly hair, handsome in his signature fedora and perfectly tied bowtie, an ebony cigarette holder clutched between white teeth. But the Cooks knew too much about his scandalous reputation with women. He had dined at the Cooks' modest family home in London along with Elisabeth Rethberg, the beautiful German soprano who starred with him on stage. They seemed constantly together, and often signed joint letters to the sisters. It was clear to the Cooks that they were having an affair.

Pinza had an eye for beautiful women. And although he was married to his first wife when he was involved with Rethberg, he still made an effort to seduce as many women as possible. His womanizing would turn tragic when, following an affair with the German conductor Bruno Walter's married daughter Gretel, Gretel's husband murdered her in revenge and then turned the gun on himself.

The sisters were pretty clear-eyed about Pinza's amorous proclivities, but they seemed to excuse him because he was such a remarkable performer. They considered him an exalted being—"sensational" in the unforgettable production of *Don Giovanni* at Salzburg. After all, they reasoned, their "operatic charmer" was stuck in a hapless marriage to his first wife, Augusta Cassinelli. "There is no use pretending that the domestic situation was a happy one, for the first Mrs. Pinza was, to put it mildly, a difficult person."[18] When she found out about the relationship between her husband and Rethberg, Cassinelli sued the dramatic soprano for $250,000 in 1935, blaming Rethberg for the "alienation" of her husband's affections. The lawsuit was filed just as Pinza was preparing to star in the Metropolitan Opera production of *Faust* as Mephistopheles alongside Rethberg, who played the role of the maiden, Marguerite. The suit was eventually dropped.

On their last day in Salzburg, the Cooks collected the photograph that Ida had left with Ursuleac and again bumped into her walking near the river. When they asked where they could hear Ursuleac sing in opera again, she told them to come and see her in Vienna. But before they could plan a trip to Vienna, the sisters traveled to Amsterdam at the end of 1934 on the advice of Rethberg, who suggested that they attend a Strauss Festival Week in the Dutch city at the end of the year. Not only would Strauss himself be conducting some of his most famous works, but Ursuleac would be performing solos from *Arabella*, which had become her most important Strauss role to date.

Ida and Louise were becoming fast friends with Ursuleac. Although she could barely speak English at the time, Ida wrote to her often. Ursuleac wrote back in her halting English, thanking the sisters for prints of the photos Ida took and for a bouquet of flowers they sent before one of her performances in Amsterdam. "Send you many thanks for the wonderful flowers and wish you a happy new year," wrote Ursuleac, whom the sisters often referred to by her initials VU or simply "Vee."

"Your letter I have read it before the performance and I was very happy to go on the stage with the thoughts from kindest friends. Could you understand my English?"[19]

They were becoming so close that Ida and Louise were among the inner circle allowed to attend Ursuleac's dress rehearsals as well as the performances during their week in Amsterdam. At the dress rehearsals they soon noticed "a distinguished-looking whitehaired lady in the audience whom we had seen once or twice with Krauss and Ursuleac in Salzburg."[20] Ursuleac introduced the sisters to her close friend Mitia Mayer-Lismann, the official lecturer of the Salzburg Festival, who gave daily talks in German and English at the Hotel Bristol the morning before each opera performance. Unwilling to share the Romanian soprano with a woman they described as an interloper, both sisters immediately dismissed the opera expert. "These people with double-barrelled names are never any good," said Louise, who had yet to attend one of Mayer-Lismann's lectures. "A lot of talk, when what one only wants is the performance."[21]

But Mayer-Lismann seemed a constant presence. They bumped into her again when they went to the Amsterdam train station to see off Ursuleac on her return to Vienna. "And then a strange thing happened," wrote Ida.[22] As the four women stood talking on the platform, surrounded by travelers with suitcases and vendors hawking newspapers, Ursuleac suddenly grabbed both sisters by the arm, and "with an earnestness and gravity that we could not quite understand" explained that Mayer-Lismann would soon be going to England for the first time in her life, to deliver a series of lectures on music. The sisters stared at each other, not quite comprehending the sense of urgency. In her broken English, Ursuleac pleaded with them to please, please look after her when she arrived. Although struck by the rather odd request, the sisters heartily agreed to do so. They reassured Ursuleac that she needn't worry about anything. They would take care of her friend. "I still see the scene on the platform of Amsterdam station as Ursuleac turned to her companion and said in a tone of somber satisfaction, 'Now you will be all right.'"[23]

The sisters returned to London and prepared for a busy 1935. King George's Silver Jubilee coincided with the first day of the Covent Garden season on May 6. Before the performance began, the King's Jubilee Message to the Empire was broadcast live from Saint Paul's Cathedral over the loudspeakers of the Royal Opera House. After thanking the British people and the empire's subjects in far-flung colonies for their good wishes on his twenty-fifth anniversary on the throne, the King seemed to allude to troubled times ahead. "Other anxieties may be in store, but I am persuaded with God's help they may all be overcome, if we meet them with confidence, courage, and unity," he said, carefully enunciating each word.[24]

Overwhelmed by the solemnity of the occasion and the King's hopeful words, Ida and Louise, happily ensconced in their gallery seats, could hardly have imagined that in a short time they would be called upon to test their own reserves of "confidence, courage, and unity."

But before those dark moments arrived there was opera, and the first of what would be their annual "gramophone parties"—the musical soirées they organized with canapés and champagne but also tea and scones, smothered in Devon cream—in their Morella Road living room. That year, the Cooks invited their gallery queue habitués who were honored with the presence of live opera stars Pinza and Rethberg. Although Ida reported that Rethberg was rather shy during the festivities, Pinza was in full charming form, regaling his listeners with backstage gossip and singing snatches of their favorite arias.

It was also during that momentous Jubilee Year that Florence Taft at *Mabs Fashions* asked Ida—her fiction sub-editress—to try her hand at a romantic serial, a suspense-laden romance that could run over several issues of the magazine. Although she was skeptical, Ida was game to give it a try, and she locked herself up in the family's attic to begin work on *Wife to Christopher*. Unwilling to publish under her real name, Ida invented a pseudonym by combining her mother's first name with her paternal grandmother's maiden name. And so the romance writer Mary Burchell was born.

Ida could easily have borrowed the plot of *Wife to Christopher* from one her favorite operas: a breathless page-turner, marked by suspense and melodrama. Vicki Unwin, with her beauty, purity, and sense of utter devotion, became Ida's first ingénue, and resembled a misunderstood Desdemona. But it was also a story about secrets shared by sisters. When Vicki and her sister Margery are faced with mounting bills for caring for their beloved dying father, Margery boldly suggests that Vicki trick a wealthy man into marrying her. Vicki spots her opportunity in Christopher Kentone, the heir to a huge fortune, who is involved with a married opera singer named Marie Renard. Vicki, who works for Christopher's father, Joseph, devises a plot that results in her becoming locked in Christopher's bedroom at night. When Christopher wakes to find the seemingly helpless Vicky in his room, he decides that he must marry her to save the young woman's reputation. But when he finds out about her betrayal, he becomes bent on revenge.

Wife to Christopher proved so successful that the fiction editor at *Mabs* suggested that Ida offer it to a publisher as a novel. She gave her the names of three publishers and Ida chose Mills & Boon, sending the serial marked for the attention of Charles Boon. The publisher responded right away, and a week later she met Boon himself in his office. The company, which had started out as a general-interest publishing firm, producing travel guides, school textbooks, and Shakespearean plays, was now focusing on romantic fiction, and Boon obviously saw raw talent in the thirty-year-old *Mabs* writer and sub-editress.

Boon, the son of a London brewer, had met his cofounder, the very proper and wealthy Gerald Rusgrove Mills, the son of a Midlands solicitor, while the two men worked at Methuen, a more established publisher. Boon, an expert in marketing and advertising, and Mills, the main investor and Methuen's former head of educational publications, set up the new publishing venture together in 1908. Among their most popular writers were Jack London, Hugh Walpole, and P. G. Wodehouse. On the eve of the First World War, they were among the first publishers in the United Kingdom to seek out talented women writers. "Men are not writing so much fiction as in past years, while the woman writer is immensely on the increase," Boon told a meeting of the Associated Booksellers in 1913.

But the company's fortunes suddenly changed in 1916. Jack London, one of their highest-grossing authors, died that year, and both principals joined the war effort, leaving the company to drift for three critical years under the stewardship of Boon's sister, Margaret. Although the firm managed to recover once Mills and Boon returned, the company searched for ways to strengthen its bottom line with a string of bestsellers. The partners began to answer the demand for romantic and escapist fiction for women and became pioneers in the genre. After Mills died in 1928, Boon continued courting prolific women writers, largely to compete with the glamorous Barbara

Cartland, who began her career in 1925 and would go on to write more than seven hundred books.

By the time Charles Boon signed Ida Cook in 1935, the firm was publishing around sixty-seven romance novels a year.[25] Ida, who had been interested in writing love stories since she had penned "A Romance of the 14th Century" as a fifteen-year-old schoolgirl in Alnwick, was overjoyed with this new opportunity, although she seemed the very antithesis of Cartland, a seductive presence who had several lovers and bore little resemblance to her virginal protagonists. Cartland was fond of wearing chiffon and throwing elaborate society parties to promote her breathless bestsellers, while Ida remained plain and no-nonsense, doing little to adopt an alluring public persona as a writer of romances.

"I am I think by nature a tale-spinner, and passionately inter-ested in people," Ida recalled years later.[26] But Ida was never alone in her tale-spinning. From the beginning, Louise was very much a partner—albeit a silent one—in the writing. The sisters would con-sult on plot and characters, and Louise would proofread and help her sister type the manuscripts. A family friend recalled that, once Ida had signed her contract with Mills & Boon, Louise helped her sister "rattle off" two books a year.[27]

Eager to head back to her attic room on Morella Road and begin her next book, Ida agreed on the spot to signing a three-book con-tract, which included *Wife to Christopher*. "'No, no,' [Charles Boone] said firmly. 'You must never sign anything like that. You take that contract home and show it to your father, and if he says you can sign it, you can.' How's that for the wicked old world of publishing? No wonder I knew from that moment I was in safe hands."[28] *Wife to Christopher*, for which Ida earned an advance of £40 and 10 percent in royalties, turned into a bestseller for Mills & Boon. After her initial success, Ida began to mine her opera-world adventures for material for future books.

Romance in the Mills & Boon universe of the 1930s was based on what Boon called "wholesomeness." Authors were encouraged "within the limits implied by 'wholesomeness,' to make their storylines as erotic as possible. A common scene, usually at the beginning of the novel, was the moment when the heroine senses an unmistakable attraction to the hero. 'Electricity' was often in the air."[29] Ida never veered from that chaste line: "I truly don't think I have ever let a girl of mine do anything that I wouldn't like to see a girl of that age do, or if she does, she's punished."[30]

In later years, John Boon, one of the sons of the cofounder of the publishing house, said that the key to the company's success was never looking down on the books they produced. "We never despised our product. I think this was highly important. A lot of people who publish romantic novels call them 'funny little books' that make a bit of profit. We never did that. We never said this was the greatest form of literature, but we did say that of this form of literature, we were going to publish the best."[31]

Mills & Boon released *Wife to Christopher* with a pink-and-grey cover featuring a drawing of a frightened blonde woman in an alluring, sleeveless, satin nightdress with a tall, square-jawed, and menacing man in a robe glaring down at her. Ida dedicated the book to her new friend Viorica Ursuleac. "To my Dear V. U. who lent me her initials to bring me luck, and to whom I now offer my first book as a very small tribute to a very great artist." In addition to Ursuleac's initials, Ida drew on Clemens Krauss for the character of Christopher Kentone, who shared the conductor's overbearing personality and, of course, his initials.

Amid all this excitement over the publication of Ida's first book, Mitia Mayer-Lismann finally arrived in London, and to safety. The

Cooks, who had promised their new friend that they would "look after" Mayer-Lismann suddenly found themselves spending a great deal of time with her. She was, they both pronounced, quite charming. The sisters were also suitably impressed with her knowledge of German opera. Still, it wasn't until they took her on a sightseeing tour of London's great churches that they began to see why Ursuleac had entrusted her to their care. At Westminster Abbey, Mayer-Lismann asked if it was a Protestant or Catholic church. When she asked the same question under the dome of Saint Paul's, Ida wondered where the conversation was going and boldly asked Mayer-Lismann a rather personal question.

"Are you Protestant or Catholic?"

"I?" said Mayer-Lismann, rather surprised. "Didn't you know? I'm a Jewess."[32]

CHAPTER 4

The Flat

Ida had spied the large construction site advertising London's newest housing complex, Dolphin Square, from her seat on the bus as she made her way home from Fleet Street to Victoria Station, where she regularly caught the train to Wandsworth.[1] She was determined to have an apartment at Dolphin Square, and one day she simply walked from Victoria Station to inquire in person, immediately putting down a £10 deposit on a large one-bedroom flat. Ida had convinced Louise that they needed their own place in central London—a pied-à-terre to entertain their opera friends, especially now that Ida was well on her way to becoming an established author, a woman of some means.

There was also something distinctly American about the well-ordered blocks of flats that must have resonated with both women after their sojourns in New York. Unlike most London bedsits that were dark and stuffy, the apartments at Dolphin Square were airy and light filled. Many overlooked the complex's manicured gardens and the Thames. The developer also showed prospective tenants plans for ground-floor retail shops. The new residents at Dolphin Square wouldn't have far to go for all their needs. Here was a modern development that lent itself to convenience and ease of living—a place of wide vistas that carried a sense of possibility in its architecture.

It wasn't difficult to imagine the delightful parties they would throw in the apartment, big enough to cram in dozens of their friends. Perhaps now they could invite even more of their fellow opera aficionados who happily endured all sorts of weather to queue up with them for tickets, sitting on their canvas camp stools outside Covent Garden during the season. At Dolphin Square, everyone would be able to gather around the sisters' beloved gramophone to listen to their growing collection of opera records. Maybe Pinza might again be persuaded to attend and tell his risqué stories. Ida and Louise were so enchanted by the social possibilities that the Dolphin Square flat held for them that they were among the first to sign up for a rental at the redbrick apartment blocks, which were still under construction.

They might not have known it when they signed the rental agreement, but the inspiration for Dolphin Square actually came from their beloved New York City. It was U.S. developer Frederick Fillmore French who bought the tract of land in Pimlico in 1933 that would become Dolphin Square. French envisioned a British version of his Tudor City and Knickerbocker Plaza, Manhattan rental-apartment complexes featuring hundreds of units that the Frederick French Company had built for middle-class New Yorkers in the 1920s and 1930s. French's plans for a mid-rise housing complex in the City of Westminster—each apartment block was to be ten stories tall—was dubbed one of "the most ambitious schemes for London in years" by the *New York Times*.

But two years after he bought the leasehold on the property from the Duke of Westminster, French's company found itself on the verge of bankruptcy, forcing the real-estate baron to sell the London parcel to a competing British developer. Richard Rylands Costain would go on to complete French's vision—a housing development of 1,250 flats. Most of the units contained three rooms—a bedroom, reception room, and kitchen. Apartments ranged from the one-room Henley Suite to the seven-room Windsor Suite that also featured maids' quarters. "London's Residential Landmark of the Future," invited prospective tenants to "a game of 'squash,' a plunge in the pool...a lift to your home!" according to a notice in *The Times* of London. Bureaucrats, lawmakers, and even spies lined up to rent the "highly desirable" apartments which were within walking distance of government offices, including the headquarters of the British security services MI5 and MI6.

The sisters found themselves in exalted company. Among the 476 early tenants were Margaret Lockwood, the most popular screen actress in Britain at the time, and David Burghley, the Conservative politician and Olympic runner. Charles Henry Maxwell Knight, the chief "agent runner" for MI5, also lived at Dolphin Square. He managed to infiltrate both communist and fascist groups from a series of flats at Hood House that doubled as his home and offices. Among Knight's most famous targets was his upstairs neighbor in Hood House, Sir Oswald Mosley. A former Conservative Member of Parliament and the leader of the British Union of Fascists, which he founded in 1932 after meeting the Italian leader Benito Mussolini, Mosley rented two large units directly above Knight's flats. That same year, the married Mosley began an affair with Diana Guinness, née Mitford, one of six aristocratic sisters whose political escapades in the 1930s and 1940s seemed to mirror the deep fissures that would tear apart the twentieth century.[2]

When they weren't immersed in opera, Ida and Louise, now both in their thirties, continued to live a quiet life with their parents at the family home on Morella Road, where Ida wrote her romance novels on her typewriter at a small desk in the attic. Dolphin Square was strictly reserved for their other life of lively opera gramophone parties but also increasingly of intrigue and drama.

In addition to Galli-Curci and her husband Homer Samuels, the sisters were still very close to Pinza and Rethberg, who became frequent visitors in the early days at Dolphin Square. "There is much excitement over here over Mrs Simpson," wrote Rethberg in a letter from New York dated December 20, 1936, ten days after King Edward VIII announced his abdication to marry his American lover, the twice-divorced socialite Wallis Simpson. "But all my sympathies are with King Edward."In the same letter, addressing "Miss Ida," Pinza regretted that the couple's schedules would not permit them to attend the Cooks' gramophone parties over the next year, suggesting that they all meet somewhere in Europe. Perhaps Salzburg? "I am also very sorry about what has happened to your King and feel he will regret his step soon," wrote Pinza, concluding with "[his] very best wishes."[3] Not long after, in another letter to Ida, Rethberg alluded to troubling times in her native Germany: "Everything seems like a terrible nightmare."[4]

Indeed, after their encounter with Mitia Mayer-Lismann on her visit to London, the sisters had slowly come to realize that life in Germany was becoming increasingly difficult for Jews. Their new friend had told them that Jews had little protection under the law and were rapidly becoming noncitizens. "But don't you think this will pass?" asked Louise while the sisters were shepherding Mayer-Lismann around London on that first visit. "I mean—it's all so silly."

But Mayer-Lismann assured them that it wasn't silly. "If Hitler becomes even more powerful and is able to do one quarter of what he has written down in *Mein Kampf* it will be a bad time for the Jews. We had a friend already who—disappeared."

"Disappeared? Disappeared where?"

Mayer-Lismann said she didn't know. Perhaps he went to jail or to a concentration camp. All she knew was that the friend was taken by the Gestapo and never heard from again.

"Do you mean he was arrested?" asked Ida, still unable to grasp what Mayer-Lismann was saying.

Mayer-Lismann had no reply.

"But one has to know where people go when they're arrested," insisted Ida. "Surely there's a trial or something? Habeas corpus and all that sort of thing. It's against the law to take them away and keep them away without trial."

Mayer-Lismann told the sisters that such legal niceties no longer applied to Jews in Germany. "And my husband says it's just the beginning. He says the time is coming when there will be no law for the Jews."

"But I never heard of such a thing!" cried Louise, the good, law-abiding bureaucrat. "This is the twentieth century!"

The sisters were so rattled by their conversation with Mayer-Lismann that Ida suggested they end their sightseeing tour and go for coffee to come up with a plan to help her. "The coffee [wasn't] very good, but the talk [was]," recalled Ida who began to plot how she and Louise were going to bring Mayer-Lismann permanently to safety in London.[5]

For the first time the sisters started to learn from their guest about work permits and visas "and how one gets out of one country and into another." They also learned that there was opposition to Jews leaving Germany, and that unless they had international banking connections, the "transfer of money [was] virtually impossible and dangerous." Goods were equally difficult to transfer out of the country, often subject to the whim of the Nazi officials dealing with the case, Mayer-Lismann told them. She explained that she had come to England in the hope of finding work as a lecturer at a college so that she could obtain a visa to leave Germany with her family. But the process would take time, and in the meantime she had to return to her home in Frankfurt. "And wait and wait and wait," noted Ida.

Just before Mayer-Lismann left for Frankfurt am Main, Ida told her that the sisters would do more research on her situation and write to her regularly. Mayer-Lismann quickly cautioned them against sending any letters, noting that they were often opened by Nazi censors.

"Opened?" said an outraged Louise. "But that's against the law…"

But, as Mayer-Lismann had tried to explain, the laws in Germany no longer protected Jews.

"Well, then," said Ida, "we'll just have to come and visit you in Frankfurt in a few months' time and talk things over."[6]

And as they gradually became aware that they could no longer rely on any rational explanations for the growing discrimination against Jews in Germany, Ida and Louise would begin to envision another purpose for the gramophone party flat: "a clearing house…for the people whom we brought to England."[7]

After the successful publication of *Wife to Christopher*, Ida began work on the other two books that she had promised to deliver to Mills & Boon—a contract that would renew itself for the next five decades. She was never under any illusions about her work. "You don't even mind when people come up to you—as they frequently do—and say, 'Of course, I don't read *your* sort of stuff.'"[8] She knew she wasn't writing literary masterpieces and that her romances appealed mainly to the secretarial crowd, the kind of young women who read *Mabs Fashions* and cut out the dress patterns. "It used to wound me very much when I was young. But now I don't mind a bit. I just look them in the eye and say, 'No? And you can't write it either, can you?' Then they fade away."[9]

It wasn't long before Ida found herself making more money from her writing than she could ever have imagined. Ida, who had never handled more than £5 at once, suddenly found her income rising exponentially. From just over £4 a week, she suddenly started to earn advances in the hundreds of pounds.

The sisters started to travel to Germany and Italy more frequently for opera, faithfully attending performances given by their new friends Krauss and Ursuleac. They briefly fantasized about spending their new-found wealth on cars, jewelry, and fur coats, and even talked about Louise eventually retiring from her civil service job.

But as Jews began to be publicly persecuted, the sisters were also conscious of another, worthier use for Ida's sudden windfall.

"I was intoxicated by the sight," wrote Ida, referring to her ability to earn significant amounts of money. "And—terrible, moving and overwhelming thought—I could save life with it. Even now, I can hardly think of it without tears."[10] For suddenly, these two rather sheltered English women were gradually understanding the full horror of what life was like for Jews in Germany. "We didn't know—imagine! In these days we didn't *know* that to be Jewish and to come from Frankfurt am Main in Germany already had the seeds of tragedy in it."[11]

Months after their meeting with Mayer-Lismann in London, they visited her in Frankfurt, where for the first time the sisters saw a shop with "JUDE" plastered over the window and "an SS man at the door with a gun, making people pass along and forbidding them to enter."[12]

During that visit the Cooks were thrilled to be invited to supper at the Mayer-Lismann home with Krauss and Ursuleac. But a foreboding overshadowed the meal as "something like panic" struck the family after Mayer-Lismann's brother, an investment banker, was delayed at the border returning from a business trip to Paris. He arrived twenty-four hours later, "very shaken" because he was taken off the train at the frontier "and searched to the skin," said Ida. "Then he was kept under arrest, but finally allowed to continue his journey. There was no explanation of why he was arrested or why he was released." When they heard the story after Mayer-Lismann's brother arrived, the sisters again responded with incredulity. Surely, one could complain? The question provoked little more than "a pale smile" from the dinner party guests. "Least said, soonest mended," noted Ida. "He is free now, for which everyone is uneasily thankful."[13]

The 1935 Nuremberg Laws, which excluded German Jews from Reich citizenship and prohibited them from having sexual relations with Aryans, did not define Jews only on the basis of religious beliefs. Anyone who had Jewish grandparents was deemed a Jew whether or not they actually practiced Judaism.

And even if they had converted to Christianity, they were still considered Jews under the race laws.

Such was the case of Mitia Mayer-Lismann.

Mitia Lismann was born on June 3, 1883, in Saint Petersburg as violence against Jews erupted in a series of pogroms. The brutality emerged after the assassination of Czar Alexander II by Russian revolutionaries in 1881. When Alexander III succeeded his father, he set about reversing all his father's liberal reforms and stoking anti-Semitic rhetoric that blamed Jews for his father's assassination; he sought to unite Russia under a single language and the Christian Orthodox religion. Jews had long been discriminated against in the empire, and the new czar saw an opportunity to either kill them all off or force them out of Russia.

In 1882 the passage of the so-called May Laws forbade Jews from living outside the Pale of Settlement, an area in western Russia where most Jews were forced to stay. The new laws prevented them from entering into any lease or mortgage agreements, and they were later barred from holding government jobs or working as doctors and lawyers, while strict quotas were placed on entrance to high schools and universities. At the same time, Russian soldiers went on a series of bloody rampages, destroying Jewish businesses, raping Jewish women, and killing thousands. As a result of the continuing violence, more than two million Jews left the Russian Empire between 1881 and 1914. Among them was Lismann's family, who escaped to Germany, settling in Frankfurt am Main.

Lismann was of Jewish origin, but her family was completely assimilated into an intellectual, cosmopolitan circle who cared more about classical music and art than about religion. She displayed musical talent from an early age and began piano lessons in 1889 at the age of six. She trained as a teacher and finished her exams in June 1910. A year later, she married Paul Mayer, a businessman, and on April 17, 1914, their daughter Else Mayer-Lismann was born. The couple also had a son—Fritz Mayer-Lismann—who died in January 1933, two days after Hitler came to power.

In 1931, when her husband's company fell on hard times, Mayer-Lismann began teaching piano at the Hoch Conservatory. A year before the Nuremberg Laws were enacted in 1935, Mayer-Lismann also started to give lectures in English and German, mostly to tourists who frequented the Salzburg Festival and the Frankfurt Opera. By the time she had distinguished herself as an opera lecturer, Mayer-Lismann and her family socialized with a circle of friends that included Richard Strauss, German soprano Adele Kern, and Clemens Krauss.

While in Salzburg during that difficult summer of 1934, Mayer-Lismann worried about her family. She confessed her growing anxiety to Ursuleac, to whom she had become extremely close, and Krauss over dinner at a "quiet outdoor restaurant along the riverbank." She also told them that she was going to England to give an opera lecture and while there would try to explore possibilities for leaving Germany.

Krauss suggested that Ursuleac should introduce her to the Cook sisters. "What about your two English adorers, the Cook *Mädels*?" said Krauss, using the German phrase for "lass" that he frequently used to describe the sisters. "Can't you make use of them?"[14]

Life in Germany for the Mayer-Lismann family became progressively worse. By 1936 Mayer-Lismann, then fifty-two, was prohibited from continuing most of her professional activities. Officials at the Conservatory told her she would only be allowed to teach Jewish children. With her husband out of work, the family began to rent out rooms in their home on Im Trutz Frankfurt Street, 27, in order to survive. Mayer-Lismann was one of thousands of talented and well-respected Jews forced out of their professions after Hitler targeted culture in Germany. Music and art were placed under the control of Goebbels's Propaganda Ministry, whose mandate was to rid German culture of Jewish influence, control the media, and place the arts in the service of furthering the Aryan "glories" of the Third Reich. Overnight, so-called "degenerate" artists, the modernists who had flourished in the Weimar Republic and whose works were often blistering critiques of fascism and authoritarianism, were deemed enemies of the state, and many were rounded up and sent to concentration camps as political prisoners.

Goebbels purged cultural institutions of Jews and Nazi Party opponents, creating the *Reichsmusikkammer*, or Reich Music Chamber, in 1933. The goal of the Berlin-based institute was to promote German music and musicians, such as Beethoven, Wagner, Brahms, and Bach. Music by classical composers who were born Jewish, such as Felix Mendelssohn and Gustav Mahler, was banned, as were compositions by Claude Debussy, who had married a Jew. Jazz, swing music, and modern works by composers such as Alban Berg, Igor Stravinsky, and Paul Hindemith were labeled "degenerate" and forbidden.

Else Mayer-Lismann was the first refugee saved by the Cook sisters. *Yad Vashem Archives*

During these increasingly desperate times, Mayer-Lismann placed her trust in the Cook sisters and her well connected music-world friends. And surely she could continue to count on Krauss, who was a rising star in Nazi Germany.

At the beginning of their friendship with Krauss, the Cooks could scarcely have imagined how much their favorite conductor was a figure of intrigue in both Austria and Germany—beloved by Hitler but openly hated by some of the titans of classical music who saw him as a dangerous threat. Ferociously ambitious, Krauss was determined to become a star. Besides, he needed the money. Following a bitter split from his first wife, Margarethe Abraham, Krauss was ordered by an Austrian divorce court to pay more than half his salary of 4,000 schillings per month to support his two children, Oliver and Oktavian. After his marriage to Ursuleac, he was also helping to raise her daughter, Nadja.

Like Strauss, he eschewed politics and was devoted to his art. He had little patience with bureaucracy and made enemies of those he considered of lesser talent. He was not above firing even the most popular singers and musicians if they did not meet his criteria for excellence and reassigning long-established operatic roles. He did little to discourage open hostility against him, which had been building for years in Vienna where opera-world worthies accused him of being a Nazi and a traitor, especially after he took over from Strauss at the Salzburg Festival in the tense summer of 1934. He came in for even more criticism when he attempted to organize a tour of South America for the Vienna State Opera a year later—a move that critics saw as further sabotage because the trip would probably conflict with the Salzburg Festival. "Repercussions of Salzburg intrigues and jealousies quiver through the first autumnal stirrings of the Vienna music season," noted Herbert Peyser, the classical music critic for the *New York Times* in the autumn of 1934. "The storm center of hypotheses and discussions is Clemens Krauss, whose personal prestige was not advanced by the late course of events at Salzburg. Today one even gathers that his foothold in Vienna is scarcely as secure as was hitherto imagined."[15]

In fact, on the opening night of Beethoven's *Fidelio*, starring German soprano Lotte Lehmann, at the Vienna State Opera in September of that year, Krauss was pointedly snubbed by Austria's new chancellor, Kurt Schuschnigg, who presented the singer with a large and ornate wreath on stage. "In this ostentatious gesture many people discerned an implicit slap at Herr Krauss, officially administered," said Peyser.[16] Lehmann, adored in Austria where she had long been associated with the Vienna Opera, made no secret that she couldn't stand Krauss. In fact, whenever she was passed over by Krauss, Lehmann leaned on Schuschnigg to intervene. "Such was the intrigue that if Ursuleac got a role Lotte Lehmann did one of her famous hysterical scenes with Schuschnigg," wrote one observer. "[She] complained to Schuschnigg that he [Krauss] was a Nazi."[17] In Austria, belief in Krauss's perceived Nazi leanings was so widespread that he and his wife were under constant police surveillance. After the Dollfuss assassination, while the couple were in Salzburg, their apartment was searched by Austrian police.[18]

Annoyed by the petty jealousies and constant challenges to his artistic vision in his native country, Krauss looked to Germany to bolster his career. He had already demonstrated that he had few qualms about taking over the posts vacated by colleagues who were either routed by the Nazis or resigned in protest at their rule. Such had been the case over *Arabella*, the first opera the Cooks saw Krauss conduct at Covent Garden in May 1934. Behind the scenes, Krauss was called in to substitute for German conductor Fritz Busch at the Dresden State Opera when Busch was fired over his very vocal opposition to the Nazis a year earlier. Strauss, who had dedicated *Arabella* to Busch, was incensed by the Nazis' backstage meddling in the opera. Members of the Dresden opera company were pressured into signing a letter critical of Busch's talents, but a more complicated scenario suggested that Busch was actually being groomed by the Nazis to take over the Berlin State Opera. The move was ultimately blocked by Wilhelm Furtwängler, Germany's greatest conductor, who did not want to compete with Busch for prestige in Berlin. In addition to his leadership of the Berlin Philharmonic, Furtwängler was also musical director of the Berlin State Opera.[19]

Like Strauss, Furtwängler was obsessed with his art and believed the Nazi regime wouldn't last. Emboldened by his appointment, along with Strauss, to the Reich Music Chamber in November 1933, Furtwängler continued to openly criticize the regime. He refused to give the de rigueur "Heil Hitler" salute at the beginning of performances. He blasted Hitler for his anti-Semitic policies and refused to fire Jewish musicians from the Berlin orchestras he controlled. He resolutely held on to his longtime Jewish secretary, Berta Geissmar.

But he wasn't prepared for the unbridled ambitions of Clemens Krauss, whom he considered a minor talent who was unable to "relate to the great German music." Naive and stubborn, Furtwängler, who was alternately described as "a visionary" and "a musical genius," was ill-prepared for Nazi meddling in his artistic decisions when Krauss was rumored as the leading candidate to replace Busch in Berlin. Furtwängler was sure the Nazi menace would blow over. In the meantime, he would do his best to stay the course and focus on his life's work. "Every German of standing today is facing the question whether he wishes to maintain and carry through with his position or not," he told a friend in 1934. "Having opted for the affirmative, he somehow *has* to make a practical pact with the ruling party, or else, he *will* have to go."[20]

However, these "practical pacts" were simply unrealistic when it came to Nazi thugs. Furtwängler's own artistic defiance against the Nazis would end up stalling his career and paving the way for Krauss's entrée into the upper echelons of German culture. For instance, despite the Nazi edict against Hindemith, Furtwängler went ahead and included one of his operas in the 1934–35 Berlin opera season. The announcement that *Mathis der Maler* would be featured as part of the new season lineup had immediate consequences. Goering ordered the removal of the offending work about the Renaissance painter Matthias Grünewald and his battle for artistic freedom set against the backdrop of repression during the Protestant Reformation. Hindemith's message that the opera mirrored his own struggle for freedom of expression under the Nazis was not lost on the National Socialist hierarchy, which quickly banned the work. Hindemith was married to a Jewish woman, and while many of his friends were prominent leftists, he considered himself apolitical. Nonetheless, he remained a Nazi target.

"When did the head of a State ever interfere with details of a theater repertoire?" complained Geissmar, who was eventually forced to leave Germany. "It was as if Mr. Churchill suddenly sent a message to Covent Garden telling Sir Thomas Beecham what to do, or Mr. Roosevelt asked the Metropolitan to put on a certain opera while prohibiting another."[21]

But Hitler couldn't help himself. Like the Cooks, he was fascinated with opera and recognized the power of its spectacle as an important propaganda tool to extol the glories of the Third Reich. In the first volume of *Mein Kampf*, Hitler wrote about his formative experiences of opera. As a twelve-year-old, he attended a performance of Richard Wagner's *Lohengrin*, becoming instantly enamored of the nineteenth-century composer: "In one instance I was addicted. My youthful enthusiasm for the Bayreuth master knew no bounds." After quitting school at sixteen, he spent much of his free time going to the opera.[22]

Opera was deemed such an important symbol to the Nazi regime that Wagner's *Die Meistersinger von Nürnberg*, an ode to the glory of medieval Germany, was performed at the Berlin State Opera in March 1933 in a ceremony to commemorate the founding of the Third Reich. The following year, Hitler ordered the reconstruction of Nuremberg's opera house, and the third act from Wagner's opera was performed at the 1934 National Socialist Party rally in the medieval city, where it was filmed for the propaganda movie *Triumph of the Will* and conducted by Furtwängler. In its final lines, the hero might be describing Hitler's state of mind in the 1930s: "Honor your German masters…even if the Holy Roman Empire should dissolve in mist, of us there would yet remain Holy German art!"[23] Furtwängler himself possibly believed he was upholding "Holy German art" when he tried to resist lowbrow Nazi edicts against Hindemith, writing an impassioned letter to the press about artistic freedom and taking a strong stand. He even denounced Hitler as "an enemy of the human race" for interfering in the opera season and went ahead and boldly conducted a public performance of music from Hindemith's opera in the autumn of 1934. Furtwängler's very public defiance infuriated the Nazi hierarchy, and by December 1934 the Nazis had forced the great conductor to resign from all his official positions.[24]

Krauss, a much more malleable successor, was waiting in the wings.

On December 10, 1934, Krauss recorded in his diary: "second interview in Reich Chancellor's [Adolf Hitler's] apartment."[25] Krauss, who had been hanging about in Berlin, was immediately engaged as director of the Berlin State Opera in place of Furtwängler, noted Geissmar in her own diary. "This we were informed was by Hitler's special request."[26] Later, when Krauss made his Berlin debut, it was Goering who personally introduced him to the audience.

"He possesses a certain cold elegance and a technique that is not without interest to experts, but beyond that he has nothing, not even the slightest, to offer and he lacks even a trace of force and warmth," noted Furtwängler of his rival.[27] However, Furtwängler admitted that Krauss had something that was perhaps more valuable: he understood "the advertising machinery and the art of cultivating personal relationships."[28]

Despite the widespread suspicions of Krauss's strategic allegiances with the Nazis, these clinical decisions had successfully launched his career in Austria and would take him to the pinnacle of success in Germany. For Krauss, the Berlin posting was simply a stepping-stone to more greatness, and he promptly moved to the city, taking his wife and other prominent singers from the Vienna State Opera, forcing many to break their contracts. This bold act inflamed his critics and further marked him as a traitor to Austria. "Clemens Krauss is now enthroned at the Berlin State Opera, mantled in all sorts of Jovian powers and prerogatives," wrote the classical music correspondent for the *New York Times* in February 1935. "He lost no time in asserting his rights of sovereignty."[29] Outwardly, at least, Krauss began to follow the Nazi Party line when it came to degenerate musicians. He publicly badmouthed the work of Alban Berg, whom he had once championed. He made a point of denouncing "the fallacies of atonality" and "the fruitless musical experiments of the moderns."[30]

Krauss became increasingly sidelined, hated by Berlin's diehard opera fans who demanded the return of Furtwängler. The *New York Times* noted: "The Nazi chieftains who with all sorts of enticements, lured Krauss away from the Vienna Staatsoper nearly two years ago to fill the berth of the Berlin State Opera precipitately vacated by Furtwängler, found themselves unable to cram him down the throats of the Berlin public and before long there was talk of shipping him somewhere else."[31]

Adding to Krauss's isolation in Berlin, the Nazis forced Krauss's protector Strauss to resign his presidency of the Reich Music Chamber after they intercepted a letter he wrote to his Jewish librettist Stefan Zweig in the summer of 1935. In the letter, Strauss told Zweig "that he was only playacting" as the president of the Reich Music Chamber "to prevent the worst from happening."[32] After Nazi censors seized the letter, the Gestapo visited him at his home in Garmisch in southern Germany to compel him to resign and to cite ailing health as his reason for stepping down. Strauss complied although he wrote a letter to Hitler to beg for his job back. Hitler never replied.

"I consider it my duty to warn you," began a letter from Strauss to his protégé in the autumn of 1935. "Indirectly, I learned in a Berlin meeting that the minister [Hermann Goering] pronounced himself very ugly about you. You cannot fight with the clueless, so be careful."[33] Clearly, Krauss was getting grief from all directions. And while he was beloved of Hitler and Goebbels, the volatile Goering was still not yet one of his supporters.

But Krauss's incredible rise continued despite that lack of backing, and in 1936 he was awarded the greatest artistic prize in Germany: the Bavarian State Opera in Munich. The Bavarian capital, where Hitler had founded the Nazi Party, was to be a centerpiece of Nazi culture, which Hitler hoped would come to rival the Salzburg Festival. He commissioned a sweeping reconstruction to overhaul the city's transit system, create grand new government buildings, and renovate the Bavarian State Opera house. Krauss, whom Hitler had come to recognize as "a brilliant organizer," was put in charge of the opera as both general manager and music director. In his new role at the Munich Opera, Krauss was set to receive 400,000 Reichsmarks in annual operating costs—a staggering amount, equivalent to nearly $20 million today.

Krauss's critics were further incensed. Furtwängler, for one, could not understand why the conductor, who in his opinion "has failed in the face of Berlin audiences," would be given such an important promotion. "He is not in a position to really fill Wagner, not to mention Beethoven and the classics. And the most important part in the new Germany—Munich—is to be handed over to this man!"[34] Still, Krauss had his work cut out for him in Munich. "It is also said that he will return from time to time to Berlin and conduct there," wrote Peyser of Krauss's new appointment. "All of which cannot disguise the fact that his Berlin sojourn was a fizzle. Will he be much more acceptable to the good people of Munich who, in the course of more than a decade, developed a strong affection for conductor Hans Knappertsbusch and would like to have him back, irrespective of his political intransigence?"[35]

Knappertsbusch's intransigence took the form of openly insulting the Nazi Party and producing *Lucedia*, an opera by the American composer Vittorio Giannini. The Nazis accused the beloved conductor—who was a blond, blue-eyed giant of a man and had been at the helm of the Munich Opera for fourteen years—of favoring foreign talent at the expense of German artists. As such, he was forbidden to conduct in Germany. The Nazi Party additionally claimed that Knappertsbusch, a leading interpreter of Strauss and Richard Wagner, had openly insulted the Nazi Party when he inquired if a German diplomat in the Netherlands had been forced to join the party in order to secure his future. It was an odd turn of affairs for a man who, on the surface, appeared to be the very epitome of the perfect Aryan. Before his falling out with the Nazi Party, Knappertsbusch had moved in nationalistic circles and had even refused to perform in Paris because he still considered France an enemy as one of the victors of the First World War. In 1933, after several of his colleagues left their posts for political reasons, he said that he would rather "toil in a quarry than leave Germany."[36] However despite his loyalty, Knappertsbusch ran afoul of the Nazi Party, largely because Hitler had never liked him.

Ursuleac and Krauss watched the drama over Knappertsbusch with a great deal of concern. They understood that the Nazis would use even the most minor offences as a pretext to rid the country of those who did not support them. And they knew that if they wanted to save Mayer-Lismann, and perhaps others, they would accomplish nothing by pleading their cases with members of the ruling party.

After Mayer-Lismann approached the couple for help in 1934, they knew they had to be careful. And clever—more so than their Nazi censors, neighbors, police, and the press. "Give nothing of yourself in writing," Krauss was fond of saying, rarely recording anything controversial on paper.[37] Most importantly, they would have to carry out any subversive activities—namely the saving of their "undesirable" friends—in the shadows. And in silence, which carried its own dangers.

After Mayer-Lismann's visit to London in 1935, the Cooks became keenly aware of the nightmare that was descending upon Jews in Germany with the application of the Nuremberg Laws.

On March 7, 1936, the same day that Hitler's troops marched into the Rhineland, Jewish violinist Bronislaw Huberman wrote an extraordinary letter to the *Manchester Guardian* denouncing the Nuremberg Laws as "this document of barbarism" and blaming intellectuals for not standing up to Hitler. "Before the whole world I accuse you, German intellectuals, you non-Nazis, as those truly guilty of all these Nazi crimes, all this lamentable breakdown of a great people."[38] Huberman, who was among the first musicians to leave the Reich after the Nazis came to power, accused his peers of appeasement of an evil regime—the same response that the Allies adopted when the Germans so flagrantly violated the terms of the Treaty of Versailles by sending troops into a demilitarized zone. Huberman, who would go on to found the Palestine Symphony Orchestra later that year, continued: "It is not the first time in history that the gutter has reached out for power, but it remained for the German intellectuals to assist the gutter to achieve success. It is a horrifying drama…"[39]

The gutter was also reaching out in London. It was happening in the city's impoverished East End, where on October 4, Oswald Mosley and his black-shirted followers staged an anti-Semitic march, denouncing Jews as "rats and vermin from the gutter." Although more than one hundred thousand local residents had petitioned the government to stop the fascist demonstrators, who had been openly planning their protest for weeks, they were rebuffed when police sent more than seven thousand officers to make sure the marchers were undisturbed. Between one hundred thousand and five hundred thousand local residents (news reports differ widely) joined together to block the fascists in what came to be known as the Battle of Cable Street. Armed with broken furniture, chamber pots, and other improvised weapons, Jewish and Irish neighbors joined forces under the leadership of leftist groups to rout the fascists. Even children rolled marbles on the street to trip up police horses. Shouting, "They Shall Not Pass"—a nod to the Spanish Republicans who resisted General Franco earlier that year—the crowds forced out Mosley and his supporters.

Although the gutter mob was temporarily defeated in London, they were triumphant in Germany. To their credit, both Krauss and Ursuleac saw what the gutter was doing in the Reich early on, when Ursuleac asked the Cooks to help Mayer-Lismann.

"Louise and I would never have started our refugee work without the encouragement of those two, and we could never have maintained it without their help," wrote Ida, recalling that when they arrived in Frankfurt to help the Mayer-Lismann family, they began to formulate a plan to help them.[40] Opera was central to the plot, and they would use their love of the art form as an excuse to visit their new friends in the Third Reich. On that first visit, the Cooks were met at the train station by Mayer-Lismann herself, who held out two tickets to that evening's opera performance featuring Krauss and Ursuleac.

And so the work began, with almost no preparation except the promise of great opera, which was their cover when they crossed into the Third Reich to interview their Jewish refugees. If anyone asked, they were simply opera fans, journeying to attend "Krauss and Ursuleac's superb performances." And that is what they would tell the border guards. But it would require both courage and ingenuity, and, as 1936 came to a close, Ida and Louise found themselves entering an international stage to perform in a real-life drama that was part farce, part tragedy.

CHAPTER 5

The Operas

"**M**y dear Cook girls!" began the cheery letter in German from Viorica Ursuleac, inviting the sisters to a much-anticipated June 1937 performance of Wagner's *The Flying Dutchman*, conducted by her husband—one of the centerpieces of his new residency at the Bavarian State Opera house in Munich. "It would be wonderful if you could come for this performance."[1] It was an innocent-enough missive full of the details of Ursuleac's hectic operatic schedule—one that had her rehearsing for *Fidelio* in Hanover one day, then immediately traveling to Munich and Nauheim for a series of concerts, before heading to Berlin for a performance of *Tannhauser*, and appropriately culminating with the June performance of a Wagner opera about an accursed sailor who spends years at sea trying to get home. "Always on the road!" she wrote in the May 23 letter, lavishing praise on Louise for learning German so quickly. "Thank you very much for your kind lines, especially for the good German of Louise. Her German is really very good."[2] Louise, the diligent bureaucrat, had taken it upon herself to learn the language when she and Ida became serious about saving Jews. "Many of the people spoke English, but

Louise gradually was able to interview those who spoke only German," wrote Ida.[3] Of course, Louise's German also came in handy when communicating about their complex mission with Ursuleac, who spoke only halting English.

On that first trip to Frankfurt to visit Mayer-Lismann, the Cooks had worked out a plan with Krauss and Ursuleac not only to use opera as a cover for their trips to the Third Reich, but also to spend their days meeting other Jews planning to escape and plotting how they could help them spirit some of their assets to England.

Although the invitation to *The Flying Dutchman* seemed simple enough, the letter was just one in a series of ruses created by the soprano, Krauss, and the Cooks to give the sisters an excuse to make the journey from England to Germany in order to coordinate their refugee activities. Should Reich censors ever attempt to intercept the correspondence as they did with Strauss's letter to Zweig, there would be nothing except opera schedules and an invitation to a premiere. What could be more innocent than two British opera fans so committed to the art form that they thought nothing of traveling to Germany on their days off? The Nazi hierarchy would surely understand this devotion, for who wouldn't want to hear great music conducted by a master and sung by Viorica Ursuleac, an operatic superstar?

During that summer visit to Munich, the sisters spent their days in secret meetings with Jews desperate to escape. At night, they gratefully took their seats—next to the "high Nazis"—in the theater. On the evening of Saturday, June 12, 1937, the sisters were relieved and exhilarated to be watching their friend in the role of Senta, the daughter of a Norwegian sailor who symbolizes redemption for the wandering Dutchman. "Although Strauss roles were her specialty, Ursuleac was also a splendid Mozart singer, the best Senta in *The Flying Dutchman* we ever heard."[4] In *The Flying*

Dutchman, Senta leaves her betrothed, Erik, and promises undying love to the mysterious sailor. Senta's devotion is the Dutchman's only source of salvation, with the power to lift the curse that casts him to the waves every seven years. They may not have realized it right away, but the Cooks became modern-day Sentas to the Jewish refugees in Germany, accursed under Hitler. In many ways *The Flying Dutchman* would become a leitmotif for the next few years of their lives.

The more the sisters embarked on "those feverish visits"[5] to Nazi Germany to interview would-be refugees, the more they understood that they were the final hope of salvation for these Jews. And it didn't take very long for their fame to spread through the Jewish underground. In addition to Senta, the sisters may have drawn inspiration for their undercover work from *Arabella*, Strauss's three-act opera about two sisters who shift identities and manipulate situations to achieve their goals.

Like characters in a farce, the Cooks entered the Reich from one border and exited absentmindedly from another. They hammed up their roles as themselves—obsessive opera groupies who would stop at nothing to attend the performances of the great Viorica Ursuleac. Ida's steady income from her book sales allowed them to stay at the finest hotels in each of the cities they visited—which were in plain sight of all society. "Clemens Krauss told us that a good underground trick to avoid suspicion was to stay at a hotel frequented by the Storm Troopers' officers," said Ida,[6] who frequently booked rooms at the Hotel Adlon in Berlin and the Vier Jahreszeiten in Munich. If they were lodging among the high-ranking Nazis then no one would suspect these women of daring to defy them. "If one is right in the center of the gang like that no one could suspect one of helping Jews," they reasoned. "We knew them all by sight—Goering, and Goebbels, Himmler and Streicher—even Hitler from the back."[7]

In fact, it was at the Vier Jahreszeiten that Nazi Foreign Minister Joachim von Ribbentrop, a wealthy former wine merchant as well as a former ambassador to the Court of Saint James, ogled the very Aryan-looking Louise across the breakfast room.[8] Louise, blonde and with luminous white skin, was always the more feminine and demure of the sisters. She took extra care with her appearance and never went out in public without applying a coat of red lipstick, recalled a friend. While she wasn't a beauty as a young woman, she was tall and striking, towering over her younger sister but decidedly more fragile.

Yet despite the uncomfortable reality of their situation, surrounded by Nazis, the Cooks were possibly for the first time imbued with a sense of purpose and counted themselves lucky to be in a position to aid people in such dire need. "Oh, blessed light romance that kept the money rolling in. We spent our time during the week pounding on doors in London, begging for guarantors for these desperate people. It was hard work. Lots of English thought that the Government ought to admit refugees and perhaps build camps for them, but when it came to personally guaranteeing their welfare, it was another story. We made endless telephone calls and visits."[9]

They had started the refugee work with Mitia Mayer-Lismann simply because she was the first Jew Ursuleac had introduced them to who desperately needed their help, although it would be nearly two years before they were able to secure her safe passage to London. In the meantime, there was her twenty-three-year-old daughter Else Mayer-Lismann who became the first refugee to occupy their Dolphin Square flat in 1937. "I was the last Jew—really the last—in Germany who was allowed to take a state examination in music at Dr. Hoch's Conservatoire in Frankfurt am Main in 1937," recalled Else Mayer-Lismann. "After my diploma, which did not allow me to teach…I left Germany a week after the examination for England….My escape was very easy."[10] Although she was a gifted music student, Else

Mitia Mayer-Lismann was an opera scholar from Frankfurt and the first Jew the Cooks ever met. *Yad Vashem Archives*

had little future at the elite conservatory where only 1 percent of Jews could be retained as staff. When half the conservatory choir walked out in protest when faced with a Jewish teacher, the Mayer-Lismanns knew their daughter had to leave the country.

The Cooks discussed ways to get Else Mayer-Lismann out of the country at her mother's elegant dinner table in Frankfurt where they had been invited to lunch on another visit to Frankfurt. One of the guests was inquiring about the fate of an elderly friend who had just died and someone else mentioned how sad it was that he was forced to die without the aid of a nurse. The Cooks were shocked and asked why this had been the case.

"Well, don't you see, there wasn't a Jewish nurse available and no Aryan nurse over the age of forty-five," came the response.

The sisters stared in bewilderment, even though they had been repeatedly told about the Nazi edicts that stripped Jews of their basic rights.

"Haven't you heard of the Nuremberg Laws? Under them no male Jew must be nursed by an Aryan nurse under the age of forty-five," someone said rather impatiently.

"But why not?" asked the sisters in unison.

"Don't you understand the implication? No young woman is supposed to be safe with a Jewish man."

It was what Ida called "the obscene cynicism of that insult" that brought everything home to them as nothing else had.

And as they sat at that sophisticated Frankfurt dining room table, both sisters burst into "furious tears and cried and cried" while their anxious hosts tried to comfort them. "It's so ridiculous—so odious," blubbered the sisters. "Things can't *be* like that!"[11]

But they were.

Else Mayer-Lismann was one of the lucky refugees, admitted to Britain under a provision that allowed Jewish refugees to settle in the country if they were students, industrialists, noted academics, or established artists. Unable to obtain a visa for a music student, the Cooks ingeniously managed to get her into the country as an apprentice chef. At the time, cooking was much more in demand than music, noted Ida.[12] Stefan Zweig was welcomed in 1935 under the same program, as were Jews who had the means to invest in the country and create much needed jobs. The government also wanted immigrants who could enhance Britain's prestige in some way or fill particular occupations. Most importantly, the difficult economic times meant the new immigrants needed to be able to provide evidence that they would be able to support themselves.

"We weren't playing God," Ida said, referring to how the sisters decided who to help. "It was more like gambling at Monte Carlo."[13] As Ida was to quickly realize, "the Jew who had a practical skill—an electrician or an engineer—sometimes made it ahead of the intellectual. The one who had converted all his material assets into diamonds or what-have-you and was able to demonstrate to his English guarantor that he would not become dependent on him had it over the man and his wife who were still clinging—as though furniture were a part of life itself—to their bedsteads and family portraits."[14] In other words, their predicament was not enough to save them—they needed to have some kind of worth. And money, assets, or valuables—all could mean life.

As early as 1933, the Jewish community in London began mobilizing to lobby the government to allow Jews into the country. The Board of Deputies of British Jews set up a series of aid agencies at their offices at Woburn House, determined to provide financial help and other aid to Jewish refugees so that the government had no excuse to turn them away. After Hitler had come to power that January, the British government accepted only a modest number of refugees. By April, as the country began to be faced with hundreds of German Jews clamoring to enter, elected officials were forced to come up with a more coherent policy, especially as local Jewish organizations pressed for change. But with rising unemployment in the country, the government feared that extreme right-wing groups such as Mosley's British Union of Fascists might seize on a sudden influx of Jewish refugees to whip up anti-Semitism.

The same was true of the United States where Congress had previously passed a law in 1924 setting immigration quotas from each country. The quotas were designed to "protect" American racial stock by limiting the number of immigrants from Asia, Africa, and Jews from Europe. With the advent of the Great Depression, the U.S. government sought to make sure that immigrants did not become a financial burden on the government. In 1933 the U.S. government issued only 1,241 visas to people applying from Germany, even though there were 82,787 people on the waiting list from that country, according to statistics compiled by the United States Holocaust Museum in Washington, D.C. Despite an increasing demand, only an average of 7,000 visas were issued to German citizens—most of them Jews—between 1934 and 1937. The waiting list continued to grow in that period, with an average of more than 88,000 Germans seeking a visa.

As Else Mayer-Lismann arrived in England and settled into their Dolphin Square flat, the Cooks researched the various ways in which they could bring others to Britain. It was hard going at the beginning, as there were limits on the numbers that they could bring in on student visas and domestic permits. Those who sponsored refugees from Germany had to sign guarantees in which they pledged to the British government that they would pay all of their expenses. Although the Cooks personally undertook financial responsibility for Else Mayer-Lismann and others, their own funds were limited. As their refugee work continued, they prevailed upon friends and community groups to help sponsor others.

Like Else Mayer-Lismann, Friedl Bamberger was twenty-three when she arrived in London and moved into the Cooks' Dolphin Square flat in the early part of 1938. The families of the two young women knew each other from Frankfurt am Main, where Bamberger had been a student of Mitia Mayer-Lismann and the girls had attended the same high school together. Bamberger finished high school after the Nazis came to power. As a Jew, she could not enroll in university where she had hoped to study journalism and law. Her father, a wealthy merchant who owned a chain of men's clothing stores, died of a heart attack in spring 1934. "The difficulties, threats and denunciation to which he had been exposed by the Nazis had proved too great a strain on his already weakened heart," said Bamberger. After his death, "all I wanted...was to leave the country."[15]

She found her escape in Rome where a cousin—the movie director Max Ophüls—was working on a film. He offered her a job in his cutting room and an opportunity to apprentice as a film editor. Backed by a small monthly allowance from her mother, Elisabeth Bamberger, Friedl Bamberger left for Italy. But barely a month after arriving in Rome, Ophüls fell out with his producers and left for Paris to work on a new project. "Almost at the same time my allowance was stopped by a new government decree." Although her mother suggested she return to Germany, Bamberger decided to stay, and "by sheer bluff and by false pretenses," she managed to obtain small jobs in the film industry, mostly as a German translator.[16] But even in the years when Italian leader Benito Mussolini considered Germany an enemy, anti-Semitism and nationalism were on the rise in Italy just as they were in Germany. "Although the Italians responded to the Nazi racial dogma with contempt and cynicism, the doors of employment nevertheless became shut to a German Jewess," said Bamberger.[17]

Life in Italy soon proved untenable. Bamberger, who had dislocated her knee while skiing in Germany, was in almost constant pain because the joint had loosened over time and "the cartilage kept slipping out at the slightest provocation and each time when this happened I was immobilized for days." She knew she needed surgery but had no way of paying for it in Italy. To make matters even more complicated, she had fallen in love with an Italian reporter, Ruggero Orlando, a fierce opponent of Italian fascism who was barred from working at any newspaper or radio station. "Unemployed, living in a state of precarious freedom, he wanted to leave Italy as much as I did," Bamberger said.

The plan was for her to return to Germany and have surgery on her knee at her mother's expense, and then meet Orlando in Paris where Ophüls had settled to make films. Orlando pawned his photo equipment to buy Bamberger a train ticket to return to Frankfurt. But it was an ominous arrival. As soon as her train entered German territory her passport was confiscated by border guards. It would be returned to her, the officers assured her, if she was able to obtain a visa to travel to a foreign country. "My mother was still living in Frankfurt, held captive by exorbitant tax requests which she could not pay before having realized all our estate," said Bamberger. "I settled down in her apartment, had my operation and waited for my French visa." The answer came in due course: "Working permit refused, visa refused." Trapped in Frankfurt, Bamberger heard Nazi paramilitaries, known as "brownshirts" because of the color of their uniforms, outside her windows every night, "howling about 'the Jew blood splashing from our knives.'" She despaired.

A month after the French visa fell through, Mayer-Lismann invited the Bambergers to lunch with the Cooks at her "half-dismantled apartment." With her daughter Else safely installed in London, the rest of the family was preparing to join her there as soon as they could leave.

"I knew who the Cooks were," said Bamberger. "Their name and fame had already spread through the Jewish community of Frankfurt and of other German and Austrian towns as well. To be able to meet them was in itself a privilege, a source of hope, a possible chance of salvation." She was hesitant and nervous as she waited for them to show up for lunch. "I had expected that the sisters would watch me, scrutinize me, look me over, but there was nothing of the sort. They just seemed to accept me as a casual acquaintance."[18]

For their part, the Cooks had difficulty understanding Bamberger's English as she had learned only a few statements by rote, and she spewed out what she needed to say in one piece. "She was really keyed up to a high pitch of nerves," observed Ida. "As we listened, one certain thing emerged. She wanted to lean on no one. She was prepared to do any work, live at any level, sacrifice anything, in order not to take more than the barest necessities." After Bamberger's little speech, Ida turned to Louise in silent acquiescence: there was no doubt between them that they would help this young woman escape to England.[19]

"When I left the Mayer-Lismanns' house my life had changed," said Bamberger. "I was to go to England. The Cooks were going to enroll me in a language school so that I could enter on a student's permit—the only kind of permit still available…I don't think it had taken them five minutes to work out this solution to my seemingly insoluble problem."[20] But the visa did not allow Bamberger to work in England, a situation that caused her a great deal of anxiety. She didn't want to be a burden on the Cooks, and she could no longer rely on her mother for an allowance. With almost no understanding of the English language, how was Bamberger going to survive? The sisters came up with a plan. Once her English improved, Ida would rewrite some of her stories as screenplays so that Bamberger (with her film world contacts) could sell the movie rights. "She must have been aware that the chance of selling film rights is one in a thousand," said Bamberger. "I knew then, as I know now, that the whole scheme was merely designed to allay my scruples."[21]

Friedl Bamberger left Germany for England on February 22, 1938, after paying a Reich flight tax of 4,500 Reichsmarks or \$1,800, and a special Jewish levy of 18,000 Reichsmarks or \$7,200.[22] "I was in London, going to school, living in the Cooks' flat, receiving from them a weekly allowance, protected by them and their friends," said Bamberger, who was so worried about incurring too many costs that the Cooks suffered "serious anxiety" over her well-being.[23] As Ida noted, "We could not make her eat enough because she wanted to cost us as little as possible."[24]

Friedl Bamberger and Else Mayer-Lismann were among the luckiest of the Cooks' refugee cases, spirited out of the Reich before the brutality escalated after the Nazis annexed Austria.

■   ■   ■

On the weekend of March 12–13, 1938, the Nazis consolidated their hold on Austria. Days before, when Chancellor Schuschnigg got wind of the possible coup attempt against him, he called for a meeting with Hitler, hoping that he could maintain Austrian independence. Hitler refused to meet him and forced the Austrian chancellor to appoint Nazis to his cabinet. On March 9, Schuschnigg called for a plebiscite on the issue of the annexation, and two days later he resigned under pressure from the Nazis. He was placed under house arrest until the end of May when he was moved to a tiny room in the Hotel Metropole where the Gestapo had set up their headquarters. He was forced to clean latrines with a towel the Nazis had given him for his personal use.

With the Austrian chancellor out of the way, Hitler had made sure that Mussolini was on his side and would not block his efforts to take over the country. On March 12, German tanks and troops began to cross the German-Austrian border on their way to Vienna. In many places, the Nazis were greeted by cheering crowds of Austrians. Under the headline "Hitler Strikes Again," the *New York Times* reported that "Austria, long denied an opportunity to throw in her lot with Germany when both these nations were democratic states, now falls victim to a Germany in which...tyranny is master."[25]

In Britain, an editorial in the *Yorkshire Post*, which was viewed as the mouthpiece of Anthony Eden, former foreign secretary, noted that Germany's behavior in Austria would only serve to embolden Hitler and that Britain's weak words of protest to the departing Nazi ambassador von Ribbentrop were delivered too late.[26] In fact, on March 11, as British leaders learned of the ultimatum that Germany had delivered to Austria a day before the annexation, von Ribbentrop had attended a farewell luncheon in his honor at 10 Downing Street, hosted by Prime Minister Neville Chamberlain. That same afternoon, von Ribbentrop returned to Berlin to assume his new position as foreign minister.

Faced with the imminent invasion of Austria by the Nazis, the British did what they had done when Hitler invaded the Rhineland— nothing.

It didn't take long for violence to erupt against Jews after the Anschluss, the annexation of Austria. Less than twenty-four hours after the country was incorporated into the Third Reich, the Gestapo and Austrian Nazis went on a rampage looting and destroying Jewish businesses and synagogues. "For the first few weeks the behavior of the Vienna Nazis was worse than anything I had seen in Germany," wrote radio reporter William Shirer, who covered the Anschluss. "There was an orgy of sadism. Day after day, large numbers of Jewish men and women could be seen scrubbing Schuschnigg signs off the sidewalk and cleaning the gutters. While they worked on their hands and knees with jeering storm troopers standing over them, crowds gathered to taunt them."[27] Hundreds more Jews were "picked off the streets" and put to work cleaning public toilets. More than 1,700 suicides were officially reported in Austria in the days before the Anschluss, although the real number was probably much higher as the media was heavily censored. "I myself from our apartment in the Plosslgasse watched squads of SS men carting off silver, tapestries, paintings and other loot from the Rothschild palace next door," Shirer wrote, adding that during the mêlée SS officer Heinrich Himmler and Gestapo chief Reinhard Heydrich began setting up the Mauthausen concentration camp so that they would not have the trouble of shipping prisoners all the way to Germany. The new camp was only two hours west of Vienna.[28]

Tens of thousands of Jews clamored to leave the country, and the British consul general in Vienna reported that his building was "literally besieged every day by hundreds of Jews."[29] By April, British authorities created a new visa system that required that Jews obtain their entry visas before leaving the Third Reich. Thousands of

Austrian Jews applied to leave for Britain in the days and weeks after the Anschluss, including writer Elias Canetti, George Weidenfeld, who would later become a celebrated publisher, and the neurologist and founder of psychoanalysis Sigmund Freud who escaped with his daughter Anna and wife Martha.

On April 26, the Nazis' "Decree for the Reporting of Jewish-Owned Property" came into effect. The new law required all Jews in the Reich to register any property valued at more than 5,000 Reichsmarks (about $2,000 in U.S. currency at the time or $34,000 today). Jews were required to register everything from land to furniture, artwork, and life insurance. Three months after the law came into effect, the German finance ministry registered more than 7 billion Reichsmarks worth of property from seven hundred thousand Jews—assets that the government prepared to "Aryanize," a euphemism for widespread theft.

In Vienna, German-Austrian SS officer Adolf Eichmann, a former itinerant vacuum cleaner salesman who had joined the Nazi Party in 1932, worked with his assistant and "right-hand man" Alois Brunner to expel as many Jews as possible from Austria. Amid the grandeur of one of the plundered Rothschild palaces in Vienna, Eichmann's newly created Central Agency for Jewish Emigration began issuing exit visas to Jews who had managed to find other countries that would take them in. All Jews who planned to leave Austria needed a stamp from Eichmann's organization in their passports. Some also needed passports. The stamp and the passport were only issued in exchange for the surrender of all their valuables. Jews were forced to give up their stocks, savings accounts, jewelry, homes, land, and vehicles if they wished to leave the country. Within a few months, Eichmann and Brunner had dispatched more than 150,000 Jews out of Austria. Later, Eichmann headed to Prague and Berlin to set up similar offices, and Brunner would be assigned to Vichy France and

Slovakia to organize the deportation of hundreds of thousands of Jews to death camps.

In the summer of 1938, while Eichmann and Brunner were busy setting up the bureaucratic machinery to rob Jews on their way out of Austria, Ida Cook was drumming up support for her refugees in England after she and Louise and their immediate circle had come to the end of their own financial resources. "I had never before in my life spoken in public, but I thought, 'This is my chance! And I'm not sitting down until I've said all I want to say!'" she recalled of the first time she spoke at a conference on refugees in London.[30] After that, Ida took every opportunity to speak before church and community groups in order to raise awareness of the situation in the Reich and persuade people to offer personal guarantees in order to allow Jews to enter the United Kingdom.

As she frequently did in an emergency, Ida fell back on her roots in Northumberland. At a meeting of the Alnwick District Association at the Imperial Hotel in Russell Square in May 1938, Ida made sure she was the first item on the organization's agenda: "Miss I. Cook Talks on a Visit to Germany."

"She spoke ... of the spiritual slavery engendered by a controlled press, controlled radio, censorship of letters and telephone calls, unrivalled system of espionage and 'informing' and persecution of most forms of religion," noted a report in the *Alnwick and County Gazette*. She also described how censorship and "carefully prepared news films" informed Germans' views of the outside world. "They were told and many believed that there was a worldwide shortage of anything they themselves lacked, such as butter; they understood that bitter political unrest existed in every country but their own."

"Miss Cook recounted how she was seriously questioned about the 'terrible outbreaks of typhoid' which swept London. With difficulty she was able to reconcile this picture of London 'bringing out the dead' with the relatively small outbreak of typhoid in Croydon." Nonetheless, that "relatively small outbreak" did cause forty-three deaths and infected nearly three hundred people in the London suburb in the autumn of 1937, according to news reports.

Ida ended her presentation with her most important point: "The almost unbelievable persecution of the Jews." No doubt Ida wanted to leave her audience with an image of the brutality aimed against so many who were part of "Germany's musical, artistic and literary lights." In a powerful conclusion, Ida asked her audience "what was to happen to a country which was systematically driving overseas all the best brains of the race, by the simple process of making it impossible for everyone to live there if they had sufficient intelligence to question the official order of things?"[31] She knew she "had struck a vein of gold" with her public entreaties, as after her lectures she was often inundated with offers to help bring Jews to safety.[32]

Ida also headed to Hyde Park Speakers' Corner, standing on a wooden crate in frigid temperatures and summer heatwaves describing her and Louise's latest trips to Germany and Austria to anyone who would listen. "I was talking to a crowd of about 50 persons when I felt someone jog my elbow," she told an interviewer. "I looked down and saw a sleazily dressed young man. I had no way of knowing whether he was with me or against me. I shook him off but he kept tugging at my sleeve." Later, the man asked permission to speak but Ida continued to cut him off. "No, no, that's not allowed! Get your own crowd!" she admonished. But he was not to be dissuaded. "He jumped up on the box when I stepped down, however, and he said, "I just want you to know that I have just escaped from Germany and everything this lady says is true. They are getting ready to slaughter the entire Jewish community. Please! You must help others to come here."[33]

■   ■   ■

"Mein Führer, Allow me to take the liberty of writing to you on a matter that has kept me busy since you brought, Mein Führer, our glorious country home to the Reich," began the bold and obsequious letter from Clemens Krauss to Adolf Hitler on April 25, 1938. Krauss went on to apologize for bothering the very busy chancellor of Germany and now Austria during this crucial time when so many "innumerable vital questions need to be resolved" but, in his opinion, the very future of the Vienna State Opera was at stake. "I am Viennese and, following the voice of my heart, I would ask you to reinstate me," he wrote. "I led this institution for five years before you gave me my assignment to work for the Reich."

His high-risk direct appeal sought more funds for the Munich Opera and to merge the two institutions under his leadership. Krauss was unhappy with the management of the Vienna Opera under Erwin Kerber and conductor Bruno Walter, a German Jew, whose original surname was Schlesinger. This, despite the fact that he himself had been appointed artistic director by Kerber in 1936. "Vienna and Munich are each, in their own way, the leading cities of the now united southern cultural sphere of the Reich," continued Krauss. "Both cities…must claim their leadership role in opera," and he described Vienna as "radiating German culture far beyond the borders of the Reich." Ever self-aware and calculating, Krauss openly acknowledged that his proposal "could easily be interpreted as a manifestation of excessive ambition or crude self-praise," but, he insisted, "I am strengthened by my firm conviction, that in the years to come, in the interests of the peaceful development of the Munich and Vienna operas, competition would be unfavorable to both, and a common artistic leadership would be more economical and undoubtedly more advantageous." He signed his letter "with deepest veneration and gratitude."[34]

Krauss was initially rebuffed, although he continued to make guest appearances throughout the Reich and continued to add to the prestige of the Munich State Opera. In addition to Ursuleac, he had secured baritone Hans Hotter for Munich. Although Hotter, one of the greatest Wagner interpreters, refused to join the Nazi Party, he was a favorite of the Führer's.

However, Krauss's maneuvering gradually worked. By the summer of 1938, he was well on his way to entering that rarefied circle of Hitler favorites—a position of power that would enable him to secure safe passage for Jews to England, for which he would always need the Cooks.

"Before we left Germany each time, he [Krauss] would get us to tell him which dates we wanted covered," said Ida. That way they could easily bluff their way through frontier interviews with inquiring border guards. Krauss would arrange for opera performances in the cities where the Cooks needed to meet refugees. If they had to be in Munich on a certain date, he would let them know ahead of time the opera he was planning to stage there. "If he was in a good mood, he would let us choose our opera."[35]

But the sisters were increasingly less motivated by opera itself. They now fully understood, and had seen, how Jews attempting to leave both Germany and Austria would have to surrender all their valuables, pay thousands in flight taxes, and only take out of the country the pittance of ten Reichsmarks if they were emigrating. "A great many nasty remarks have been made about so-called rich Jews who fled the Nazis and took their millions with them," said Louise. "It is so absurd. There may have been a few who were shrewd enough in the early 1930s to salt some escape money away in Swiss banks. But the vast number just had to sell everything they owned and convert it into assets that could be smuggled. Furs and jewels. That was about it."[36]

And so within these limitations the sisters made their plan. It started with the jewelry and furs—anything they themselves could wear across an international border. In the months leading up to the Second World War, Ida would describe the sisters' "bosoms quivering with smuggled jewels."[37] They guessed that set against their very modest clothes, the diamond brooches, gold pendants, and bracelets would simply look like so much cheap costume jewelry—far too ostentatious to seem real. "I was wearing a six-and-eleven penny Marks & Spencer jumper—of jacquard satin, with glass buttons down the front," said Ida. "And I thought: *If I plaster this on top and can make myself come out with my coat open, it wouldn't possibly be anything but Woolworth's.*"[38]

Of course, their big fear became the "black guard" as Ida referred to them—the SS guards who would suddenly board the trains at frontier checkpoints to crack down against smuggling. "We were a little frightened," Ida confessed after one harrowing situation as they were leaving Germany.[39] Both sisters had sat bolt upright as a group of SS officers lingered in the corridor outside their compartment for what felt like a full half-hour.

Covered in strings of pearls, diamond necklaces, their sweaters plastered with bejeweled brooches, their bosoms rose and fell as Ida and Louise tried desperately to still an overwhelming sense of fear. They wore bracelets and a Swiss watch each, and their hands sparkled with the dazzling rings that they could fit over their thinnest fingers. Their handbags were filled with the rest of the jewelry that they had promised to spirit out of the country. Worried that the guards would ask them to open their bags, they had come up with a cover story. They were going to launch into their "nervous British spinster act and insist, quite simply, that we always took our valuables with us, because we didn't trust anyone with whom we could leave them at home."[40]

They had practiced the routine time and again. "It's rather good," said Louise. "There's absolutely no comeback on it."

"No," said Ida. "They can say, 'How ridiculous!' or 'What sort of a family have *they* got?' or 'Silly asses.' But they can't say, 'That isn't true.' Provided we never take earrings for pierced ears of course."

They flatly refused to take such earrings—the pearl studs, the gold loops, the dangling emeralds, and the Cartier platinum– and diamond-chandelier-like bijoux that were a favorite of film and theater stars in the 1930s. The thought of having their ears pierced, even for their good cause, was too awful to contemplate. Ida claimed not to have the courage to do it, and Louise grew faint just thinking of the pain, which she imagined was worse than having a tooth out. They may have been only amateur smugglers, but Ida and Louise were no fools, and they were not going to get caught at the German border loaded with earrings that they could never wear themselves.[41]

The furs could also have tripped them up. When their refugees asked them to transport their furs back to England, the sisters realized that they would need British labels sewn into the coats. As Louise noted:

> Any of the furriers would have given us labels, but nothing looks newer than a new label in an old coat....So we went around London appealing to well-dressed women to rip labels out of their coats. Once they caught on, it was quite a fad. We used to go direct from the airport or train station to the home of the prospective refugee. There we would rip off the German labels, sew in the London ones, pin on the jewellery, stuff our suitcases, and go on to the hotel.[42]

Each of the sisters would try on the fur coat to see who looked best in it, and then they would enter their grand hotel lobby "in a state of innocent magnificence."[43] It was an exhausting, almost military, exercise, and they made sure to check in to their luxury German and Austrian hotels with overstuffed suitcases, looking the very picture of moneyed international travelers. "We came into the Cologne airport each Friday evening with practically empty suitcases, shivering in our tweed suits," said Ida. "And we went across the Dutch border on Sunday wearing furs, sparkling with jewellery and scarcely able to drag our bags. We were smuggling out people's lives."[44] As soon as they landed in London, Ida took the valuables to deposit boxes they had rented at British banks, and Louise went to work.

Smuggling Jewish cash out of the Third Reich, however, was a bigger problem.

■   ■   ■

"Would you be so very kind as to have two stalls reserved for us for both the *Ariadne* performance and the *Palestrina*?" wrote Ida to Erik Maschat on June 9, 1938. "We can just manage the weekend nicely if we leave here by the last aeroplane to Cologne on Friday evening and then come by the night train to Munich."[45]

During the summer opera festivals in Munich, organized by Krauss, Ida would put together trips for dozens of English opera fans. "I used to constitute myself 'manager' even to the point of dealing with all the financial arrangements."[46] For this purpose, she co-opted the very efficient Erik Maschat, Clemens Krauss's personal assistant in Munich, who managed all Krauss's affairs and who was a member of the Nazi Party. For Ida and Louise, he was a useful, if unwitting, accomplice to their scheme and a great alibi. Krauss had instructed him to secure tickets for any opera they wanted to attend in Germany and Austria.

In the same letter, Ida asked Maschat if the dates on the leaflets for upcoming Salzburg performances were correct: "If you will kindly let me know about this I will send the order for the tickets right away because, as we want something like 80 tickets I expect we had better not wait until we come to Munich on the 9th before we order them."[47] Ida would pay for the tickets and all the German and Austrian travel arrangements for the British opera fans with cash collected from the Jews she was helping to leave Austria and Germany. "Then, when we returned home, we credited these people with the equivalent in English money, thus transferring some of their capital without any cash ever passing the frontier." As Ida herself noted about her foray into money laundering: "If we were not exactly breaking the law, I suppose one might say that we were bending it rather sharply."[48]

Following the summer trip to Munich in 1938, Ida continued the correspondence with Maschat, even suggesting that in order to publicize the upcoming opera seasons he should send leaflets to the German consulate in London, whose address she happily supplied. "I think it really would be a good idea if they would put leaflets of the festival in the waiting room there," she wrote, every bit the intrepid fan of German opera. "Everyone who comes in there definitely intends to go to Germany, and I should imagine that a sight of the festival leaflets would make them decide to include Munich in their trip!"[49]

As Ida schemed to bring as many Jews as possible to safety in England in the summer of 1938, U.S. president Franklin D. Roosevelt convened an extraordinary conference at Evian to deal with the Jewish refugee problem brought on by the Anschluss. Delegates from more than thirty-two countries met at the grand Hôtel Royal in the French spa town with its stunning views of Lake Geneva, to discuss how they would respond to the growing refugee crisis. For nine days, delegates made noble speeches about human rights but stopped short of actually agreeing to take in any persecuted Jews. In fact, most of the delegates addressed the refugee issue without even mentioning the word "Jew."

Such was the case with American envoy Myron C. Taylor, an industrialist, who set the tone of the conference when he said that the international meeting was playing out against a backdrop of "serious unemployment in many countries."[50] The head of the British delegation, Lord Winterton, stated the obvious when he observed that "the question was 'not a simple one.'"[51] British Jewish groups were not happy with his leadership, for he was known to be pro-Arab and "out of sympathy with the Jews in general."[52] If Jews had hoped that he would suddenly facilitate immigration into the United Kingdom or Palestine, they were disappointed. In his opening remarks Lord Winterton declared that Britain was not a country of immigration and that asylum was something that could only be granted "within narrow limits."[53]

Nearly all the delegates to the conference said they were unable to help because of strict immigration quotas and a worsening global economic crisis. Taylor simply reinforced what was already the policy of the United States, which was to combine the German-Austrian quota to a total of 27,370 refugees a year. In 1938 the United States took in "only 17,868 refugees, and the quota was never to be filled in any single year across the duration of what remained of the Third Reich."[54] In the end, only a handful of countries stepped up to the plate. The Dominican Republic offered to take in Jews, but only if they arrived with huge amounts of cash. "It is plain enough that if Hitler would allow German Jews to take abroad the wealth that belongs to them and that if the nations possessing large territories would receive the German Jews, there would exist the elements of a gigantic operation which would have every chance of a large measure of success," noted a reporter for the *New York Times*. "But neither of these conditions has been met. The Germans of the Third Reich not only show no disposition to cooperate with the conference, but the Nazi press ridicules it."[55]

The Evian Inter-Governmental Conference gave the Nazis even more ammunition to go after the Jews. For now they knew that the world was unlikely to lift a finger to stop the persecution. One Nazi magazine featured a cover story deriding the conference and calling for the removal of all gypsies and Jews from Vienna, referring to them as Bolsheviks and spies. After the Evian conference, Goebbels was quick to emphasize its utter failure. He said that Germany was content to let any Jew exit the country who wished to leave, provided that he had a destination that would accept him irrevocably and issue the appropriate paperwork—and with the caveat that Jews could not take any of the Third Reich's wealth with them.

But where would they go? "Where can a million persecuted Jews and others go now from countries which seek to get rid of them?" asked an article in the *New York Times*. "And where can perhaps another million find refuge from lands which in the future may try to get rid of them?"[56]

Ida and Louise understood that the time for talking and international conferences where nothing but platitudes were exchanged was over. They knew they couldn't help the millions, but they could save *some* lives. "Everything had to be done in such a hurry—such a terrible hurry," said Ida. "There was no time to think or to argue." There was little time even for prayer. "If you can pray on the run. I think you have to listen quietly to an answer to a prayer. But there was just no time."[57]

CHAPTER 6

The List

I n the days after Kristallnacht in November 1938—during which the Nazis had gone on a forty-eight-hour rampage, torching Jewish businesses and synagogues and rounding up Jewish men for the concentration camps—Ida decided to travel alone to Frankfurt am Main. Louise had already used up her annual leave from her civil service job, and she was also feeling rather unwell, so Ida had no choice but to travel solo. She had urgent business on behalf of Irma and Ilse Bauer, an Austrian mother and daughter whom she had never met. With all other stratagems exhausted, as a last resort Ida was determined to enlist the aid of the British consul general in Frankfurt am Main, whom she had met briefly through the Mayer-Lismann and Bamberger cases.

Days earlier, Ida had received a telephone call in London from the Austrian Aid Committee concerning the Bauer women. Herbert Bauer, who had recently escaped to England, was worried about his mother and sister who were still stuck in Vienna. Both had been turned out of their flat and were living in a friend's basement. The

Irma Bauer, one of the women saved by Ida and Louise from Vienna. *Yad Vashem Archives*

Ilse Bauer, Irma Bauer's daughter. Ida Cook traveled alone to Frankfurt on the eve of the Second World War to try to save mother and daughter. *Yad Vashem Archives*

daughter, Ilse Bauer, then twenty, had received a domestic visa to travel to England, but the mother, Irma Bauer, fifty-five, had been denied the same visa by British diplomats in Vienna because of a rheumatic knee.

Ilse Bauer, who was engaged to marry a non-Jew, had tried to escape to Switzerland where her fiancé had recently fled. After having his tonsils out, her fiancé had insisted that he must spend time in the mountains to recuperate. With a great deal of difficulty, he managed to get permission to go for two weeks and had left for Switzerland vowing never to return. He made arrangements for his fiancée to be secretly rowed across Lake Constance, but on the night she was to depart, the boatman was arrested and Ilse Bauer was stuck.[1]

These two Jewish women were in dire need, their relative's desperation audible on the phone. Could the sisters get Ilse out of Vienna, and did they know anyone in the British diplomatic corps who could possibly reverse the decision on Irma's visa? Without thinking, Ida suggested that the Bauers meet her in Frankfurt, where she would try to persuade the British consul Robert Smallbones to look over the case. It was worth a try to meet him in Frankfurt if the Bauers were willing to travel. The women happily acquiesced, very willing to use their remaining money on what seemed a half-baked plan. "This rather doubtful offer was accepted with a fervour that told me it was their only hope," recalled Ida, who embarked alone on what would one day be called "Ida's little piece."[2]

After Kristallnacht, the Bauers were anxious to leave Austria by any means.

> My mother and I remained in Vienna in a desperate plight
> as the Gestapo was rounding up all Jewish persons and sent
> them away to concentration camps. We managed to hide
> out until we got word from my brother in London that
> Miss Ida Cook had presented herself at the Austrian Aid
> Committee and had asked if she could be of help, where-
> upon she was told of the difficulties Austrian refugees had
> encountered in getting visas to England, on which their
> lives depended.[3]

Ida barely had time to make arrangements. She didn't even own a thick winter coat for the trip and had no idea where the Bauers would stay in Frankfurt. With Friedl Bamberger's help, the women were temporarily installed with her mother at a flat that Elisabeth Bamberger rented after the Nazis took over the family's sprawling home. Else Mayer-Lismann loaned Ida her winter coat.

Ida was deeply nervous about heading to Germany on her own in those volatile days in the wake of Kristallnacht. "It gave me rather a helpless feeling to go alone just at this time," Ida confessed. "Louise became ill, and I went to Germany all by myself."[4] What would she do without her older sister? Louise was the quiet, calm one, the one who spoke fluent German and was rarely flustered. Would Ida be able to pull off the "nervous British spinster act" on her own?

To make matters worse, the sisters had read every detail that the British newspapers carried about the violence and carnage that had taken place throughout the Reich during Kristallnacht. Ida and Louise had pored over reports of the state-sanctioned pogroms against Jews in the Reich in retaliation for the assassination of a minor German Embassy official in Paris. Ernst vom Rath was shot five times at point-blank range by seventeen-year-old Polish Jewish refugee Herschel Grynszpan on November 7, 1938. Two days later on November 9, vom Rath died of his wounds in hospital, and the Nazis unleashed their murderous revenge against Jews in the Third Reich.

Travel to the area was now more dangerous, and SS guards might not be so tolerant of a flaky opera fan if they caught Ida trying to save Jews and smuggle jewelry across the border. "I had occasionally got by in a tiresome situation by playing the poor dumb Britisher who determinedly knew no word of German," said Ida, admitting that the "the more I thought of the trip, the less I liked it."[5] But there was no backing out. She had said she would go, and two lives hung on her word.

Just before she left for Frankfurt, Ida was also asked to bring out a valuable diamond brooch which represented "someone's entire capital." If she could possibly take it over the border into England, the jewelry would make it possible for its refugee owner to obtain a guarantee to stay in the country. "It was too late to say no," recalled Ida. "So I said yes. And off I went."[6]

Mitia Mayer-Lismann, who was now also living in the Dolphin Square flat, having arrived in London with her husband after being sponsored by the Cooks, gave Ida a list of Jewish friends and acquaintances in her old city for whom Ida "was to bring some words of reassurance and hope." Across the top, "scribbled in a moment of deep emotion," were the words "God bless you and help you."[7]

Ida, who spoke only a few words of German, was more exposed without Louise, and especially without the pretext of attending an opera that winter of 1938. "I was warned that if war broke out while I was there, I would be interned for the duration. I remember taking a good, hard look at my dark blue British passport and thinking it was rather precious."[8]

After fetching the desperate mother and daughter who met her at the Bamberger flat, Ida headed directly to the British consulate on Guiollettstrasse, convinced that as a British subject she would gain easy access to the top diplomats. "On this occasion...I waited over an hour, holding my British passport which friends had assured me would do instead of the 'queue number' which every Jewish applicant had," she said.[9] But the British passport was of little use at the diplomatic mission, teeming with weary and frightened families, many of them sitting amid bulging and hastily packed suitcases. Ida found herself surrounded by hundreds of weary Jews who occupied every available inch of floor space in the waiting room, spilled into the immaculately manicured garden, and lined up outside the main door.[10] After Kristallnacht, they were too afraid to remain at home, where they feared marauding bands of Nazis and phalanxes of the Gestapo were waiting to arrest them, and had gathered a few necessities, prepared to camp out at a friendly foreign consulate for as long as it took to obtain the necessary documents to leave Germany.

Ida, a veteran of queues, would never be able to cut this line of "old men, clutching their hats in shaking hands, [and] women with the tears only just held back."[11] Yet that is precisely what she attempted when she spotted a very harried Arthur Dowden, the British vice-consul, in a hallway, determined to use the authority that came with her dark blue British passport. "Presently Mr Dowden came to his office door and I asked if I might speak to him, adding that I had come from England to do so. He glanced at me and then round the room. 'I am sorry,' he said, 'but many of these people have been waiting since seven o'clock. You must come back this afternoon and take your turn.'" Ida was momentarily taken aback, but his sense of fairness had a profound effect on her and those around her. "He was right, of course, and I shall never forget the impression it made on the cowed, broken, hopeless people in that room. In this house, and this house only, they had their rights. I very willingly withdrew."[12]

It was then that she began to watch a graceful young girl—could she be a consular employee? wondered Ida—whose name she never learned, but whose courtesy and measured calm instantly impressed her. "Behind her surged a crowd of terrified, pleading, eager people. She left them all to talk for a few minutes, then, having procured silence, she sorted them out into their various groups, telling each where to go and ending with—"The rest follow me." Like children they streamed confidingly after her."[13] Back in the waiting room, the girl listened to each desperate refugee "as though this case, and only this case, were the important one. No wonder there were often little bunches of flowers pushed silently into her hand, or humble little parcels left for her afterwards."[14]

The consulate was a haven for desperate Jews. "Those who came there hungry and in need—no Jew was allowed to buy food for nine days—were fed," said Ida, describing one of the Nazis' many anti-Jewish measures after Kristallnacht. "And I understand that the

Vice-Consul even went through the streets, with food in his car, to feed those in want." One Jewish refugee recalled that she arrived at the consulate desperate to get her husband out of a concentration camp. "It was too terrible for one even to cry," said the woman. "Then at last I went to the British Consul to see if he could help me. And the first thing they asked me at the consulate was, 'Have you had anything to eat today?' I hadn't, of course—I was too worried to think of food. And, before they did anything else, they fed me with coffee and sandwiches, as though I had been a guest. And then I cried."[15]

Robert Townsend Smallbones, then fifty-four, was in charge of the consulate. He was away in London on diplomatic business when the Nazis started their Kristallnacht rampages in Germany and Austria. But as soon as he got a call from his wife about the dire situation in Frankfurt, the veteran diplomat with a reputation for compassion and humanitarianism sprang into action, setting up urgent meetings in London with Jewish community leaders and government officials. Working from a table at the Savoy Hotel, the balding, bespectacled diplomat summoned officials from the Home Office, which was responsible for immigration, and demanded to know what they were doing about the persecuted Jews. Worried that letting thousands of Jewish immigrants into the United Kingdom would cause economic hardship, Home Office bureaucrats had already turned their backs on the issue.

But Smallbones had a mission of his own. After a hastily convened lunch meeting with Jewish philanthropist Otto Schiff at the Savoy, Smallbones drafted a plan that allowed Jews to circumvent British immigration quotas and seek temporary residence in Britain for up to two years while they awaited their immigration visas for other countries, including the United States, whose quota system would only allow a handful of Jews into the country at any one time. Under the so-called "Smallbones Scheme," the applicant would be granted a visa that was guaranteed by a bank or a responsible person in the United Kingdom.

In London, Woburn House began to be overwhelmed by requests from Jews in Germany frantically searching for ways of escape. Volunteers from the Board of Deputies of British Jews received thousands of letters seeking help every day. The community set up the Jewish Refugees Committee in early 1933 under Otto Schiff, a Frankfurt-born banker who had helped thousands of Jewish refugees after the invasion of Belgium in 1914. When Hitler came to power, Schiff's organization helped thousands more settle in Britain by providing housing and other services. The nonprofit body also aided others who were passing through Britain on their way to more permanent residence in other countries. Schiff promised the Home Office that his organization would undertake all the expenses of maintaining the refugees who arrived from the Third Reich and look after the needs of all the refugees who entered under the plan.

Smallbones worked out the details with American consular authorities in Germany to make sure that applicants who were waiting for American visas would eventually be allowed admission to the country. "I submitted this at once to the Home Office and was authorized the same afternoon to introduce this system in my district," said Smallbones. "The Foreign Office was to be asked to send corresponding instructions to the Passport Control Officer at Berlin and to all my colleagues in Germany."[16]

Before taking up his post in Frankfurt in 1932, Smallbones already had a reputation as both an upstart and a visionary. Having joined the British Foreign Service in 1910, he was posted as viceconsul in Portuguese West Africa (present-day Angola) where he took a stand against slavery, having witnessed firsthand the horrors of indentured servitude in the country. Later, during a posting in Bratislava in the early 1920s, Smallbones, known as "Bones" to his foreign service colleagues, was very critical of official Czechoslovak policy towards its minorities and spent much of his term there making tours of Slovakia, prompting angry Czech authorities to complain that he was overstepping the bounds of diplomatic service.

When Smallbones was finally sent to Frankfurt after postings in Liberia, Angola, and Croatia, he felt that he had finally landed in a civilized place. But he seemed to have little idea of where he had just settled as he naively described Germans as "habitually kind to animals, to children, to the aged and infirm" in a communiqué to the Foreign Office. "They seemed to me to have no cruelty in their make-up."[17]

Kristallnacht shook him to the core. After his brief sojourn in London, Smallbones returned to Frankfurt in time to witness scenes of incredible brutality and deprivation. As he made his way through the city, he reported having seen a group of Jews forced to kneel and place their heads on the ground. When some of them vomited, "the guards removed the vomit by taking the culprit by the scruff of the neck and wiping it away with his face and hair."[18] These Jews were later taken to Buchenwald and some were beaten to death. Over the next several days, Smallbones and his deputy Dowden took action, driving to concentration camps to demand the release of incarcerated Jewish men, after the Nazis had ordered the arrest of all Jewish males between the ages of sixteen and eighty.

Once the Home Office gave him the go-ahead for the Smallbones Scheme, they set to work immediately preparing visas. His first task was to present the plan to the Gestapo. At its headquarters in Frankfurt, Smallbones, elegant in his pince-nez and bespoke suit, informed his Gestapo contact that the British government was prepared to help Germany get rid of most of its Jews. The Gestapo agent was dubious and at first resisted any cooperation. He told the British diplomat that the thousands of Jews incarcerated in concentration camps couldn't possibly deal with any legal niceties while they were behind bars. Besides, no Aryan lawyers would dare to represent them. "We had a fierce argument and I started shouting in the proper German manner," Smallbones recalled. "When I jumped up and said that my proposal to help Germany to be rid of some of their Jews was off, and that I would report by telegram to my government, the Gestapo bully collapsed and we made an agreement."[19]

He had set a Herculean task for himself and his staff, working eighteen-hour days to issue as many visas as possible. He even enlisted his entire family to help with the influx of refugees. His daughter Irene—"a pretty girl in her teens"—worked as his secretary, and this was the composed figure who greeted Ida and the distraught Bauer women when they returned later to the consul's private home to plead their case after office hours.

"Could you explain the case to me first?" the nineteen-year-old asked Ida. "We're all in on this, and sometimes it saves Daddy a few minutes if I or Mother hear a case first."[20] Irene had already witnessed enough to know that the Jews who came to seek her father's help were fighting for their lives. An avid equestrian, she had recently come across rows of dead Jews hanging from trees on one of her rides on the outskirts of Frankfurt. She had also tried to intervene—brandishing her horse whip—when Gestapo agents dragged a Jewish man off a city street. Those images would haunt her for the rest of her life. But they also drove her to action, especially when hundreds of Jews began gathering outside the doors of the consulate on the night of November 9, the first night of Kristallnacht. With her father away in London, Irene and her mother, Inga, took it upon themselves to allow everyone who was seeking refuge from the Nazis to stay at the consulate, working all night to provide them with food and reassurance.

Ida left the Bauer women in the living room and walked into the meeting with the consul general's daughter alone. When Ida explained the Bauers' case, Irene Smallbones agreed that it was a matter that her father needed to deal with personally. Minutes later, Ida walked purposefully into Smallbones's home office prepared to fight for the Bauers. "Once more, I told the tale, and by now it sounded pretty good to me. But, at the end, Mr. Smallbones said, without hesitation, 'I'm sorry. It's quite outside my province to reverse the decision of another consul.'"[21] Ida was shocked, and pleaded with the consul, appealing to his well-known sense of humanity. "And afterwards, Mrs Smallbones herself pleaded the 'human' side of my case while her husband gravely weighed up official necessity against the demands of humanity. And how he tried to make humanity win."[22] Besides, Ida was not about to take no for an answer. "They've come all the way from Vienna....I *can't* go out and tell them there's no chance."[23]

Moved by the force that was Ida Cook, Smallbones came up with a plan to contact the chief British consul in Berlin to tell him that while Irma Bauer's visa had been refused in Vienna on health grounds, he was perfectly convinced that her health had been restored. Ida even took it upon herself to persuade a doctor to sign a declaration saying the rheumatism had been cured. However, Smallbones had no idea how long such a decision might take or whether it would be approved at all. In the meantime, Ida and the Bauers were forced to wait in Frankfurt. "At any rate, optimistic though I tried to sound in my report of events, they both wept on the way back," said Ida. "And so did I finally."

They waited for more than a week. "Each day, we went to the Consulate. Each day, we learned that no reply had been received from Berlin."[24]

As she sat in Frankfurt with the worried Bauers, Ida began to despair. She would have loved to have taken off to Munich to meet

Krauss and Ursuleac and perhaps take in an opera, but the refugee work had been very expensive. Even though she was making more money than she had ever dreamed of with her writing, "the newfound wealth [was] otherwise engaged" in helping her refugees.[25] In London, Ida and Louise continued with their old habits: they made most of their own clothes, traveled third class, and queued up for the gallery seats during the opera season.

Now, in Frankfurt, Ida had to provide for the Bauers, who had spent most of their savings fleeing Vienna. Stuck in cold, dark Frankfurt on the eve of winter without Louise and with few people she could speak to because she could barely understand the language, Ida suddenly felt that everything was out of her control. She tried as best she could to comfort the Bauers, but they must have sensed her anguish.

There was nothing to do but wait.

■　　　■　　　■

The list was prepared in violet ink in a tight cursive hand. Mitia Mayer-Lismann, who had once been among the most important piano teachers at the renowned Hoch Conservatory, had written the names and addresses of Jewish friends and the families of her former music students who were still stuck in Frankfurt am Main. In addition, Mayer-Lismann had contacts in the resistance—former students and music-world confidants who were risking their lives to help Jews escape. Among them were two half-Jewish sisters whose childhood home, a stately townhouse on Arndtstrasse, not far from the Frankfurt Opera, was used as a clandestine meeting place where Ida and Louise were able to interview prospective refugees without fear of being caught.

Pauline Jack, an opera singer and voice teacher, along with her sister Gertrud Roesler-Ehrhardt often worked with the American

Friends Service Committee, a Quaker relief organization, in order to smuggle Jews out of Germany and into neutral Switzerland. Like Mayer-Lismann, Jack was affiliated with the Hoch Conservatory, and after the Nazis came to power she could only teach "non-Aryan" students. Although Jack, her architect husband, and her parents fled Germany in the summer of 1939, Roesler-Ehrhardt continued to live with the eldest of her four children at the house on Arndtstrasse, which doubled as a safe house for members of the resistance and once even served as a chapel where a Catholic priest administered the last rites to Jews who had been practicing Catholics for generations, before they were deported to Poland.[26]

The German sisters forged an underground relief network with Ida and Louise, who later came to rely on their home as an important meeting place to plan their operations. Ida provides only vague descriptions of the Frankfurt home in her memoir and never names the brave women who risked everything to help persecuted Jews, although one of them—Pauline Jack—would be among the guests on Ida's *This is Your Life* broadcast after the war. On several occasions, Ida and Louise interviewed up to fifteen refugees at a time in that room. "They came, poor souls, all keyed up to tell their tale," recalled Ida. Each refugee had about half an hour to convince "two utter strangers" that their case was worthy. "They stumbled on...searching frantically in their inevitable leather cases for papers, with hands that shook so that they could sort out nothing."[27]

Armed with Mayer-Lismann's list of contacts, Ida ventured out into the city, determined to speak to even more desperate people. Frankfurter Strasse was a leafy residential street of grand art deco mansions in nearby Offenbach am Main, on the left bank of the River Main. Number 116 was the Basch family home. "The first shock was the sight of a wonderful Venetian mirror, now splintered," recalled Ida. "One of the SS men had thrown a hammer at it. They had tipped over the cabinets of glass and thrown them down the stairs. The grand piano had been hammered, the notes torn out of the keyboard."[28] A museum-quality Dutch painting that once had pride of place on a living room wall had also been hammered beyond recognition by the SS. The living room was still littered with shards of glass and pieces of wood. On the second night of Kristallnacht—November 10—fifteen Nazis "forced their entry into the house and smashed most everything," recalled Lisa Basch.[29] Her father, an industrialist and prominent member of the Frankfurt Jewish community, had been dragged away by the Gestapo and interned at Dachau.

Oswald Basch was eventually released after a British business acquaintance was able to guarantee a visa for him in the United Kingdom. By the time Ida, accompanied by Elisabeth Bamberger, knocked on their door, Oswald was preparing to leave Germany and hoping to join his two sons who had already emigrated to the United States. His head was still freshly shaved from his time in the concentration camp, and his wife Helene complained to the visitors about standing ankle deep in broken glass after the pogroms, recalled Elisabeth Bamberger. A married daughter was also in the process of leaving the country. Only Helene Basch and the couple's second daughter Lisa, then twenty-six, were stuck with no prospects of escape. Despite their situation, the family had invited Ida and Elisabeth Bamberger to dine with them. "Drinks were offered and the daughter appeared with a tray containing one liquor glass, one champagne glass, one eggcup and one water glass," recalled Elisabeth Bamberger. "This was all the drinking vessels left in the super-wealthy cultured and well-ordered household."[30]

Ida decided to help the family on the spot. "I loved them on sight," she said, promising to find a guarantor for Lisa Basch and her mother—yet another mother and daughter—to travel to London. "Though she had never met us before...[Ida] invited my parents and me to her apartment in Dolphin Square, London, to await our American quota," said Lisa Basch. "For myself Miss Cook had approached a Member of Parliament to guarantee my years in England as she herself had guaranteed for too many already."[31]

Ida also spent a great deal of her efforts during that week in Frankfurt trying to help Mayer-Lismann's brother Carl to leave the country. Carl Lismann was sixty-six years old and partly blind when she went to visit him in December 1938. "Owing to his age or some inexplicable oversight, he had been missed in the great round-up of Jews in November, and we were anxiously busy on his case now, trying to get him out before attention was drawn to him," said Ida. Perhaps Lismann was overlooked because he lived in a small apartment in a house that was undergoing renovations and was partially blocked by scaffolding, which gave the place an uninhabited appearance. During that difficult week in Frankfurt, Ida would sometimes dine with the man she came to call Uncle Carl. "With a low light, carefully shielded, and thick curtains drawn, we would sit there talking of the past and the future—although seldom of the problematical present."[32]

The "problematical present" was simply too much for everyone to bear. In London, the *Jewish Chronicle* and other newspapers were filled with ads from Jews in Austria and Germany seeking guarantors. "Urgent Appeal! Would noble-minded people assist Viennese couple to come to London," read one ad. "Capable for every kind of housework; knowledge of English, French and Italian; wife, excellent cook and good dressmaker." Another notice advertised "Viennese pastry cook, Jewish, seeks position in business or private; very urgent."[33]

At the British consulate in Frankfurt, Smallbones and Dowden practically lived at their desks for the next several months, urgently authorizing tens of thousands of travel visas for Jews. Exhausted, Smallbones's nerves were shattered after he found out about the case

of someone who had died in a concentration camp because a member
of his staff had failed to get his signature on an official form that
promised the prisoner a visa. A mixture of determination and guilt
drove him on.

The rest of the consular staff was also frantic, feeding the thousands of Jews who descended on the building. "I was told by grateful
Jews in Frankfurt that during the worst of the troubles the consulate
was thrown open day and night, and even in the garden in the rain
all night hundreds of desperate people stood who felt safe there
because that little square of ground was England," noted Ida.[34]

Although Smallbones and Dowden were able to issue 48,000 visas
under the Smallbones Scheme, turning the British consulate into what
Ida would later describe as "one shining oasis in a desert of horror
and despair," they were unable to help Irma Bauer.[35] After more than
a week of daily visits to the consulate, there was still no answer from
the British Embassy in Berlin. Unable to return to her home in Vienna,
Irma was now stuck in Frankfurt, waiting for the sound of jackboots
on her street.

After an agonizing deliberation, Ida decided to act, and told the
Bauers that Ilse Bauer needed to accompany her back to London
immediately before her own visa expired. Mother and daughter would
have to be split up while Irma Bauer awaited her visa in Frankfurt.
"It was a hard decision for them to make: to separate after all they
had been through together," said Ida.[36] Ilse Bauer was deeply worried
for her mother: "She had to stay behind in Frankfurt without means
and at the mercy of the Nazis."[37] But Ida left Irma Bauer with
Elisabeth Bamberger in Frankfurt, gave her a list of other friends she
could contact if she needed help, and gave her most of the money she
had left.

On a snowy winter morning in December 1938, Ida and Ilse Bauer
left for London. Ida, who had promised to return with the valuable

brooch that represented a refugee's entire financial guarantee to stay in London, affixed the "great oblong of blazing diamonds" on to her Marks & Spencer sweater. "Trembling a bit," she escorted Ilse Bauer across the border.[38]

■   ■   ■

Following the November pogroms, life became even more intolerable for Jews in the Third Reich. Not only were they expelled from their jobs, but they were banned from high schools and colleges—a sinister development that was reported on the front page of the *New York Times*. The law banning Jews from educational institutions had been in the works for a while, but Nazi officials used the assassination of vom Rath as the excuse—the same one they used for the state-sanctioned violence of Kristallnacht—to expedite the prohibition. "The...nefarious crime of the Jew [Herschel] Grynszpan demanded immediate action because German children could no longer be expected to work together with Jews in high schools and their installations," pronounced Bernhard Rust, Minister of Science, Education and National Culture. The prohibition also applied to students in elementary schools.[39]

Other restrictive government measures followed. Although they might have seemed relatively tame compared with throwing people into concentration camps, they effectively excluded Jews from any semblance of normal life. By the end of 1938, the Reich National Bank forbade Jews to sell stocks. The president of the National Socialist Motor Corps dissolved the Jewish Automobile Club, which had been created after Jews had been expelled from the larger Automobile Club. Jews were also forbidden from securing international customs passes required to drive outside the country. "The effect of this measure is that Jews will no longer be able to cross the border by automobile," noted the *New York Times*. In a subsequent dispatch, the paper's Berlin correspondent wrote: "Having attained a position of power in which it feels able to defy world opinion, the National Socialist regime has embarked on what it considers its final and decisive battle with world Jewry."[40]

As Smallbones and his staff worked day and night to help Jews leave Frankfurt, other rescue efforts were also underway. Nearly a month after Kristallnacht, British aid groups along with their counterparts in Austria and Germany began to organize so-called "Kindertransports" to bring Jewish children under the age of seventeen to safety in the United Kingdom. The British Committee for the Jews of Germany and the Movement for the Care of Children from Germany raised money and guarantees for children, many of them orphans and others whose parents were in concentration camps. The children were admitted without visas provided that British foster parents could be found to guarantee their stay. Once the "refugee crisis" was over, the children would have to return to their countries of origin.

After the first successful Kindertransport to Britain, notices began to appear in Jewish newspapers about meetings to seek guarantors for children. One advert in the *Jewish Chronicle* for a public meeting at Stoke Newington Town Hall, set for Monday, the twelfth of December, urged readers to act immediately: "To be silent means to acquiesce," adding, "SAVE THE CHILDREN" in bold, black, capital letters.[41] Between 1938 and 1940, more than ten thousand children would travel by train from Germany, Austria, and later Czechoslovakia to ports in the Netherlands in order to board ships for Britain. When the Nazis agreed to the evacuation of the children, they did so on condition that they would not clog up German ports.

In addition to the children, thousands of Jewish women were admitted to Britain on domestic servant visas even though many of them had never done any kind of housework in their lives. The United Kingdom also admitted five thousand Jewish men who had been released from German and Austrian concentration camps as "transmigrants" on the understanding that they would eventually go back to their countries when it was safe to do so.

As thousands of refugees of all ages descended on Britain, more and more bedraggled and exhausted Jews arrived at the Cooks' Dolphin Square flat. At one point, there were fifteen people sharing the one-bedroom apartment. "Often we, the younger ones, slept on the floor of the elegant three-room apartment," recalled Friedl Bamberger. "Some of the refugees were on their way to the U.S., others had come to live in England, others again did not know where they were going save that it was not into a concentration camp." Some of the wretched figures Ida and Louise had known for some time, others "they had never seen except in a photo. Yet all were their guests."[42]

Bamberger's Italian fiancé Orlando arrived in London in 1939 having agreed to become Italian state radio's correspondent in Britain.[43] Later, he would join the BBC after it began broadcasts to Germany and Italy, and he became a popular broadcaster. He had a flair for words, though his use was idiosyncratic, French and English mingling strangely with his gushing Italian.

In the early days Orlando was unable to marry a Jewish woman because he worked for the Italian government, but at least the couple could now live in the same city and enjoy their freedom.

Slowly, some of the refugees who were determined to stay in London began to find work. Mayer-Lismann and her daughter found jobs as music teachers at the Club of the Three Wise Monkeys, a "rather classy" boarding school in London, noted Ida.[44] Mayer-Lismann also became a lecturer at the Glyndebourne Festival Opera, which had been mostly founded by refugees from Germany, including conductor Fritz Busch after he had been expelled by the Nazis from Dresden in 1933.

Else Mayer-Lismann often sat in on her mother's lectures on Mozart and other operatic composers. It was an apprenticeship of sorts, which would one day allow her to continue in her mother's footsteps and rise to prominence in the United Kingdom.

After returning from Frankfurt am Main with Ilse Bauer, Ida "kept running from one government office to the next, filling in applications for entry, underwriting affidavits," noted Bamberger. "She toured the country describing in lectures and public speeches conditions in Nazi Germany and calling for help."[45] If individuals could not afford to offer a guarantee for a refugee, Ida would prevail on entire congregations to pool their finances and ask the clergyman to sign the documents that would allow a Jewish refugee to live in the United Kingdom, out of harm's way.

Despite all her work, Ida still had no idea how she was going to get Irma Bauer out of Frankfurt. After Ida left the German city, Elisabeth Bamberger's landlord, who denounced her to the Gestapo, demanded to know "about the two English ladies" who always visited. "Recently, they left with a suitcase," he said.[46] Elisabeth Bamberger had given Ida some of her daughter's clothes to take back to England and now realized that her movements were increasingly under scrutiny by the Gestapo.

At the beginning of 1939, the Cooks and their refugees closely followed the grim news reports from Germany and Austria. "The news of ever mounting Nazi brutality, the sorrow for those who had stayed behind threw an all-embracing shadow over the minds of those who, like me, had reached safety," said Bamberger. "The world seemed dark and humanity frightening and despicable."[47]

On March 15, 1939, the Nazis took over the remainder of Czechoslovakia. The move effectively ended the policy of appeasement, and by the end of March, British Prime Minister Neville Chamberlain vowed to protect Poland if Germany dared to invade the country. As the world moved closer to war, Ida and Louise grew increasingly frantic about the persecuted Jews who still remained in Germany and Austria. "To make it even more harrowing, the whole thing was really a fight against suicide as well as murder," wrote Ida,[48] who worried that refugees left without hope of escape would rather die than suffer Nazi abuses.

As late appeals for help were made, the sisters' list grew. In addition to the Baschs and Irma Bauer in Frankfurt, Ida was also asked to save Ferdinand Stiefel, a fifty-one-year-old accountant and tax expert who was the former owner of a property-management firm and a chemical company. When friends told Ida and Louise his story, Ida once again returned to the febrile atmosphere of Frankfurt to interview him—this time in the company of Louise.

In 1936 both of Stiefel's businesses had been Aryanized. He managed to find work as a superintendent of one of the properties his company managed and continued in his leadership role in the local Jewish community, sitting on the board of the Jewish hospital and acting as president of the city's main synagogue. In 1938, on the second night of Kristallnacht and as most of the city's synagogues went up in flames, Gestapo agents stormed the family's rental apartment on Jahnstrasse to arrest him. They took him to Buchenwald, where he languished for a month before his wife Getta could show proof that the couple had been granted visas for the United States. He was released "under the condition to leave Germany in a certain time," but in fact the Stiefels needed to wait three years for their American quota numbers to come up. "Friends of ours told the Misses Ida and Louise Cook of the predicament of my father," said his daughter Friedl Marburg.[49]

Ida, who had exhausted her own network of guarantors, wrote an appeal in the *Christian World* newspaper. When Ida sat musing at her typewriter searching for the perfect title, Louise interjected, "Call it

Friedl Marburg. *Yad Vashem Archives*

'Will Somebody Save Me?' That's all these desperate people in the center of Europe are trying to say to an indifferent world."[50] Under Louise's dramatic headline Ida set out to write about Stiefel's case "in such a way that someone, somewhere, would feel an urge to help."[51] By that point, the sisters' "grim education" had transformed them from "light-hearted and naïve" young women to active volunteers, determined to save as many lives as they could. Aware that few understood as they did, they saw that their appeals often fell on deaf ears.

They were "really rather frightened sometimes," admitted Ida, years later, referring to herself and Louise in the third person in the film treatment she wrote about their relief efforts. "But no one is going to stop them. It takes a war to do that. They've learned quite a bit about the world and human nature. The worst side of it and the best."[52]

The day the article appeared in print, Charles Graham of Dunfermline, a town in the west of Fife, sent a telegram to Ida and Louise in London "stating clearly and coolly that he and his wife would guarantee" Stiefel and house him for the necessary three years. The sisters were ecstatic.

Ida and Louise headed to Frankfurt almost immediately to meet Ferdinand Stiefel. But when they showed up at the apartment on Jahnstrasse, they met with a surprise. Stiefel was married. Unaware of this when they began working on Stiefel's behalf in Britain, the guarantee from the Grahams had only covered the husband, a reality they explained to his dejected wife Getta. Despite the family's wealth and connections—Getta Stiefel's grandfather Josef Goldschmidt had built Europe's first bicycle factory in Neumarkt—they had run out of options. Remaining outwardly calm, Ida and Louise promised—somewhat hopefully—to find her a guarantor, preferably one close to Dunfermline.

The sisters then urged the Grahams to take in both Stiefels. In response, the Grahams insisted on traveling to London in order to meet the Cooks in person. "They were a middle-aged couple, in very moderate financial circumstances, who traveled over three hundred miles to London and three hundred back again—all within twenty-four hours—just to discuss how they could best help two people they had never seen," recalled Ida.[53] The Grahams told the Cooks they could only afford to guarantee the husband, but in the end agreed to take both husband and wife, provided that Ida and Louise could find someone to pay a pound a week for the wife's upkeep. Again, the Cooks sacrificed just a little more of themselves, with Ida offering to pay out of her own pocket for Getta Stiefel's maintenance in Scotland.[54] Getta Stiefel was so moved by the generosity of the Cook sisters that she "prayed for them every day until the day she died," her daughter recalled. Thanking Ida and Louise for saving her life, "was almost the last thing she said" before she died, said Marburg.[55]

Despite this success, the Cooks were facing a vanishing window in which to save lives. Irma Bauer was still stuck in Frankfurt, and the situation was looking increasingly hopeless after her visa as a domestic worker had been refused. The Smallbones Scheme had failed her. "We had to start all over again," said Ida, "to try and get her out on a guarantee as an elderly person who would not be permitted to work." As Ida was having lunch with a friend at an Oxford Street restaurant, a woman at a nearby table was rather brazenly listening in on their conversation. She approached their table and asked if she could help. Although she had at first wanted to become a foster parent for a refugee child arriving on a Kindertransport, she agreed to take on Irma Bauer, a middle-aged woman with a bad knee. Irma Bauer's guarantor was found quite by accident—a stroke of sheer luck that Ida herself would never have concocted.[56]

With Irma Bauer on her way from Frankfurt, Ida and Louise focused on the remainder of the Stiefel family in Germany. Friedl Marburg's older brother Walter Stiefel was stuck in Berlin where he lived with his Christian wife. Their five-year-old daughter Elfriede Stiefel had been bundled on to a Kindertransport in May 1939 and was already living with a family in London. During the journey when the Gestapo boarded her train for inspection at the frontier, she knew that Jews were not allowed to have valuables, so she took off a small ring that she found in a Christmas cracker and sat on it to protect it from the Nazis. Now Walter Stiefel, a leader of the anti-Hitler underground for the last several years and publisher of an anti-Nazi newsletter, was on the run, forced from safe house to safe house every few days. His life was in danger and he needed an exit.

Ida and Louise had no idea of his underground activities when they agreed to help him. To them, he was just another persecuted Jew in need of their immediate assistance even if they thought his choice of rendezvous curious. Through one of his underground contacts, Stiefel managed to get a message to the Cooks to meet him at the ornate Anhalter Train Station, the main terminus for trains arriving in the center of Berlin from other parts of Germany and Austria. They would recognize him as the man standing at the station holding an English-language newspaper. But on the appointed morning, the Nazis had banned English-language media and no such newspapers were available for sale anywhere in the city. Walter stood around the cavernous station carrying a Swedish-language journal under his arm, and completely missed his meeting with the Cooks, who failed to recognize him. In such tense times it wouldn't have been wise for them to approach strangers to ask their identity, so the Cooks returned to the grand Adlon Hotel on Pariser Platz, a short walk from the Brandenburg Gate.

Modelled on the Waldorf Astoria in New York City, the Adlon was among the city's most luxurious hotels—a center of Berlin high society and a meeting place for foreign dignitaries after it opened its doors in 1907. Patronized by Enrico Caruso, Thomas Mann, and Marlene Dietrich, it was also used by the Nazis for some of their glittering soirées.

Although it was well known that the phones at all luxury hotels in Berlin were tapped, Stiefel took the risk of calling the Cook sisters in their room and arranged to meet them on a street corner. He would pick them up in a taxi, he said.[57]

The Cooks had managed to get a guarantee for Walter Stiefel and his family from an accountant, Tom Walton, in Altrincham, a town near Manchester in the north-west of England. Walton would also eventually take in Ferdinand and Getta Stiefel after Dunfermline became "a protected area" in the United Kingdom, forcing all "aliens" to move to other places and prohibiting the Grahams from hosting Germans. Walton turned out to be "the most wonderful, warm-hearted employer" who provided the Stiefels with a cottage on his small estate, "and there were even hot water bottles in the bed for them when they arrived."[58]

But on that last trip to Berlin, Ida and Louise got a glimpse of what happened to Jews who weren't so lucky. The sisters left Berlin from the same imposing central station where they showed up for their aborted meeting with Stiefel. As they stood waiting for their train, they saw hundreds of bedraggled men, women, and children. They didn't know it, but these were Polish Jews, many of whom had lived their entire lives in Germany but who had never needed to obtain German citizenship. Now they were being expelled from the country by the Nazis, who used their undefined, foreign status as a pretext to get rid of as many of them as possible. They were being shipped to Zbaszyn, a Polish town on the German border. The deportations of more than ten thousand Polish Jews began in October 1938 and continued through the summer of 1939. Among the first families to be expelled from Germany was the Grynszpan family whose son Herschel had taken out his rage on the Nazis by shooting vom Rath in Paris. The passengers would end up at the Polish border town stuffed into a makeshift transit camp fashioned out of an abandoned flour mill and filthy army barracks. Most had had only minutes to dress before they were hauled from their homes and herded into the train carriages headed for the Polish frontier. Many could not even speak Polish. The trains would stop six miles from the border, and the deportees would be forced to walk the rest of the way.

"We boarded a train in Berlin and saw people herded along the lower end of the platform," recalled Louise. "It was a cold, rainy day and many were in dresses or shirt sleeves, carrying bundles on their shoulders. Always the bundles! And the strangest things inside them. You'd think they would have a survival kit—things like honey, dried meat, Aspirin, matches. But no, the bundles contained sentimental memoirs—photo albums, favorite books, lace scarves."[59]

Appalled by what they were seeing at the train station, Louise was so outraged that she forgot her reticence and didn't stop to think about how she would be perceived. She simply addressed the train master in her best loud German: "What on earth is going on down there?"

"He shrugged and said, 'Only Jews.'"[60]

CHAPTER 7

A Friend in Downing Street

Bill Cook was Ida and Louise's younger brother. A man of twenty-nine, he worked as a civil servant and maintained a close relationship with the inseparable sisters. Perhaps moved by the helpless plight of Jews in Austria, or perhaps shocked by seeing Ida crying—possibly for the first time in his life—it was he who stepped up quite suddenly to offer a guarantee to bring a refugee couple to safety in London during the blurred summer of 1939. In his own muted fashion, Bill didn't discuss his reasoning or try to comfort his older sister who seemed to be breaking down under the strain of the refugee work. The Cooks were very practical people, and in keeping with that family tradition, he simply offered the solution that had eluded Ida and Louise for several weeks. "You can take my Post Office savings book if you like and a statement: I'm a permanent civil servant. See if they accept a guarantee for the two of them from me."[1]

The Cook sisters were ecstatic and set about filling in the paperwork to allow Bill to be the sponsor for Georg (who had changed his name from Jerzy to something more Teutonic) and Gerda Maliniak, a Polish Jew and his Aryan wife, who were virtual prisoners in their

Vienna apartment and in grave danger of being rounded up by the Gestapo. "But I knew no pipsqueak official would accept it," wrote Ida. "I had to get to one of the big men who would take the responsibility for accepting an irregularity."[2] The Maliniaks had simply waited too long to apply for British visas, largely because Ida and Louise were hard pressed to find them a guarantor.

It was Mitia Mayer-Lismann—now building her own network of powerful friends both in the London Jewish and classical-music communities—who arranged a meeting with Sir Benjamin Drage, a wealthy businessman and philanthropist. It had been to Mayer-Lismann that Gerda Maliniak had first sent a letter begging for help shortly after the Anschluss. Sir Benjamin was also the head of the Guarantee Department at the Board of Deputies of British Jews, which, alongside several other Jewish non-profit organizations, had moved from Woburn House to larger office space in Bloomsbury House. On the eve of world war this functioned like a busy command center with dozens of volunteers answering phones, filling in official forms, and organizing Kindertransports and other relief efforts for Jews trapped in the Third Reich. Ida was a familiar face at Bloomsbury House, where she had successfully organized the Kindertransport that brought the Maliniaks' daughter, Ingeborg Daisy, to safety weeks before.

Ida had never met Sir Benjamin Drage, who was one of the highest-ranking volunteers of London's premier Jewish aid group. Despite his hectic schedule, Sir Benjamin told Mayer-Lismann that he would be delighted to see Ida, who was by now well known in Jewish relief circles. With no time to lose, Ida managed to get a meeting the following day. "I was prepared to pull out every organ-stop in my voice to make the best effect, and no star actress had her role better prepared," recalled Ida of the moment she walked into Sir Benjamin's office on a summer afternoon in August 1939.

Sir Benjamin, then sixty-one, was "stone deaf," and Ida had to tell her story into a small radio set on his desk. It was an awkward situation, and she wasn't entirely sure that Sir Benjamin had any idea what she was saying. "And yet, appliance or no, he gave every detail the utmost perfect attention." He immediately sent an assistant to fetch the Maliniaks' file and completed all the paperwork in front of her. The assistant who stood by Sir Benjamin's desk seemed horrified by his actions, arguing that it wasn't proper procedure, but Sir Benjamin was not to be dissuaded by bureaucratic niceties.[3] Ida had succeeded in communicating the urgency of the situation. There were lives to be saved, and no one was going to tell him what to do.

Sir Benjamin was also deeply concerned about the plight of Jewish refugee children. On July 4, *The Times* published his letter seeking an amendment to the 1926 Adoption of Children Act, the law that had prevented child refugees from obtaining British citizenship: "We owe much in the past to the admission of refugees in this country. The children we are educating at present are the pick of Germany and Austria. Cannot we make use of these brilliant youngsters who are full of gratitude to the country that has saved them? [It] would be a blessing to them and a great advantage to England."[4] Later, he and his wife Etta would offer their sprawling weekend estate on the outskirts of London—Weir Courtney—to house refugee children brought to safety on Kindertransports.

When Sir Benjamin handed Ida the file with its thick sheaf of papers, he told her, "From this point, it has to go to the Home Office where, in the ordinary way, it will take four weeks more....If you have any sort of government string to pull, pull it now."[5]

Ida used Sir Benjamin's telephone in order to call Charles Harris, the husband of the Cooks' best friend, Emily, with whom the sisters spent nearly every Christmas. Fortunately, Harris was at his desk at 12 Downing Street that particular moment.[6] Ida would never name her Downing Street source for fear that Harris would lose his position as private secretary to the government Chief Whip if he were caught helping her to circumvent the system[7]—what both sisters liked to refer to as "sharply" bending the rules. In September 1939, Harris was appointed as assistant to the Parliamentary Secretary of His Majesty's Treasury.

"Well, of course, there is nothing I can do for you officially," Harris told Ida over the phone, "but can you get hold of the name of the Home Office official who would deal with this case in the ordinary way?"

Ida prevailed upon Sir Benjamin to supply her with the information, and Harris agreed to make the important call on Ida's behalf, triggering immediate action at the Home Office.[8] Ida then rushed out of Bloomsbury House to hail a cab to the Home Office. Sir Benjamin accompanied her out of the building, and then insisted upon paying her cab fare—"for luck." But it was more than luck. Ida was broke. She had spent "all the lovely romance money for the time being."[9]

It was late afternoon, and the "hidebound' official she met at the Home Office seemed completely unmoved by the plight of the Maliniaks and was looking forward to going home. Realizing that his desire to pack up and leave for the day was her "best card," Ida refused to leave his office until she had what she needed. When the bureaucrat finally confessed that the Maliniak file had been lost in the system, Ida boldly told him that he needed to find it. Even before Bill Cook had pledged to sponsor the couple, a file had been opened to obtain a domestic permit for Gerda.

"But suppose we don't find the file?" asked the bureaucrat.

"You've got to find it," said Ida off-handedly. "You've got all night, haven't you?"

The bureaucrat reluctantly agreed, and Ida sent a cable to the Maliniaks in Vienna telling them that their British visas were on the way.[10] It was a lie, of course, but it was meant to instill hope in the hapless couple, who, for all Ida knew, were on the brink of starvation, too afraid to have left their home in search of food. Although she knew that everything could still go wrong, she refused to give up, trusting in British expediency, goodwill, and justice—the same principles her parents had instilled in the Cook children. Ida had done everything that she could for the Maliniaks. Surely now they would be saved.

But early the next morning at the Cook family home in Morella Road, Ida and Louise stared at the devastating telegram they had just received from Vienna: "Georg not at home. Helpless. Gerda." Ida and Louise were dumbstruck.

"Well, they've got the husband," said Ida when she called the Home Office official shortly after the telegram arrived. "What are you going to do before they get the wife?"[11]

■   ■   ■

Before he was arrested by the Gestapo in the summer of 1939, Georg Maliniak had been assistant conductor and chief coach at the Vienna State Opera under Clemens Krauss. The master conductor, who first hired Maliniak when he was director of the Frankfurt Opera in 1923, took the young man under his wing, guiding what then seemed to be a very promising music career. Maliniak soon became indispensable to Krauss. In fact, when speaking of Maliniak to the Cook sisters, Krauss paid him a rare compliment, calling him "probably the finest operatic coach in Europe."[12]

Maliniak was born on December 1, 1895, in Warsaw. His father, Jakob, was an accountant at a sugar refinery, and one of his distant relatives was Solomon Herschel, the first Chief Rabbi of Great Britain. A promising music student, Maliniak made the move to the Austrian capital at the height of the First World War to study under some of the most important composers of the day. He counted both Franz Schreker and Alban Berg among his teachers, both of whom were musical giants in the Weimar Republic, which saw a renaissance of German-language arts and culture during the period between the end of the First World War and 1933 when the Nazis rose to power. Schreker's works were among the most performed after those of Richard Strauss, while Berg's *Wozzeck* was considered one of the finest operas of the century following its premiere at the Berlin State Opera in 1925. Despite their critical acclaim, both these musicians' illustrious careers would come to an abrupt end in the Third Reich. Schreker's works would cease to be performed because of the composer's Jewish background and Berg's compositions were deemed too modern.

Although Maliniak would also go on to suffer marginalization and discrimination, during the Weimar years his future seemed assured. In 1922, when he was twenty-seven, Maliniak garnered rave reviews when he made his debut as a conductor at the municipal theater in Graz. "A new man appeared at the conductor's podium, with very expressive gestures," wrote a critic in the *Neues Grazer Tageblatt*. "With the overture…the conductor and his orchestra received rapturous applause.…Certainly a remarkable initial success."[13]

While he was working as Krauss's deputy in Frankfurt, Maliniak met Ellen Gerda Rissler, whom he married in June 1928 when she was already three months pregnant with their daughter. Public records show that Maliniak, then thirty-three, changed his religion to "evangelical" Christian, presumably to marry Gerda, who was not Jewish.

When Clemens Krauss had agreed to take the role of conductor in Vienna, he demanded that Maliniak work with his singers. Krauss was planning to stage *Wozzeck* the following year and Maliniak was considered one of Berg's best interpreters, skilled in the staging of what is considered a difficult and very complex work—the story of German soldiers billeted in a small town during the First World War. The Vienna premiere of Berg's opera, which also benefited from the participation of the composer, was to be the highlight of the 1930 spring season. It proved to be a resounding success. Berg himself declared, "I have never heard my work done to such perfection." And he singled out his former student, Maliniak, for special praise. "I hasten to thank Kappellmeister Maliniak, who did great services at the rehearsals."[14]

Such critical success was surely a factor in the extension of Maliniak's contract at the Vienna Opera. Originally signed to a three-year term in 1929, Maliniak's relationship with the company was extended twice, until 1938, by which time he became not only responsible for coaching the opera singers but also began to take on more administrative responsibilities. He followed Krauss to the Salzburg Festival too, winning effusive praise for a 1935 production of Mozart's *Cosi Fan Tutti* (Maliniak being also an expert in Mozart).

But the critical praise also engendered bad feeling among lesser talents in the vipers' nest that was the Vienna classical-music community before the Second World War. Like his boss, Maliniak was a victim of nasty gossip. The attacks against Maliniak began in 1932, a year before the Nazis came to power in Germany. At first, they seemed harmless enough—the wild ravings of opera-world colleagues, jealous of his proximity to one of Austria's most critically acclaimed conductors. "The activities of the so-called opera coach Maliniak, the special confidant of the director Krauss, who...propagates him as deputy director, are also highly problematic," wrote Otto Stieglitz, the head of the "claqueurs"—audience members organized to clap or boo—at the Vienna Opera in the early 1930s. "Mr Maliniak was a mediocre...student of the Vienna Academy and since then has been dragged along everywhere by Clemens Krauss." Stieglitz denounced Maliniak in his blistering July 1932 attack in *Das Forum*. He called on opera management to cut conductors' fees by 50 percent and curb "the relatively high salaries of certain assistants such as Herr Maliniak."[15] But the reality was that Maliniak never commanded a high salary and seems to have struggled to make ends meet throughout his career in Germany and Austria.

After the Nazis marched into Vienna on March 12, 1938, life for the Maliniaks became virtually impossible. "The very next day after the Anschluss on entering the Opera House, groups of members and onetime colleagues and friends of my husband's turned their heads away, thus ignoring him completely," recalled Gerda Maliniak. "After two or three more days like this a letter from the Kulturministerium arrived, informing my husband, that according to new regulations, his services were no longer required and that his salary would come to an end on such and such a day." Under the Nuremberg Laws, neither Maliniak nor his Aryan wife were permitted to work after the annexation of Austria. Gerda Maliniak was classified as a "first degree Mischling" (half Jewish) and could only be restored to Aryan status with full rights of citizenship if she divorced Maliniak.

Maliniak's music-world friends soon told him about a teaching position in the music department of De Paul University in Chicago. "We saw the American Consul General who seemed to be very pleased for us," said Gerda Maliniak. The Maliniaks applied for an "out-quota" visa for Polish citizens and waited anxiously for an answer from Washington. "We began with preparations, growing impatient at the same time," said Gerda Maliniak. "Then we were summoned to the American Consulate General where we had to hear to our utter dismay that the special visa could not be granted."[16] U.S. immigration authorities had determined that in order to enter the United States as a professor, Maliniak needed to demonstrate that he had held the job in Vienna. But by that point not even the influential Krauss could do much to help his former deputy, at least in any official capacity.

"Suddenly I remembered Mitia," recalled Gerda Maliniak. "Our friend Mitia Mayer-Lismann...was already well established in London at that time. To her I wrote in my last desperation and implored her to help. Had it not been for her, we would never have met our dear Ida and Louise."[17]

The Cooks had written to the Maliniaks immediately and began to organize their escape from Austria. On their way to Vienna, however, Louise had such a violent toothache that the first thing they had to do was find a dentist. "This delayed us terribly," recalled Ida, who didn't speak enough German to call the Maliniaks and tell them they would be late for their meeting. "Gerda sometimes described to us how they sat there, watching the clock, the table laid with everything nice they could think of to impress the English ladies who MIGHT help. They talked nervously, hopefully, hopelessly—and finally were utterly silent, looking at the sandwiches and the cakes."[18]

"They won't come now," said Maliniak.

But just when the family had lost hope, Ida and Louise arrived at the Maliniaks' flat on Stiegengasse and made plans to help them.

Kindertransport would be arranged for Ingeborg Daisy, and Louise suggested they should advertise for a domestic servant for their own flat in London to help Gerda Maliniak. But worried that the position could easily be filled by a local, they needed to come up with a different proposal. Gerda Maliniak suggested that they advertise for someone who knew all about cooking for diabetics—something she was skilled at doing for her own husband. Still, detail-obsessed Louise worried that they couldn't pull off the lie because neither of the sisters was diabetic. "Oh, don't get so bogged down in *detail*," said Ida. "We might have diabetes for all we know. Anyway, we're just talking precautions."[19] The Cooks returned home, filled with optimism.

But weeks after the Cooks put the plan in place, Maliniak received the order to report to the local police station. He and his wife dutifully attended, confident in their explanation that visas were on their way from Britain where they would join their daughter. Ignoring this, the Gestapo agents arrested Maliniak on the spot. "They shouted at me that if I stayed married to 'The Jew' I am regarded as a Jewess myself," said Gerda Maliniak, adding that the Gestapo gave her a *stillsweigende*— permission to remain in the country for ten days before they would arrest her and take her to a concentration camp.[20]

Gerda Maliniak tried to find out where they had taken her husband, but no one would tell her. Despondent, she began to walk home. There was nowhere else to go because Jews were barred from hotels, boarding houses, and all public buildings. But before she could reach their flat on Stiegengasse, she bumped into her sister-in-law who lived nearby and had come to warn her that a group of Gestapo agents were outside the Maliniaks' building, seemingly waiting for her return.

For the next two days, Gerda simply "lived on her feet," walking through Vienna, too afraid to go home for fear of ending up at a concentration camp herself.[21] She telephoned her sister-in-law for news, but she told her that the Gestapo had returned at intervals looking for her. She walked to the British consulate to inquire about the visas, but the clerks were not aware that the documents that would allow them to leave Austria were already on their way. After she received the crushing telegram, Ida's call to the Home Office bureaucrat in a state of high anxiety had done its work. Gerda Maliniak rested for a few hours in the lobby of the consulate, and then was told she had to leave, probably because consular personnel found it difficult to cope with the large numbers of Jews who now descended on the building every day.[22]

Gerda, who was Polish by marriage, eventually made her way to the Polish consulate and managed to secure permission to travel to Warsaw, where her mother-in-law lived. As the wife of a Polish national, she was easily granted leave to enter the country. "I then broke up completely but eventually had to pull myself together and escaped into Poland."[23] Gerda Maliniak didn't dare return to her apartment to pack. She called her sister-in-law and asked her to meet her at the train station to help her buy a ticket to Warsaw. They bade each other a "quiet farewell," never expecting to see each other again.[24]

"She was so tired she was beyond common sense," said Ida. "She expected the Gestapo to take her off the train at every stop. A kindly, grey-haired conductor asked what ailed her, and she poured out the whole story. He said, 'Give me your papers, and I'll take care of everything.' He gave her an orange. She fell asleep expecting him to betray her, but feeling there was no further point in fighting to stay alive. When she awoke, she was in Poland."[25] The conductor returned with her passport, bearing the immigration officer's stamp: "Look, the stamp is on it. You are over the frontier and free."[26]

She stumbled out of her train compartment and looked out of the window as a beautiful summer morning began to unfold. "She always [said] it was like looking at the morning of the world, when everything was fresh and innocent and untouched," said Ida. "She was free and it was like being born again."[27]

When the conductor brought her a tray with breakfast, Maliniak gave him her handbag and told him to take whatever he needed for payment. But the gray-haired gentleman returned her bag. "No, madam, the breakfast is my pleasure. You are going to need all your money."[28]

A week after Gerda made her way to her mother-in-law's home in Warsaw, Maliniak managed to leave the concentration camp by signing a declaration that he would return immediately to the country of his birth. While it's not clear how Maliniak was able to leave the concentration camp, Krauss appears to have used his influence with the Austrian Nazis. "We are inclined to think that Krauss made energetic representations on his behalf, for much later we saw strongly worded letters from Krauss in his opera house file on the Maliniak case," said Ida.[29]

"It shows that one should never despair," said Gerda Maliniak. "One should remember that miracles still happen. And one should not forget them or take them for granted when they do happen."[30] The couple were happily reunited in Warsaw, where they contacted Ida and Louise. Ida called the Home Office bureaucrat, who telegraphed the new visas to the British consulate in the Polish city, and the Cooks also sent them the funds for their ship passages.

It was a difficult leave-taking. Even in those terrible times, when war was on the horizon and Jews were being arrested by the Nazi secret police throughout the Third Reich, Maliniak and his wife had little idea of the horror that was yet to come. Anxious to flee and be reunited with their young daughter in England, they said goodbye to Maliniak's mother.

It was the last time they would see her.

The Maliniaks crowded into the Dolphin Square flat with the other refugees as Ida and Louise set about helping them find a permanent residence in London. Their first task was reuniting them with their child, Ingeborg Daisy. This was no easy task, for the family who fostered the little girl no longer wanted to give her up to her parents. Although the Cooks eventually persuaded the foster parents to return her to the Maliniaks, the experience of many of the Kindertransport children was anything but seamless. Ingeborg Daisy was one of the lucky ones.

"In London, they took constantly [*sic*] care of us three," recalled Gerda Maliniak. "To my delight, we got Inge back from her foster parents when war broke out....Ida and Louise always helped us along."[31]

In between their refugee work in the spring and summer of 1939, there was also the opera season at the Royal Opera House where Pinza and Rethberg were reprising their roles in *Don Giovanni*, under the baton of Sir Thomas Beecham.

Anyone flipping through the white souvenir program with its ornate, orange, royal coat of arms might just happily embrace the message on the royal garter written in old French: "*Honi soit qui mal y pense*"—Spurned be the one who thinks of evil. The audience in the Royal Opera House on those glorious summer evenings in June must have been hard pressed to imagine a world where evil reigned. After all, in between the synopsis of the opera were glamorous ads for "Tosca Eau de Cologne" which promised to dispel "all fret and fatigue," and Elizabeth Arden's "party makeup expert who brings to life before your eyes a new and ravishing face; a perfect evening which lasts from early evening to—early morn." The advert featured a silhouette of a bare-shouldered opera guest wearing long black gloves and a tiara.

While Sir Thomas conducted Wagner's *Tristan und Isolde*, the last of that season's operas, on June 16, the king and queen were returning from a successful state visit to Canada and the United States, where they had dined with President Roosevelt. The Cooks were reunited with Rethberg and Pinza, although the Dolphin Square flat was now too crowded with refugees to hold their usual gramophone parties.

Still, the sisters were worried. They heard reports of a moral abdication in the treatment of refugees around the world. The MS *St. Louis* had set sail in May from Hamburg, loaded with 937 passengers, most of them Jewish refugees, en route to Havana. When the Cubans refused to allow them to land, the ship's captain, Gustav Schroeder, embarked on a frantic mission to Canada, the United States, and back to Europe to find countries that would allow the refugees to disembark. The ship returned to Antwerp on June 17. Britain agreed to take 288 refugees while the remainder were dispersed between France, Belgium, and the Netherlands. When the Nazis invaded these countries, and rounded up the Jews, many of the *St. Louis* refugees ended up in concentration camps.

Following the opera season at Covent Garden, the Cook sisters were on their way back to Berlin. They returned to London wearing jewelry belonging to the city's most famous milliner, Alice Schreiber, desperate to find her a guarantor so that she could leave the city immediately. Schreiber used to make the crown princess's hats, and when the Nazis came to power von Ribbentrop's wife became one of her best customers, along with Magda Goebbels, the wife of the propaganda minister.

At one point, Annelies von Ribbentrop suggested that she could make sure that Schreiber would be able to keep her hat shop in Berlin. She simply had to divorce her Jewish husband.

Schreiber, whose husband had just managed to escape to Holland, adamantly refused and courageously replied, "I think perhaps it is better I keep my husband and lose my shop."[32] The following day, von Ribbentrop's manicurist arrived to inform Schreiber that the wife of the Reichminister of foreign affairs would no longer be visiting her shop in person and wished to have all her hats delivered. Fixing the envoy with her piercing "hyacinth-blue eyes," the milliner briskly retorted, "Please tell Frau Ribbentrop that I may be a Jew, but I don't do business by the back door."[33]

And so the shop was Aryanized, and Schreiber was out of work when a friend put her in touch with the Cooks, to whom she told her troubles. Schreiber had tried to join her husband in Holland, only to be turned away at the border. In her despair, she fainted, and when she recovered consciousness she was on a train headed back to Berlin and a grim future.

Ida and Louise agreed to smuggle her jewelry into London, plastering brooches on to their Marks & Spencer dresses and doubling up the diamond and pearl rings on their fingers. They stuffed their handbags with pendants, bracelets, and even more rings. When they saw the German guards board their train and linger outside their compartment, they tried to keep calm, prepared—if questioned—to resort to their tried and true "nervous British spinster act."

And while they did indeed manage to smuggle Schreiber's jewelry into England, bringing her to safety was a harder proposition. As they began making the usual inquiries with the Jewish relief agencies, Emily Harris invited them to tea. Emily and Charles Harris—their "friend[s] in Downing Street"—had also acted as guarantors for Lisa Basch and her mother. Now, as they sat around a dining room table laden with tea cakes, scones, and Devon cream, Harris introduced the sisters to a friend who wanted to do her part to help the Jewish refugees and was willing to act as a guarantor but didn't know who to contact to offer her services.

Ida immediately launched into Schreiber's situation, and Harris's friend—whose name Ida never divulged—would, with her husband, provide the guarantee for Schreiber's time in England. Schreiber was dragged out of Berlin with a month to spare before the war started, but alone. Her husband would neither escape nor survive the war.[34]

■   ■   ■

"I Jewish of both Polish and German nations," began the letter in halting English that made its way to the Cooks from the Zbaszyn refugee camp in the spring of 1939. "My parents were taken away since six months. I have 16 years of age. I look not so much for help as for hope." The letter writer, who was interned at the Polish border with Germany (where the Nazis had dispatched thousands of Polish-born Jews the year before), went on to say that he had an immigration quota number for the United States but that "it will not be ripe" for another three years. Could the Cook sisters possibly help him? "It is hard to keep alive here without encouragement," he wrote.[35]

The conditions at the camp were appalling, and many of the older refugees had died. Those remaining lived in converted horse stalls. Although from January 1939 the Nazis allowed many of the refugees to return to Germany in order to liquidate their assets and hand them over to the Reich, they did so sparingly, allowing only a hundred Polish Jews back to Germany at a time. Hundreds still remained at the makeshift camp in the summer of 1939.

It's unclear how the letter made its way to 24 Morella Road, "but news traveled quickly and by strange paths when there was any hope of safety involved."

Ida wrote back to the boy and promised to do what she could to help. She began by speaking from the pulpit at a local church group, and three weeks later the clergyman called to say that they would agree to guarantee a child for three years. "It was such...an unexpected offer out of nowhere," said Ida.[36]

She rushed to Bloomsbury House, and excitedly thrust the boy's paperwork at the young clerk who had helped her in the past. "The girl clerk who usually processes these cases was by now a good friend," Ida explained. "She hurried through the application forms as quickly as she could scribble. Then she raised her pen and said, 'Oh, how terrible. We have just had an order stating we cannot accept anyone with a U.S. quota higher than 16,000. This boy's quota number is 16,522.'"

Ida recalled how she spoke to the "perfectly charming young girl, in what I am afraid was a terrible voice, 'My dear, I just am not going to write to this boy and tell him to stop hoping. You must think of something!'"

The clerk stared "helplessly" at Ida and "her eyes began to fill with tears."

"I snapped!" Ida said. "Enough of that. You aren't in a concentration camp! Look in your silly rule book, and find us a way out!"

The girl clerk turned to Ida with a solution "a few minutes later."

"Miss Cook, I've got it! I'll write you a predated letter—say a week ago—asking for these missing papers. That will start this case file several days before the new rule. He'll be eligible."[37]

Ida and Louise found out that the boy had received his British visa while they were on their last trip to Germany in the summer of 1939. It would prove the only good news on that sad last trip to get refugees out of Germany.

In August 1939 the sisters met a German woman—a Christian—in Frankfurt am Main. Her Jewish husband had been interned at the Dachau concentration camp after the Kristallnacht pogroms. The woman had refused to divorce her husband, and, as a result, she was prohibited from holding a job. She made a little bit of money by cleaning the homes of people who were brave enough to hire her, but her cash was running out, and her children—three boys and a little girl—were obviously malnourished when the Cooks visited.

The husband had been released but was so ill after his brutal treatment at Dachau that he was interned at the Jewish Hospital on Gargenstrasse. The Cooks knew that there was little they could do to help the woman and the children leave the country, but they promised to find a way and gave the woman most of the cash they had left before returning to England.

They also promised to visit her husband at the Jewish hospital, where only two Jewish surgeons remained on duty. One of them had a septic thumb and could no longer operate. "It was a strange and terrible experience," recalled Ida, as she made her way through the wards of sick and dying men—all of them victims of Nazi concentration camps where "every patient had been made ill deliberately." When they reached the woman's husband, they could barely look him in the eye. "It seemed to us that he was obviously dying, and though fairly interested in our assurances that we would do what we could for his children, he appeared to have passed any expression of deep emotion."

The sisters were shaken and angry as they stepped into the bright sunshine of Gargenstrasse, with Ida confessing a "fervent and personal desire to have a hand in killing those responsible for what we had left behind." The feeling gradually faded when the sisters finally heard through their network that their "Polish boy" would soon be on his way to safety in England.[38]

But there was another logistical headache. With war looming in the summer of 1939, every boat out of Poland was booked with thousands of refugees. The boy could not travel through Germany by train in order to leave from a German port. The only chance left was for him to obtain passage on the Kindertransport boat that was sailing from Poland on August 29. He could travel as one of the escorts in charge of the children, if the Cook sisters would send him his passage in advance. Two weeks before war broke out, the Cooks left Germany, and telegraphed the money as soon as they reached their home in London.

They had no idea if the boy had made it on to the ship that sailed from the Polish port at Gdynia.

The last Polish Kindertransport arrived in London three days before war was declared. The SS *Warszawa* carried eighty-three Polish

Jewish children from the Zbaszyn refugee camp. Most of their parents had already been murdered.

Ida and Louise were so nervous about their Polish boy that they headed down to the London docks to see if he had made it. Clutching a small, black-and-white passport photo of the boy, Ida scanned the crowds of children "carrying their little bundles and gazing around on a strange world." The Cook sisters stood in the heat for what seemed like hours, and then "Suddenly there he was!" shouted the usually reserved Louise. "He came across the dock with a big, lanky stride, like one of your American cowboys. He had blond curly hair and grey eyes. He wasn't carrying so much as a knotted handkerchief. And he was smiling!"[39]

Two days later, on September 1, the Nazis invaded Poland. Two days after that—on September 3—Neville Chamberlain took to the BBC to announce that the British ambassador to Germany had handed a final note to the German government that morning giving the Nazis an ultimatum: if they did not withdraw their troops from Poland at 11:00 a.m., a state of war would exist between the two countries. "I have to tell you now that no such undertaking has been received and consequently this country is at war with Germany," Chamberlain declared.[40]

The Cooks knew that war would be the end of their refugee mission, and it was also the end of opera at Covent Garden. Ida later typed a brief note and affixed it with a red paperclip to the program that the sisters bought when they had been to see Rethberg and Pinza in *Don Giovanni* in June before she put it away with all her other opera keepsakes: "The last two performances at Covent Garden before the season and the plans for the next season—which never materialized."

Opera sets and costumes were put in storage, and the Royal Opera House was shut down. Over the next few months, the Cooks' treasured venue—the scene of so much emotion—underwent a dramatic transformation. Parquet flooring was installed, a bandstand was created behind the proscenium arch, and the floor where the stalls had been was raised to the level of the stage. It re-opened in December as a dance hall for servicemen, with twice daily dances and "refreshments at popular prices."

Perhaps anticipating a lengthy war, Mecca, a chain of ballrooms, took out a five-year lease on the Royal Opera House.

CHAPTER 8

The Bombs

The declaration of war on September 3, 1939, ushered in months of boredom and isolation for Ida Cook. For the first time in their lives, Ida and Louise were separated when Louise's office evacuated their employees to Wales for a year. They only saw each other fleetingly, on occasional weekends. As Ida confessed, "We loathed it, both feeling that bombing was preferable to evacuation any day."[1] With no Louise, no opera, and only sporadic news from her opera friends, Ida was taciturn and uninspired. After the intensity of the previous year—in which the sisters traveled almost constantly between London and Austria and Germany in pursuit of their refugee work and opera—Ida was suddenly at a loss as to what to do with her time. And during the seven months of the "Phoney War" following the occupation of Poland that saw almost no fighting or bombing, Ida found it almost impossible to write. In Louise's absence there was no one with whom she could discuss her romantic plots and characters; there was no one to help type and proofread her work.

The political situation grew bleaker although certainly more agitated in the spring of 1940 as Hitler's troops marched into Denmark and Norway in April. The invasion of Norway provoked a crisis in the British Parliament, and Neville Chamberlain, whose doomed foreign policy of appeasement had allowed Hitler the strategic upper hand, was forced to resign after he lost a confidence vote. Conservative Member of Parliament Leo Amery seemed to voice the concerns of that entire chamber when he invoked Oliver Cromwell's celebrated speech: "You have sat too long here for any good you have been doing. Depart, I say, and let us have done with you. In the name of God, go."

On the same day that the Nazis began the takeover of Belgium and Holland—May 10—Winston Churchill, First Lord of the Admiralty, became Prime Minister. In his speech to his new cabinet Churchill famously declared: "I have nothing to offer but blood, toil, tears and sweat." He repeated the same phrase in Parliament. He went on to describe the dark period ahead and promised to "wage war against a monstrous tyranny, never surpassed in the dark, lamentable catalogue of human crime." Ida, who had seen for herself that "catalogue of human crime" for the last few years, became a passionate supporter of the new prime minister, whose faith in toil, tears and sweat resonated deeply with her and Louise.

And Churchill meant business. Less than two weeks after he took office, his government began to crack down on Fifth Column Fascists with the passage of the new Treachery Act on May 23. The legislation effectively banned the British Union of Fascists, whose members had increasingly engaged in acts of sabotage and espionage since the Cable Street Riots. The group's followers had damaged phone booths to prevent emergency communications during the sporadic bombing raids that took place after the declaration of war, and some were caught providing the Nazis with information on munitions factories and military installations in Britain. They had also set fire to homes and industrial buildings so that they could be more visible to Luftwaffe bombers.

On the day after the Treachery Act was passed, police arrived at Hood House in Dolphin Square to arrest the Cooks' neighbor Oswald Mosley, who was taken to Brixton Prison. His capture was seen as a victory for the Cooks' other neighbor, idiosyncratic MI5 agent Maxwell Knight, who lived in apartment 608, Hood House, while the Mosleys occupied two flats at 706 and 707.

After France fell to the Nazis on June 22, the refugees crammed into the Cooks' flat saw a whole new set of neighbors moving into Dolphin Square. Members of the Free French government under exiled General Charles de Gaulle set up offices and residences in the apartment block. De Gaulle had escaped to the city when the Nazis overran Paris and installed Marshal Philippe Pétain as head of the Vichy government. In London, de Gaulle made a speech that was broadcast by the BBC and sowed the seeds of the French resistance movement. "I call upon all Frenchmen who want to remain free to listen to my voice and follow me," he said, calling on French professionals living in the United Kingdom, to join his cause. "Long live free France in honor and independence!"

For the residents of Dolphin Square, the presence of the deskbound warriors of Free France meant added hassles. Workmen entering the security zone set up around Grenville House were issued security passes labeled "No Go" whenever de Gaulle was present in the building.

More than a month after Mosley was taken away to Brixton, McKnight made sure that Mosley's wife Diana was also arrested for her well-known Nazi sympathies. According to MI5 reports released in 2015, the security agency considered Diana Mosley to be "far cleverer and more dangerous than her husband." On June 29, Diana Mosley was hauled away by police, having hidden a photograph of her hero Adolf Hitler under the mattress of her two-month-old son Max's crib at one of her Hood House flats before she was driven to Holloway Prison for women. She was held without charge or trial.[2]

Like the Mosleys, some of the Cooks' refugees were also interned as enemy aliens on the Isle of Man under the sweeping measures of Defence Regulation 18B, which allowed those suspected of being Nazi sympathizers to be interned or jailed without any legal formalities. Mayer-Lismann's husband and uncle were interned at the beginning of the war, as was Friedl Bamberger's fiancé, Ruggero Orlando, who was sent to an internment camp under 18B because of his ties to fascist Italy. But Orlando was quickly released after "he offered his services to the British government."

"After some delay and confusion, during which time he too found refuge in the Cooks' flat, his offer was accepted," recalled Bamberger, who was able to find a job as a translator for the British Foreign Office, earning between £27 and £30 a month. That same year, Bamberger and Orlando were married, and Bamberger became an Italian citizen. "Both of us entered government service," she said. "We married at last—an act which had been impossible until the war had severed communications with the Axis countries, for Italy, too, had adopted the Nazi ban on "mixed" marriages."[3] Their registry-office wedding was a happy occasion attended by Ida alone, Louise still being stationed in Wales.

Good news also arrived for the Basch family, who were able to finally obtain their U.S. visas and sail to New York City in February 1940. However, Mayer-Lismann was among the refugees who suffered intensely during the Blitz, both from various ailments and poverty. She remained at the London school in charge of the "war workers" while Else Mayer-Lismann and most of the students were evacuated to the countryside where Else ran the school's music department.

But once the relentless nightly bombings began in London in September, most of Dolphin Square was transformed into a militarized zone. The basement of Frobisher and Hawkins Houses became air-raid shelters, the complex's underground garage was requisitioned for an ambulance depot, and the gymnasium was outfitted as an emergency hospital. A "decontamination" center and mortuary were added later.

For several days after the start of the Blitz on September 7, there was relative calm in Pimlico. But the peace was shattered on September 22 at 11:36 p.m. when a bomb exploded at 90 Claverton Street and an adjacent building on Grosvenor Road, hitting nearby Hawkins House, which was crowded with dozens of residents, among them refugees from Germany and Austria. As sirens blared and the night sky glowed orange from the intermittent fires throughout the city, many frightened residents were instantly buried under rubble. Rescue teams were immediately deployed, arriving at the Hawkins House shelter within minutes. Crews worked in pitch-dark, hauling out the bomb victims through a single passageway that was quickly filling with poisonous fumes after a coal gas main was ruptured during the blast. Fifty-eight residents, many of them with life-threatening injuries, were rescued and taken to the makeshift hospital in the gymnasium that was only equipped to deal with superficial wounds. The remains of four people were later found in the wreckage.

In the aftermath of the explosions, the air over Dolphin Square was thick with smoke and filled with flurries of billions of white soap particles from the burning Palmolive Soap Factory that was hit on Claverton Street. The smoke, which enveloped the neighborhood, held the sweet, slightly citrusy notes of the company's famous soap bars, and after firemen arrived to douse the flames, more perfume filled the air as the water turned the burning soap into "hot froth."

"It is an indescribably strange moment when you see *your own* city on fire," wrote Ida as hundreds of thousands of Londoners were evacuated from the city. "You can read of the same fate befalling other cities and be horrified.... But when your own place starts to burn, there comes a sensation that is entirely new and incredible."[4]

With the Cooks' flat at Dolphin Square crowded with their refugees, Ida was pretty much confined to Morella Road. The first bomb to hit the street exploded in the garden of a house across the road, causing most of the Cooks' windows to blow in and part of the roof to come down. "It is strange to hear the clink of your own windows and the crackle of your own roof slates as you sweep them into the gutter," said Ida. "But oh, how soon you grow used to that too."[5]

After "a great deal of our local railway station was blown away," Ida's mother left for the city of Gloucester where Ida's brother Bill had been evacuated with his office. Her other brother Jim was "somewhere in England" waiting to be called up for service, and Ida was alone with her seventy-five-year-old father at the house, which suffered a few more hits during the Blitz. "I heard a tearing sound, and then something hit the ground like a giant mallet," recalled Ida during the second bomb blast to hit the Morella Road house. "All our front windows blew in and our back windows blew out once more. But the moment was over, and I crawled out, feeling rather as one does after a bilious attack."[6]

Ida was deeply affected by the Blitz. Nesta Guthrie, one of the sisters' best friends from opera queues at Covent Garden, was badly injured in one of the most devastating raids that destroyed her family home in Kensington in November. Ida had spent the weekend of the bombing in Wales with Louise and was shocked when she called Nesta's office on Monday morning and heard the news that she and her mother were in hospital. Her sister Jane and their father had also suffered injuries during the blasts, but they were not seriously hurt. "I stopped only to ask the name of their local hospital, put down the telephone, and set out, running," recalled Ida. "I remember running along the top of our road, unable to bear waiting for a bus."

The hospital was surrounded by rubble, and inside there were hundreds of wounded. When Ida found Nesta, she was in a room by herself, barely conscious, her face bruised and head swathed in gauze. Nesta was still in a state of deep shock and didn't recognize Ida. "Speak to her," a nurse told Ida. "See if you can hold her attention for a moment and persuade her to rest. We can't."

Ida thought quickly, and "out of the welter of shared recollections," pulled out opera, specifically their shared passion for Krauss and Ursuleac. "Nesta dear...try to go to sleep and dream of K and Vee," said Ida, using the nicknames their little group of opera devotees used for Krauss and Ursuleac.

After a few moments, Nesta replied without opening her eyes, "Yes, I will."

After spending time at her friend's hospital bed, Ida went to see Nesta's mother Annie, who seemed to be in better shape than her daughter, sitting up in bed and speaking quite lucidly to her. But Ida underestimated the sixty-two-year-old's severe injuries. Annie died the following day.

Ida visited her friend every day, and every day for weeks Nesta failed to recognize one of her best friends. Finally, after more than a month in the hospital, Nesta seemed to come back to herself. It was Ida who broke the sad news that her mother had not survived the bombing. Nesta would go on to lose an eye, and worried for months that her arm might have to be amputated. She would require months of plastic surgery to heal her head injuries.

"Never once, not even when you told me Mother was dead, or when I knew I had lost my eye and thought I must lose my arm, never once did I feel so bad as the day we signed the Munich Pact," she told Ida, referring to the agreement signed by Britain, France, Italy, and Germany that permitted the Nazi annexation of the Sudetenland and became a byword for the futility of appeasement. "I *know* now which are the really terrible things in life."[7]

Despite the constant threat of a German invasion and the danger of London during the Blitz, Ida and Louise's father, John, was the first in the family to volunteer as an air-raid warden, one of thousands of members of a civil-defense force making sure that neighborhoods were pitch-black and no lights in his vicinity were visible from the air at night. He was also responsible for monitoring the extent of bomb damage. Armed with a tin hat emblazoned with a large white *W*, a gas mask, first-aid kit, and a hooked ceiling pike used to assess destruction in bomb-damaged buildings, John Cook set out every evening during the Blitz to carry out his civic duty.

In central London, hundreds of thousands of people lined up in the late afternoons outside Underground stations which were converted into air-raid shelters at night. The subway stations, which had also been used during the First World War as bomb shelters, housed more than 150,000 residents every night. Factory and warehouse basements were taken over for communal shelters too, although most Londoners remained in their homes during the Blitz.

Ida decided she also needed to do her civic duty and signed up to be a volunteer at a shelter in London's East End. This was considered the most dangerous part of the city because it was an industrial hub—an important target for the Luftwaffe's bombers. Ida was assigned to a large shelter in Bermondsey, home to many factories, warehouses, and gas works along the Thames. Between October and December 1940, the district suffered 395 air raids.

Ida's shelter was in the basement of a factory on the Old Kent Road, near the site of the South East Metropolitan Gas Works. As night fell, she reported for duty, walking gingerly down the stone steps to the factory cellar that was filled with "a smell compounded of cement, disinfectant, Oxo, people, and sawdust." It was Ida's job to stay awake most of the night to make sure everyone was all right in the shelter, helping hundreds of people to set up their cots and distributing meals. Sometimes she helped a group of other volunteers in an adjoining sick bay. The colorful patchwork quilts sent from volunteers in the United States instantly reminded her of happier, more innocent times—those now distant autumn nights at Sul Monte with Amelita Galli-Curci and Homer Samuels in the 1920s, when Ida and Louise had used similar rustic quilts against the chill of the mountain air.

Although they faced grave danger every night in the shelter, Ida recalled a sense of camaraderie among the Cockney class in London's shabbier East End. The stolidly middle-class Ida was clearly surprised by the lower classes' stories of "unflinching courage" and sacrifice and delighted by the entertainers who volunteered to perform underground as the city was racked with the terror of falling bombs. One evening a well-known contralto who "had never been a favorite" of Ida's serenaded the crowd in the cellar, who all sang along. For Ida, who was by now a fiercely opinionated opera critic in her own right, it would rank as one of her all-time favorite concerts: "Among my own list of great performances…I must place that strange and moving occasion when 200 Cockneys sang "Drink To Me With Thine Eyes" in the cellar of a London factory and forgot that from overhead the bombs were falling."[8]

On another occasion, just before the command of "Lights Out," a group began to say their prayers out loud. "There was the murmur of a couple of hundred voices repeating the ageless words of the 'Lord's Prayer.' And the not very distant crash of a bomb lent a terrible point to the earnest petition 'Deliver us from evil' breathed from the farthest, shadowy corner."[9]

Deliverance took several months, and the nightly pounding of German bombs only grew worse. On April 16, 1941, the Nazis launched what they called a "super attack" on London, dropping hundreds of thousands of incendiary bombs from four hundred planes over the course of eight hours. That pounding of London would prove the longest concentrated attack on the city since the beginning of the war. "Flames rose on every hand, casting a sunset glow against the blackout," declared the *New York Times*'s front page the following day. "They were no sooner smothered by fire than other forked tongues could be seen licking up to frame London's slender church spires, the Houses of Parliament and other historic landmarks." Saint Paul's Cathedral was badly damaged in the April 16 attacks, and rescue crews worked through the night digging out residents buried by rubble from the relentless blasts. No part of London, and no part of society, was spared. Among the dozens of casualties was Lord Stamp, the economic adviser to the British war cabinet, killed when bombs destroyed his home. His wife, a son, and three of his servants were also killed, buried in rubble after taking refuge in their cellar.[10]

Ida holed up in her Bermondsey shelter night after night and tried in vain remain calm. The lights remained on during the frightening blasts, and many residents stifled cries or prayed. Ida tried to focus on her evening newspaper, but barely managed to read the stories, beginning each of them over and over again. She had been frightened before, but on the night that the Luftwaffe battered London with bomb after bomb after bomb, Ida convinced herself that she would not live until morning. "I remember thinking, I shall never see Mother again. I shall never hear Rosa sing again."[11] Rosa, of course, was Rosa Ponselle, and her unforgettable debut at Covent Garden on May 28, 1929, was still fresh in Ida's mind. After the performance Ida had pronounced her "the greatest singer I ever heard."[12] Since then, the sisters had taken to repeating the refrain, "There is always Rosa!"[13] when things became difficult. Of all the things that mattered in life, opera was chief among them.

Outside the shelters, rescue workers struggled to dig out the victims and extinguish the fires. "Everywhere was crushed glass, doors oftener than not blown in, everything covered in the black soot that forms a kind of war patina for London," wrote a correspondent. "Even the air itself was dusty."[14]

Earlier, Ida had a sense that she had somehow survived the worst even as more difficult days lay ahead. "As my bus went up Park Lane, I suddenly saw the wonderful, fantastic riot of purple, white and golden crocuses that, every year, burst forth at that side of Hyde Park in a glory of insolent color. It was a perfect day, and I was alive. I should have been dead, but I was alive. The sky had never been more blue, the grass more green nor the crocuses more incredibly beautiful."[15]

There were other signs that life was incredibly beautiful even in those dark days. Despite the nighttime closure of all concert and music halls during the Blitz, Ida and Louise's new friend, Myra Hess, a concert pianist, decided to organize free classical-music concerts and went in search of a suitable venue.[16] On September 16, 1939, she had written to the BBC asking for help, but when she received no reply from the national broadcaster, she called on the director of the National Gallery, which had recently been emptied of its art treasures in case of a German attack. Hess asked if she could put on lunchtime classical-music concerts there five times a week. Gallery administrators agreed, and Hess went to work. She performed at a handful of concerts, but mostly ensured that nearly 1,700 classical music performances took place without fail during the war years.

Yet life was much worse for Ida and Louise's refugees, many of whom had escaped from their own harrowing situations and were suddenly thrust into a country at war. Under stress from constant nightly bombing raids and with no news from his mother after the Nazis had forced Warsaw's Jews into a ghetto in autumn 1940,

Maliniak grew increasingly ill. A diabetic, the anxiety raised his blood sugar levels to life-threatening heights. "During the war my husband had collapsed and had to be transferred to an emergency hospital," wrote Gerda Maliniak. "He was severely suffering from diabetic [*sic*]." Adding to his stress was the fact that he had only intermittent work, especially as theaters were shuttered every night during the Blitz. "He was more unoccupied than occupied and consequently very depressed," wrote his wife.[17]

Maliniak's plight was shared by a number of middle-aged Jewish refugees who arrived in London in the late 1930s. As a Polish citizen, he was not interned like many other refugees who arrived from enemy countries after war was declared, although he did suffer from a devastating loss of professional and social status.

The situation was especially bad for male refugees who could not find work in their professions in England and were either forced to take on menial jobs or rely on their wives, who worked as domestics and cooks in order to support their families. "They suffered keenly from a loss of professional dignity: scientists forced to take employment as laboratory technicians; men who had held senior and responsible positions working as bookkeepers and office drudges; scholars and intellectuals... working as waiters or menials in the struggle to keep their families."[18]

Lore Segal, a little girl from Vienna who arrived on a Kindertransport in Harwich, could tell that adjusting to life in England was easier on her mother than on her father after they had both arrived to join her on domestic work visas. Her mother became a cook and housekeeper, and her father, the former head accountant at a large bank in Vienna, was forced to work as a butler—a job he just couldn't abide. "I think the middle-class Jewish male in Vienna did not wish to know that there was a kitchen," she said years later. "When my father passed our maid in the hallway, he would look in the other direction. And here he was supposed to be the butler." Unable to function as the butler, he was eventually relegated to gardening duties—another job he was wholly unable to do.[19]

Other refugees suffered similar fates. Alfred Kerr, a brilliant and leading German intellectual well-known as a socialist writer and theater critic for both the *Berliner Tageblatt* and *Frankfurter Zeitung*, became a virtual ghost in London. "Kerr had...interviewed Émile Zola, spoken at Ibsen's funeral, written a libretto for a song cycle with Richard Strauss, and become close friends with Albert Einstein, H. G. Wells, and George Bernard Shaw."[20] After fleeing Berlin for Nice in 1933, Kerr and his family traveled to Zurich and Paris before settling in London in 1935. At first, Kerr managed to support his family on the proceeds of a film script he had written about Letizia, Napoleon's mother. But as the money ran out, he declined into "enforced idleness" and poverty, relying on his wife, an accomplished musician, to survive. In 1948, a year after becoming a naturalized British citizen, Kerr committed suicide.[21]

Like Kerr, Maliniak had difficulty adjusting to his new life in London, and was largely dependent on his wife, who took jobs cleaning houses in order to make ends meet. In 1941, after the eight-month Blitz finally came to a close and theaters gradually began to re-open, Maliniak managed to find work on and off as an operatic coach with the Music Art and Drama Society, preparing singers for Italian and Russian opera. The job also allowed him to fill in occasionally for absent conductors.

The Music Art and Drama Society was founded by Jay Pomeroy, a brash Ukrainian-Jewish exile who made his fortune speculating on whisky stocks. Pomeroy was an ambitious impresario who was determined to take on the "snobs," as he called them, at Covent Garden, who looked down upon his New London Opera Company as an enterprise run by upstart foreigners who threatened to usurp their hold on musical theater. Rumors swirled in the British press about Pomeroy, who was portrayed as a scheming outsider who founded his company largely to help his opera-singer mistress Daria Bayan secure the best roles. "Short and stocky with dark eyes that blinked rapidly when he was thinking of a suitable reply to an awkward question," Pomeroy was clearly a threat to the established opera world.[22] While the British government had grudgingly welcomed thousands of refugees from the Third Reich, it remained an insular and suspicious establishment as a whole, and as such was threatened by such accomplished, independent, European immigrants and refugees, especially in the arts.[23]

Pomeroy managed to flourish nonetheless, and to carve out an important niche in the London opera scene during and after the Second World War. Known as "Pom" to his contemporaries, Pomeroy took advantage of the flood of talented exiles who escaped to London before and after the war to build his fledgling company. Among those new immigrants was Georg Maliniak. "Speaking a large number of languages and possessing a colossal musical erudition, Maliniak was the most invaluable member for any operatic company and the ultimate polish and finish of the singers was due to a very great degree to his experience, knowledge and fantastic ability to pass these to the singers," wrote Pomeroy.[24] In the end, Maliniak proved largely inscrutable, so quiet and reserved that few of his colleagues knew anything about his personal life. "He never gossiped, nor took part in theatrical intrigues," Pomeroy said. "He was friendly with all although I doubt whether his natural reserve ever allowed him to make deep friends."[25]

Lanky and intense, Maliniak never quite lost the rather formal, harried air of the Viennese music student. But the Vienna of his youth seemed a lifetime away. The bespectacled opera coach and sometime conductor now lived under increasingly difficult circumstances in London. In his mid-forties, an age when most musicians of his stature and experience were firmly ensconced in reputable opera companies or had taken up teaching positions at universities in Europe or America, Maliniak was again struggling to make a living. Tired, sickly, and depressed, he was under constant strain, even as the rest of his family seemed to be adapting well to life in London. The Maliniaks were eventually able to leave the Cooks' Dolphin Square apartment and find a place of their own. They moved into a modest but comfortable flat in a house on Compayne Gardens, a leafy street in Hampstead, northwest London.

Except for the Blitz, London offered relative safety. Maliniak's life was no longer in grave danger. He could walk the streets without fear of being followed by shadowy Gestapo agents. His daughter could go to school and play in a park without being mocked by other children because one of her parents was a Jew. Money was tight, but the family had true friends in the Cook sisters whom they could call on in case of an emergency. But, according to his wife, Maliniak's struggles with "terrible depression" began to overwhelm him.

■   ■   ■

The year 1942 had started out on a somber note for Clemens Krauss and Richard Strauss when they heard the news that Stefan Zweig and his second wife Lotte had been found dead in their bedroom in Petrópolis, Brazil. The suicide of one of the world's most popular writers made front page news in the *New York Times*, next to a story about Franklin Delano Roosevelt addressing U.S. troops. America had declared war on the Axis powers two months before, after the bombing of Pearl Harbor in December 1941.

Zweig had fled Vienna for London and then New York, eventually ending up outside Rio de Janeiro, where the fascist and anti-Semitic government of Getúlio Vargas had welcomed him as a famous

European writer, somehow overlooking the fact that he was a Jew. Despite being able to live without the fear of persecution, Zweig had never been comfortable with exile. "My own power has been expended after years of wandering homeless," he wrote before mixing barbiturates in two water glasses for himself and his wife. "I thus prefer to end my life at the right time, upright, as a man for whom cultural work has always been his purest happiness and personal freedom—the most precious possessions on this earth." Zweig and his wife were found lying on their bed, completely dressed, their arms wrapped around each other on February 23, 1942, a day after they died.[26]

For Krauss and Strauss, Zweig's death was a huge blow. Not only was he a close friend of the ageing composer, but he was the librettist on *Capriccio*, the opera that was to have its premiere that autumn at the National Theater in Munich. The opera, subtitled, *A Conversation Piece for Music*, was a treatise on the art form itself. When Zweig died, Strauss immediately called in Krauss to help him with the libretto. The conductor made frequent trips to the seventy-seven-year-old composer's estate in Garmisch, sixty miles from Krauss's home base in Munich, the seat of his most important work—at least as far as the Reich was concerned. Despite the war, Hitler was still obsessed with making the Bavarian capital the center of cultural life in the Third Reich. The Führer continued to have great faith in his ambitious *Generalintendent* of the Munich Opera, so much so that he called upon Krauss to lead the Berlin Philharmonic's tour of Europe—a public relations move to show off the mastery of German music, even as the country was enmeshed in a brutal war. Weeks after Zweig's death, Krauss embarked on the tour, leading performances in fascist Spain, Portugal, and Vichy France.

Hitler's backing notwithstanding, the conductor still found himself fighting for increased salaries for his singers and musicians, costumes, and stage sets. And after the German invasion of the Soviet Union in June 1941, the war began to hollow out the business of culture, as members of Krauss's staff were increasingly called up for military service.

As soldiers were being dispatched to the Eastern Front, Hitler was preparing his machinery of murder. The systematic slaughter of Jews began without any formal declaration in occupied Poland in May 1940 at the largest of the Nazi death camps—Auschwitz—where more than 1.1 million Jews from across Germany, Austria, and Nazi-occupied countries started to meet their end. The so-called "killing factory," which was expanded in 1942, boasted more than forty sub-concentration camps and was located at the crossroads of various railway routes in an isolated part of the country, surrounded by marshland, making prisoner escapes nearly impossible.

The roundup and murder of millions was organized in secret under Operation Reinhard—named in honor of SS General Reinhard Heydrich. On January 20, 1942, Nazi leaders at the Wannsee Conference pledged the destruction of every Jew in occupied Europe. They launched the so-called "Final Solution to the Jewish Question," which would put existing concentration camps to an even deadlier use and require the construction of new killing centers. The plan called for the mass deportation of European Jews to death camps in Poland.

At the same time as the Nazis were planning their final offensive against the Jews, Krauss was fighting for their apartments, many of them sitting empty as thousands were forced to flee Munich or were rounded up by the Gestapo and sent to concentration camps. On March 24, 1942, he wrote a terse letter to Hitler's private secretary and head of the Nazi Party Chancellery Martin Bormann demanding the use of the abandoned Jewish apartments for his musicians and singers, who were living in temporary lodgings in the city. The letter, which included the subject heading: "Procurement of new housing for the management board and members of the Bavarian State Opera," was critical of city officials in Munich, namely the mayor and the "Gauleiter in Charge of Aryanization": "I would like to remind you that the order granted me a year ago by the Führer and Chancellor for the artistic development of the Bavarian State Opera, also endowed me with the responsibility of dealing with the necessities of opera personnel." The letter went on to enumerate the "urgent need' for apartments for a host of employees of the Bavarian State Opera. Many staff members had arrived from other parts of Germany and were living in shared accommodation or hotels throughout Munich.[27]

By April 1, Bormann himself had written to the mayor of Munich on behalf of Hitler: "According to an order of the Führer, General Director Clemens Krauss is to address me if he has any wishes concerning the Opera...I have today reported to the Führer on the letter of the venerable director Krauss. He wishes you to consider again, whether a number of other Jewish apartments could not be vacated for the newly engaged members of the Bavarian State Opera."[28] The speed with which Bormann was deployed to do Krauss's bidding at the height of the war in Munich was a marker of the importance of the Bavarian State Opera to the Führer and to Krauss's own special relationship with members of the Nazi hierarchy. Bormann was so close to Hitler that he oversaw the renovations at the Berghof, Hitler's holiday chalet in the Bavarian Alps, and managed the Führer's personal finances.

Despite his standing with Hitler, Krauss found himself increasingly locked in a power struggle with Goebbels, who was his senior as the head of the Reich Culture Chamber. When Krauss jockeyed for more control of opera theaters throughout Germany and Austria, Goebbels, probably feeling threatened, put obstacles in his path, canceling Krauss's productions at will. In July 1944 Krauss refused to sign an extension to his Munich contract after Goebbels canceled the premiere of Strauss's new opera *Die Liebe der Danae* at that summer's Salzburg Festival even though his annual salary—80,000 marks—was double what he started with in 1937.

With daily life a challenge in Munich, Krauss and Ursuleac sought more permanent quarters in Salzburg, where Krauss had been put in charge of the summer festival in 1942. Here, Krauss landed an enormous prize for himself and Ursuleac: an apartment at the Leopoldskron Castle. The massive property had belonged to Austrian theater director and producer Max Reinhardt, who bought it in 1918 and spent twenty years restoring the grand rococo mansion to its eighteenth-century glory. Reinhardt, a Jew, clearly wanted to be close to the festival he had cofounded. But after the Anschluss, the Nazis Aryanized all Reinhardt's theaters throughout the Third Reich and seized the castle. Reinhardt, who was already working in Hollywood, managed to stay in the United States, where he died in 1943.

Goering himself had made big plans for Leopoldskron, intending to turn it into temporary housing for the Reich's greatest artists. While the sumptuous palace functioned as a guest house for important performers including Krauss and Ursuleac, it continued to serve as a glittering reception hall for Hitler whenever he found himself in Salzburg. As the industrial heartlands of Germany suffered bombing raid after bombing raid by the Allies, Krauss and Ursuleac passed the summer of 1943 in an unreal world of luxury, in company, occasionally, with the Führer's entourage, even as bombs ripped apart the Munich Opera House.

Nearly a year after the glittering premiere of *Capriccio*, which would be Strauss's final opera, Allied bombs pounded Hitler's beloved National Theater on Max-Joseph-Platz, reducing the home of the Bavarian State Opera to a pile of rubble. Only some of the outer walls survived.

A year later, Krauss wrote to Hitler directly to ask for permission for a permanent move to Salzburg after his Munich flat was bombed: "During a terrorist attack at the end of April my Munich apartment was completely destroyed. I would now like to take the liberty of asking you, my Führer, to allow me to make the apartment in Salzburg my permanent home during the winter months."[29] However, months after obtaining approval to live year-round in Salzburg, the arrangements proved untenable for the increasingly harried conductor whose nearly two-hour commutes between his jobs in Salzburg and Munich, sometimes under Allied bombardment, were now putting his life at risk. In a letter to Martin Bormann, Krauss sought permission "to buy myself somewhere in as quiet and secluded an area as possible, as I absolutely need real peace and relaxation for a few days between the extremely strenuous concert tours that are taking place under the present circumstances."[30]

By September 1944, Krauss knew he would never fulfil Hitler's grand scheme to turn Munich into the center of culture in the Reich. As Allied troops massed at the German borders, and Krauss lost more and more staff to compulsory military service, he wrote to Bormann: "As far as I myself am concerned I have to face the fact that any artistic work in Munich will be quite impossible. To inform you of this is merely my duty."[31] And as the war raged, and Krauss found himself on the wrong side of history, "peace and relaxation" continued to elude him.

Shaken, but undaunted, Clemens Krauss was still determined to carry out his mission to produce great opera, although he could hardly have failed to notice that he himself was enmeshed in the real-life drama that had become the beginning of the end of Hitler's Reich. Krauss increasingly resembled a character in one of his operas. Like the Cooks before the war, he was living in a state of tragedy and farce.

As the Nazis continued to round up millions of Jews for extermination at Auschwitz and other death camps throughout the Reich and their much-vaunted war machine began to sputter with devastating losses for German troops in the Soviet Union, ordinary Germans found themselves fighting to survive. In major cities throughout Germany and Austria, food was severely rationed, and Allied bombs fell with increasing frequency.

But Krauss surely had the private solace of the work he had done with Ida and Louise, helping dear friends, artistic collaborators, and even total strangers to escape before the chaos. What were their lives like now away from Germany and Austria? Cut off from the outside world, Krauss's only news came from Nazi newsreels. Returning to Munich to search for theaters that could still accommodate his opera productions, the bombed-out and desolate city now resembled the propaganda clips of Luftwaffe raids over London. Had those two mad Englishwomen, Ida and Louise, and the others he and Ursuleac had helped escape the concentration camps survived the Blitz and flying bomb raids over London? Had any?

Krauss himself was now deep into what his friend Zweig had described in his suicide letter as the "long night," and the dawn was nowhere on the horizon.

CHAPTER 9

The Aria

Ida knew that she would get her old life back when she found the photograph, sifting through the ruins of a friend's bombed-out home in London. "Ankle-deep in rubble," she discovered just about the only item that was still intact—a framed enlargement of the snap she had taken of Clemens Krauss and Viorica Ursuleac standing gamely in front of the fold-out canvas stools of the queue at Covent Garden on that distant spring day on the eve of the British premiere of *Arabella* in 1934. "The snap that was to draw us into the dark melodrama that had enveloped Europe," was also an image of more innocent times. Brushing aside the dirt, Ida gazed once again on Ursuleac's shy smile, the curls hidden under her white hat, and Krauss's handsome smirk, his hands planted firmly in the pockets of his trench coat. "It was dirty, of course, and the cardboard backing had been torn. But it was there, virtually intact, a symbol of the days that had been, but I believed, in that moment, would surely come again."[1]

Though so much had changed in their lives since the photo was taken, the Cooks remained very much the same. They still had the pluck and determination of the Northumberland schoolgirls about them—the ones who saved their pennies, walking to work every day and going without their lunches so that they could sail to the other side of the world to hear Amelita Galli-Curci sing.

How far away that seemed now. Galli-Curci had given up performing after damage to a laryngeal nerve made it impossible for her to hit high notes. The end of her career became painfully clear during a final performance as Mimi in *La Bohème* in Chicago in 1936. One critic called her "pathetic," and another stated the obvious when he wrote: "She lost her voice."[2]

The war made it impossible for the sisters to communicate with Galli-Curci or their other beloved opera stars. The only respite from Ida's bleak existence in those years seemed to be the lunch-hour concerts organized by Myra Hess. Louise continued to work on and off in Wales, and Ida often thought of her as she wandered through the bombed-out ruins of central London after her shifts at the air-raid shelter. She was also deeply worried about paying the interest on hundreds of pounds in loans that she had taken out to help bring refugees to the country. She was paying out half her earnings from her writing to the cases she had personally guaranteed. Many of those refugees were old and sick, and it was unlikely that Ida would ever see her debts repaid. Not that she was expecting the money back: "Either one took the risk and people lived, or one played safe and they died," was the Cooks' motto when it came to their relief work.[3] And despite their flight to freedom, some of the sisters' refugees died soon after arriving in the United Kingdom. Ferdinand Stiefel, aged sixty-three, died in the north of England in 1941, a year after leaving Frankfurt, while Mayer-Lismann's husband, Paul Mayer, died in London in the same year.

During the worst of the rationing and the bombing, Ida dared not plan for the future. Instead she lived in the past, reminiscing over the smallest details of the magnificent performances she had attended with Louise, and the larger-than-life characters they had already met.

But it was hard to escape reality. The war had changed everything. In addition to Galli-Curci's virtual retirement from the stage, Ida and Louise were surely aware of Ezio Pinza's bad luck in America. Not only had his first wife threatened to sue him and Rethberg over their affair, but in the early 1940s, after Pinza had married Doris Leak, an American ballet dancer, and was firmly ensconced as a star at the Metropolitan Opera in New York with a house in the Westchester suburbs and an infant daughter, the FBI had hauled him off to an internment camp on Ellis Island, accusing him of being a supporter of Mussolini in Italy. A month before his arrest, in February 1942, the federal government had declared all Germans, Italians, and Japanese living in the United States "enemy aliens."

On March 13, 1942, two FBI agents barged into Pinza's home in Mamaroneck through an open door and arrested him "in the name of the president of the United States." The news of the internment of New York City's biggest opera star was front page news in the *New York Times* the following day. Decades later, his granddaughter wrote that Pinza was never told what the charges against him were and was not allowed to have an attorney present at his hearings. Pinza was finally released after eleven weeks in prison and returned to his wife and baby daughter. He was only allowed to leave his Ellis Island prison on the condition that he report weekly to "a reliable U.S. citizen," in his case, his doctor. Although he resumed his work at the Metropolitan Opera, the incarceration ruined his health and led to severe bouts of depression.[4]

When would the madness end? mused Ida and Louise whenever they found themselves together. When would they all emerge from this misery and recapture the glory of the opera?

Part of the answer seemed to emerge with the discovery of Ida's timid snap of Krauss and Ursuleac—the first real glimmer of hope. For Ida's alter ego Mary Burchell, who had become so adept at crafting the happy ending, it was surely a sign that all was not lost. If they survived the war, they were determined to return to America. Ida wanted to travel to California to visit their old friends Galli-Curci and Samuels as soon as the war was over.

Perhaps they could look up Pinza and his new American wife. More importantly, they would seek out Rosa Ponselle who had moved them to ecstasy and tears during that one magical performance at Covent Garden in 1929 and had set their lives on this course.

But the war was not yet over, even as 150,000 Allied soldiers landed in Normandy on June 6, 1944. In retaliation, the Nazis launched their deadliest attacks on London since the Blitz. A week after the D-Day landings, the infamous *Vergeltungswaffen* or V-weapons—the so-called flying bombs—made their deadly debut in London. The "doodlebugs," or buzz bombs, looked like small, pilotless planes that made a distinctive buzzing sound before they fell to the ground over random targets. The bombs caused crippling damage, leveling hundreds of thousands of homes and buildings and leaving thirty thousand civilian casualties throughout Britain in their wake.

With the buzz bombs making life in London even more dangerous, Ida and Louise convinced their parents—Mary Cook had returned from Gloucester in the meantime—to sit out the rest of the war at the home of an old Duchess's School friend in Northumberland. John and Mary Cook went to live with the Douglas family in their modest home in the small North Sea port of Amble, which is about nine miles from Alnwick where the sisters attended school. The Cook parents squeezed into the three-bedroom home, with its outhouse in the back yard, for the remainder of the war.[5]

Ida and Louise got out in the nick of time. They had decided to decamp to their flat in Pimlico and left Morella Road at 10:00 a.m., just hours before a buzz bomb flattened their home at 1:00 p.m. With the help of a neighbor, the sisters returned briefly to board up what remained of the house against looters, and headed to the Dolphin Square flat with Igor, the family cat, until their home could be repaired. "When we were halfway there, it dawned upon us that *we* were the refugees now," said Ida. "Countless others had sought sanctuary in the famous flat. Now it was our turn."

■   ■   ■

When Ida Cook wanted to write to Rosa Ponselle in America after the war, she didn't let anything as mundane as not knowing her address stop her. She had read that Ponselle had married one of the sons of the mayor of Baltimore, so she addressed her letter to "Rosa Ponselle, Baltimore, U.S.A."[6]

Ponselle had asked Edward Johnson, the Metropolitan Opera's general manager, to stage *Adriana Lecouvreur* and when he refused, Ponselle, thirty-nine, and still in the prime of her career, decided to retire after nineteen seasons at the Met. So, on February 15, 1937, following a performance of *Carmen*, she left the Met vowing never to return. She gave up her New York penthouse, and settled with her new husband, Carle Jackson, who worked for his father's insurance firm, in Baltimore, where the couple built a villa overlooking the city. The Villa Pace was named for her first major operatic aria, "Pace, Pace, Mio Dio" from Giuseppe Verdi's *La Forza del Destino*. Ponselle first sang the role of Verdi's tragic Leonora opposite Enrico Caruso at the Metropolitan Opera in 1918 when she was twenty-one years old. The first lines of the aria, with notes in the shape of roses, were inscribed above the doorway of the rambling, whitewashed Tuscan-style villa, which featured large, picture windows and a terracotta roof.

But less than three months after the wedding, things had started to sour. Ida Cook's letter reached Ponselle just as her relationship with her husband was entering its final stages. In her letter, Ida wrote about what the prima donna had meant to her and Louise and how the intense hope that they would hear her magnificent voice again had sustained the sisters during the darkest days of the war. "I tried to tell her something of what she had been to us all during those three great seasons at Covent Garden, and how she had remained in the memories of so many of us when we had nothing *but* memories to sustain our courage and hopes." Ponselle was so moved that she invited the sisters to visit her and her husband at Villa Pace when they made their trip to America.

But before that, Ida dared ask for another favor: Would it be possible to phone her in Baltimore and hear that voice again? Perhaps they could call on May 28, the anniversary of her London debut at Covent Garden? Ponselle wired back almost immediately: "Will be waiting for your call. Rosa."[7]

On the appointed spring day, Ida and Louise had invited some of their opera friends and a few of their refugees for the occasion. Among the group there was good news. The Bauers were on their way to Brazil after living in Croydon since the beginning of the war, and Friedl Orlando was now pregnant and expecting her first child later in the year. Her mother, Elisabeth Bamberger, had finally made it safely out of Germany, traveling to Russia and Japan bound for Quito, Ecuador, where she was living with her son Willi Bamberger.[8] As they all gathered around the telephone at the Dolphin Square flat, Ida called "the Atlantic operator" to make a long-distance call to America for the first time in her life. At precisely 8:00 p.m. London time the operator rang back "and dead silence fell upon the room."

"Go ahead," said the operator as Ida stood nervously clutching the receiver.[9]

And then the voice—which one opera critic had described as "that big, pure, colorful golden voice" that would "rise effortlessly, hitting the stunned listener in the face, rolling over the body, sliding down the shoulderblades, making one wiggle with sheer physiological pleasure"[10]—suddenly hit Ida with exceptional force. It immediately sent her back to the canvas stools of the Covent Garden queue.

"Hello, Ida! Is that you?"[11]

And then Ponselle asked if she could sing, and the wonderful voice began clear and steady, over 3,000 miles and a vast ocean, the heartfelt aria from Verdi's *La Forza del Destino*.

> *Pace, pace, mio Dio!*
> *Cruda sventura*
> *M'astringe, ahimé, a languir; Come il dì primo*
> *Da tant' anni dura*

> Peace, peace, my God!
> Raw misfortune
> Forces me to languish
> My suffering has lasted for so many years,
> Deep as on the first day.[12]

In the fourth act of *La Forza del Destino*, Leonora, who has tried in vain to forget her South American suitor Don Alvaro who accidentally killed her father, prays to God for peace and to end her terrible suffering. But for the Cooks and their friends who stood in silent wonder around the telephone in the Dolphin Square flat, the suffering of so many years seemed to vanish in those moments as they passed the receiver around so that they could each experience even a few seconds of the glorious, golden voice.

Ida and Louise arrived in New York City on the twentieth anniversary of their first visit—January 4, 1947. Their plane was delayed so long that by the time they disembarked there was no one to meet them at the airport. But a surprise greeted them in their hotel room. "I shall never forget how it looked," said Ida. "It was a film star's room. There were flowers and telegrams and candy and cakes and letters and phone-call slips. I took one look around and began to cry."[13]

They spent "ten magical days" in the city, where they were reunited with the Basch family, the Stiefels, and Elisabeth Bamberger, who had settled in New York after spending the war years in Ecuador.[14] Ida and Louise were able to give her firsthand news of the new baby—Lucien Orlando—who was now a year old. In later years, Lucien Orlando would remind his parents and grandmother of the courage of the Cooks in saving their lives. "As a small child he often used to speculate on the fact that he would not be alive had it not been for Ida and Louise," recalled Friedl Bamberger.[15]

While catching up with their refugees, the sisters also went to the Metropolitan Opera where they saw their old friend Ezio Pinza in *Boris Godonov*. They were also reunited with Amelita Galli-Curci and Homer Samuels when they flew to La Jolla.[16]

But the highlight of that American sojourn was their trip to Baltimore to visit Rosa Ponselle at Villa Pace. Carle Jackson picked them up at the train station and took them to the estate, installing them in the *La Traviata* bedroom. Ponselle was still in the hospital, he said. No doubt, she was recovering from one of her bouts of depression. He assured the worried sisters that he would pick her up the next day. "You realize, I suppose, that Rosa's rather scared about meeting you?" Jackson told them, adding that she was worried that they would be disappointed because she was no longer the great prima donna that they expected to meet.[17]

But the two diehard opera fans refused to be put off. After all, the memory of "that dark matchless voice" had sustained them through the entire Second World War. When Ponselle arrived the next day at Villa Pace, the sisters rushed outside to greet her. She was as beautiful as they remembered her on the London stage in 1929. With her dark, wide eyes and air of drama, she "looked like a Verdi heroine." The sisters fell on their "darling Rosa" and held her in a long embrace.

"It would be unrealistic to believe in a strict scheme of reward and punishment in this life," mused Ida. Still, she was certain that seeing Rosa again was "God's reward" to her and Louise for their refugee work.[18]

CHAPTER 10

The Trial

It was the perks that would get Clemens Krauss into trouble as the war ended in Europe: the luxurious apartment at Leopoldskron, the car and the driver, and the seemingly unlimited supply of food in the midst of chronic shortages in a devastated Germany and Austria. The denunciations against the conductor had never really abated during the war, but they rose to a fevered pitch once the Allies moved into the Reich following Germany's surrender. An anonymous letter addressed to the Salzburg police, and later passed on to state authorities in November 1945, alleged that Krauss and Ursuleac even tried to obtain residence permits in Austria for their two German housemaids.[1]

The persecution of Krauss took place in Austria after the country was divided into zones of influence controlled by the triumphant Allies—the United States, France, Britain, and the Soviet Union. But in April 1945, when Soviet troops captured Vienna from the Nazis and unilaterally formed a provisional government, it seemed that Krauss was very much in favor. Russian officials asked the conductor, who had remained in Vienna with Ursuleac during the bloody siege of the city, to conduct a series of concerts for the Vienna Philharmonic.

The Soviets were keen to bring some sense of order and normality to the war-ravaged Austrian capital, and an important part of that was putting the opera and the philharmonic back to work. They seemed to have little patience for the bureaucracy of vetting the Nazis' former music-world superstar, preoccupied as they were with the reconstruction of the entire country.

In the spring of 1945, Krauss might have been forgiven for thinking that he had emerged from the war with his reputation intact, but his proximity to Hitler and the Nazi Party hierarchy soon earned him a prominent place on an American blacklist of Nazi sympathizers alongside his mentor, Richard Strauss. It didn't matter that they had never been Nazi Party members. Both Strauss and Krauss were popularly perceived to have made gains because of their ties to the murderous regime, and in the view of the American forces they needed to pay for those transgressions, especially if Germany was to truly cast off its Nazi past and move boldly into the future. The denazification inquiries set up by the Allies in cooperation with local authorities weren't exactly the Nuremberg prosecutions of high-level Nazis; but they were a way to rid Austria and Germany of Hitler's hateful ideology, although many of those attempts to prosecute fell by the wayside as the Allies increasingly focused their attention on the growing menace of the Soviet Union at the beginning of the Cold War.

Nonetheless, authorities seemed particularly keen on making an example of Clemens Krauss. "We have to judge the facts as they appeared to the public," noted a 1945 U.S. Forces in Austria communiqué. "And the fact is, that Krauss was judged by the overwhelming majority as a Nazi at this time." It was the view of the U.S. Forces in Austria that both Richard Strauss and Clemens Krauss had been particularly compromised by the Nazis.[2]

Strauss had been the first president of the *Reichmusikkammer* and had composed music for the 1936 Olympics and a hymn to honor

Germany's ally, Japan. He had even written a poem in honor of Hans Frank, a legal adviser to Hitler and the Nazi governor of occupied Poland, known as the "Butcher of Poland." The poem, which hails Frank as "the savior of Poland," was written in gratitude for Frank intervening when the composer's estate at Garmisch was in danger of being requisitioned by Nazi engineers during the war.

Admittedly, Strauss curried favor with the Nazis, but he did so in a desperate bid to protect his family. The composer spent the war years deeply worried over the fate of his Jewish daughter-in-law Alice and his "Mischling" grandchildren. After Kristallnacht, Nazi storm troopers targeted Alice and Franz Strauss's home in Garmisch. In 1942 Strauss moved with his family to Vienna, where they sought the protection of Baldur von Schirach, the Vienna *Gauleiter* and Hitler Youth leader who had promised the composer that he would do what he could to help them. But Strauss's influence in the Third Reich seemed limited to those who still perceived him as a great composer. As the war dragged on, Strauss became tiresome to high-ranking Nazis, who remained unimpressed with his connection with Jewish writers and musicians. At one point he tried to secure the release of Alice Strauss's grandmother, Paula Neumann, who had been deported to the Theresienstadt death camp. Arriving at the gates of the camp in his chauffeur-driven Horch, Strauss informed the guards, "I am Dr. Strauss, the composer." Clearly nonplussed, the soldiers at the gates ordered him to leave at once. Neumann was eventually killed along with twenty-five of Alice Strauss's other relatives scattered in death camps in Nazi-occupied Poland and Czechoslovakia.

In April 1945 when U.S. soldiers arrived at Garmisch, where the composer had returned to live in the final months of the war, Strauss introduced himself in broken English, fearing that they would immediately put him in jail or take over the estate. Instead, the Americans were star-struck and asked for his autograph. Later, American officers were even invited to dinner at the Strauss home. By November 1945, as the denazification investigators probed his connection to the Nazis, the eighty-one-year-old composer was demoralized and desperate, and his health was in decline. He fled his beloved Bavarian country estate and moved to a spa town in Switzerland, where the press continued to hound him and portray him as a Nazi sympathizer. Eventually, in June 1948, a denazification court in Munich cleared Strauss of all charges. The court concluded that he had not benefited from his relationship with the Nazis and had simply dedicated himself to music during the Third Reich.

Krauss presented another problem for the Allies. "His is one of the most difficult cases we have in Austria," wrote Otto de Pasetti, the Austro-American theater and music officer assigned to his case. "Krauss, according to our findings, is the most compromised conductor."[3]

Born Otto Freiherr von Pasetti-Friedenberg in southern Austria, de Pasetti had once worked as an operatic tenor in Graz and Vienna in the 1930s, although it's unclear whether he ever performed under Krauss. He emigrated to the United States in 1937, but found himself back in Vienna just before the end of the war as an intelligence officer for the U.S. government. Setting up his base in the devastated and divided city where he had once sung in Bertolt Brecht operas opposite his lover Lotte Lenya, he now began his probe for the theater and music section of the U.S. Forces in Austria. Of course, his knowledge of German and music made him the ideal investigator.

In November 1945 de Pasetti embarked on "the Viennese conductor problem," with a focus on Clemens Krauss, who was well known to de Pasetti as the world-renowned conductor and a favorite collaborator of Strauss. In the introductory notes on Krauss that he presented to his superiors in the U.S. Forces, he noted that Krauss was a prodigy—a musical genius who held a professorship at the State

Academy for Music and Dramatic Art by the time he was twenty-nine and who had traveled to Italy to conduct the Vienna Philharmonic in the presence of the Pope. In Salzburg, he had long directed master classes for conductors at the Mozarteum Academy. In Munich, he was entrusted with building Hitler's dream of the greatest musical empire the world had ever seen.

De Pasetti went to Munich to do his preliminary research on Krauss, arriving in the devastated city five days before Christmas in 1945 and three months after the end of the war to interview Krauss's staff at the Bavarian State Opera. The U.S. Army's Office of Military Government for Bavaria sent a notice to the administrators of the Bavarian State Theater instructing them not to allow Krauss "or any representative of that individual" to have access to the conductor's private correspondence. "The files are to be locked up and no one allowed to examine them without the express written permission of Military Government."

The profile of Krauss that emerged from de Pasetti's interviews with administrative staff and stage crew was of a highly driven professional who had "the most intimate relations with the Nazi big shots."

"He used his connections first for himself to get the best living conditions and a very high salary, and second for the State Opera in Munich, which he built up to a very high level," wrote de Pasetti, quoting Bertil Wetzelsberger, director of the Munich State Opera. "He states that the bad influence in Nazism on Krauss was his present wife, Viorica Ursuleac....He blames her for urging Krauss to leave Vienna for Berlin." Another source called Krauss "a Machiavelli type" and "a master of diplomacy" who often told his musicians that if he didn't get what he needed for the opera, "I shall go to the Führer and I shall get it." When he gave out awards for loyal service to his musicians and staff at the Bavarian State Opera, Krauss also handed out copies of Hitler's *Mein Kampf*, with his own personal dedication.

"Source knows that it was a rule that this book had to be distributed with the medals, but the personal dedication was absolutely his own free will," noted de Pasetti.

In Vienna, much of the anger against Krauss stemmed from the perception that he had abandoned the Vienna State Opera and taken away its best musicians and singers when he made the move to Berlin in 1934. "There is no doubt that his leaving the Vienna State Opera was a very hard blow to Austrian theater and music," said de Pasetti. "Whatever his reasons were for his step, the way he did it cannot be considered as fair.... The Nazi press created the impression in Germany and in foreign countries that Krauss made this step because of his sympathy with Nazism."

But Erik Maschat, Krauss's secretary in Vienna and Munich, told de Pasetti that Krauss had no choice but to leave Vienna because he was treated so badly by the state-opera hierarchy. The Heimwehr, or Austrian fascists, were also against him because they perceived him as pro-Nazi and helped to sabotage the renewal of his contract at the opera, Maschat said. Krauss's bosses at the opera privately denounced him—a fellow Austrian—for bowing to German influence after the Nazis came to power, for having conducted the premiere of *Arabella* in Dresden and maintaining guest contracts with German singers from Berlin. In Vienna, Krauss had surrounded himself with a select group of composers and performers, sparking professional jealousy among his rivals and opera divas. In the Machiavellian world of the Vienna State Opera of the 1930s, his enemies were not above labeling Krauss a Nazi when they didn't get their way.

Krauss's close friendship with Strauss, an artist he equated to "the Goethe of music," badly hurt his own reputation in Austria. After the near fiasco of the 1934 Salzburg Festival, when Strauss failed to show up for part of his own tribute, opera administrators put the blame squarely on Krauss.

When Krauss's five-year contract had come up for renewal in 1934, Vienna Opera administrators were reluctant to sign him up for another five years and offered him a one-year contract instead. They later agreed to a five-year contract with the proviso that they could get rid of him after a year. Humiliated, Krauss decided to take up Hitler's offer and move to Berlin, taking his select group of young singers he had nurtured over the years with him to the German capital. The Vienna State Opera never recovered. Krauss's abrupt resignation from the Vienna State Opera was regarded in political terms at a time when relations between Austria and Germany were extremely tense. In short, his critics charged him with betraying Austria at the most vulnerable time in the country's modern history.

But, of course, Krauss didn't have an easier time in Germany, with rival Wilhelm Furtwängler doing everything he could to derail Hitler's favorite behind the scenes. "It was his bad luck that Hitler liked him very much," said de Pasetti's report. "He was given all the power he wanted which no other musician got in the Third Reich and he used this power without scruples...Krauss was the most powerful musician within the Third Reich."[4] Heinz Tietjen, another rival, derisively referred to Krauss in interviews after the war as "Hitler's favorite, his blue-eyed boy." Tietjen, himself the subject of a denazification probe, had been the powerful artistic director of the Bayreuth Festival between 1931 and 1944.

Certainly, Krauss was guilty of using music for Nazi propaganda purposes. He was a willing tool of Josef Goebbels, conducting a concert for the Waffen-SS in 1940 and supervising radio programs in honor of Hitler's birthday. Krauss conducted *Die Meistersinger von Nürnberg* in Berlin in 1935, a performance that the Nazi Party organ—the *Völkischer Beobachter*—proudly called "a Saar celebration and a loyalty rally."[5] The opera is a paean to German nationalism and its anti-Semitic portrayal of the Jewish clerk and head of the "master singers" guild made the opera a favorite of Hitler's. Furtwängler also famously conducted the Wagner opera on the eve of the tenth National Party rally at Nuremberg in 1938.

In addition to conducting Wagner, Krauss led the Berlin Philharmonic on a tour of Nazi-occupied France, neutral Portugal, and fascist Spain and undertook travel several times with Ursuleac to Kraków to entertain Hans Frank. Given the couple's work with the Cook sisters in saving Jews from persecution, it seems impossible that they did not know that Frank, a connoisseur of classical music and opera, was directing the mass murder of the country's Jews.

As his influence grew under the Nazis, Krauss became increasingly ambitious and overzealous. Even Goebbels became annoyed with Krauss when the conductor went over his head and appealed directly to Hitler with his requests for the Munich Opera House. On March 27, 1943, Goebbels wrote of Krauss in his diary: "He has become a sovereign conductor and has appropriated airs and graces that speak absolutely against him."[6] But the nakedly ambitious "sovereign conductor" was no Nazi. That's the message that Maschat tried to convey during his interview with de Pasetti in Munich. In fact, Maschat confessed to the investigator that the reason he joined the Nazi Party in 1938 was largely because Krauss refused, and Maschat did not want to antagonize the party by working for such a maverick.[7]

Indeed, some did defend his name. The German soprano Adele Kern was among Krauss's select group of musicians and singers—the ones he brought with him from Vienna and Salzburg to Germany when he moved among the various opera houses at Hitler's request. Kern, who remained loyal to Krauss and spoke out on his behalf, belonged to the Cooks' "magic circle" surrounding Krauss and Ursuleac and was also very close to Mayer-Lismann.

Although Krauss was accepted "with high honors by Goering" when he showed up in Berlin in 1937, Maschat emphasized to de Pasetti that his old boss "helped many people and is not the bad man as he is pictured by many artists."[8] The sentiment was echoed by Rudolf Hartmann, the former stage director of the Bavarian State Opera. "He helped Jews," Hartmann told de Pasetti during his own interview.[9]

But de Pasetti seemed to dismiss the statement when he wrote to his superiors: "Source could not give any names."[10] On the Jewish issue, de Pasetti probed no further. Nor did he seem to take into consideration the glowing letter about Krauss sent to American General Robert McClure at the department of the Office of Military Government in charge of denazification in Germany and Austria from conductor Lothar Wallerstein, who had worked with Krauss for more than a decade at the Vienna State Opera and at Salzburg: "I entreat you to hasten, if possible, the rehabilitation of a great Austrian conductor and theater leader, who in my opinion is of the most vital importance to the cultural redevelopment of the Austrian opera."[11] Wallerstein, a Jew, fled Austria after the Anschluss and settled for a short time in Italy before moving to The Hague where he founded an opera school. "If he had 'close relations' with Hitler, Goering, Bormann etc. he used them only in the interest of his art," wrote Wallerstein. "In a period in which it was dangerous to protect a Jew, he wrote a warm letter of recommendation to all authoritative officials and even to the Gestapo, making to give me [sic] the opportunity to leave Nazi-occupied Holland where I was living at that time. His files will certainly contain additional proof of his deeds in behalf of many persecuted people."[12] According to Ida, Krauss "and two other good friends from the Vienna opera exerted much pressure and finally succeeded in having him [Wallerstein] released with permission to go to America."[13]

Again, U.S. authorities failed to take the lead. But where would they even begin to look for such files? Any information about the work that Krauss and his wife had done on behalf of the Jews saved by Ida and Louise was known only to a few members of that "magic circle" who were sworn to secrecy.

Even Krauss's decision to risk his own life and Ursuleac's and remain with the Vienna Philharmonic in the war-ravaged city in April 1945 during the final and brutal offensive with Soviet troops was used against him. For months, Allied bombs had pounded the Austrian capital day and night. Ruins and rubble clogged the streets, and electricity and food were severely rationed. The trams ran only at midday, if at all. By April, when the Soviets began their siege, the city was being defended by one of the fiercest Panzer divisions, who were aided by the mostly teenage members of the *Volkssturm*, a militia set up in the last desperate months of the war by the Nazi Party. Krauss's main aim in leaving the relative safety of his castle in Salzburg was to make sure that the Vienna Philharmonic and the State Opera remained together, and that none of their members be forced into conscription by the Nazis. He had done much the same with his staff and musicians in Munich during the height of the war when he stood up to the Nazi Party hierarchy to prevent them from being conscripted into the Wehrmacht. "This could be considered as heroism, but it also could have been calculation, because this acting could make good his prior activities," noted de Pasetti.[14]

In the end, Krauss just couldn't win. His enemies lined up against him, savoring their revenge.

The "evidence" against Krauss was presented to the Austrian Commission—a coterie of government ministers and professional rivals who had always envied his talent and who watched his rise to power and success under the Nazis with barely contained rage. Some of them had run afoul of the Nazis and languished in prison during the war. They were bitter, angry, and looking for a scapegoat.

The Austrian Commission concluded that Krauss had betrayed his own country. "If Krauss had really acted as an Austrian, he would have persuaded the singers to stay in Vienna." Another member of the commission bemoaned the fact that Krauss had taken eight "important singers" with him to Germany and "thus put the Viennese opera in a very difficult position." Later, as director of the Salzburg Festival, between 1942 and 1945, "he alienated it from its Austrian character." Commission members went on to denounce the conductor for taking the Berlin Philharmonic on tours of Spain, France, and Portugal, among other countries in 1942—"thus conducting in occupied foreign countries" and taking part in "National Socialist cultural propaganda." The commission also noted that "Frau Krauss was a very frequent guest in the Reichskanzlei and acted often as Hitler's hostess when he gave official parties. The position of the couple was strong and powerful during the Third Reich."[15]

Krauss and his legal representatives mounted the best defense they could under the circumstances. In a last-ditch letter addressed to commission member Egon Hilbert on December 8, 1946, Krauss pleaded: "Please listen to the testimony of those people who were my artistic collaborators. Please give them more faith than what two National Socialist functionaries wrote to each other in 1939 in order to fulfil the formal conditions of their party laws."[16]

Two days later he sent another letter to the commission, which was now accusing him of plotting with the Nazis before the Anschluss: "Shortly after my assumption as director of the Vienna State Opera in 1929, the Austrian daily newspaper of the National Socialist party published a series of violent attacks against my leadership. The management of the state opera was described as Jew-loving and that I as director was entirely in the hands of a Jew [Wallerstein]." Krauss said he sought a diplomatic way to end the attacks and appealed to prominent Nazi Party member Alfred Frauenfeld, an engineer who would go on to become an important leader of the party in Vienna, especially in artistic circles. A patron of the arts and an actor, Frauenfeld admired Krauss. Krauss said he requested a meeting with Frauenfeld and asked him to intervene with the party organ in order to end the slander against the opera. "For this reason...I met Frauenfeld several times." But the conversations were in no way related to party membership, he said, dispelling long-circulated rumors that he had sought to join the party when he reached out to Frauenfeld.

Krauss also fought to clarify his relationship with Hitler to the panel, saying that he only had three face-to-face meetings with the Führer during the twelve years of the Nazi regime. He also said he had only a fleeting acquaintance with Bormann and spoke to him twice. He denied allegations that the *Gauleiter* of Salzburg had provided him with a car and driver or extra food rations, calling it malicious gossip. Moreover, he reminded the Austrian panel that he had received permission from U.S. authorities to remain at Leopoldskron when the war ended.

As for allegations that he tried to undermine the Salzburg Festival during the war years, Krauss pointed out that he only intervened to become director "in order to save the Festival from being seized by the Berlin art policy authorities." In this way, he ensured that the festival retained its Austrian character. As an Austrian himself, he insisted that the festival be dominated by the Vienna ballet, opera, and philharmonic orchestra. He also stepped into the Salzburg Mozarteum to ensure that it would not be taken over by Nazi functionaries.[17]

But his answers seemed to fall on deaf ears. "According to the testimony of all witnesses it can be stated that Krauss was neither a member of the party nor particularly close to Nazi ideologies," the commission declared in its final report. "One of his most outstanding characteristics is his ambition. He was intent on good relations with the responsible authorities of the Nazi regime and used these primarily for his person and then also for the promotion of the opera houses under his leadership. In general, he is described as an excellent musician and outstanding opera director. According to several testimonies he behaved decently towards Jews."[18]

Just before Christmas 1946, the Austrian Commission evaluating Krauss ruled that he would be "excluded from any artistic activity for a period of two years." The ban was retroactive to May 1, 1945. The commission also banned him for five more years—until May 1, 1950—from occupying "any leading position in Austrian musical life."[19] The December 20 letter that the commission sent to Krauss noted: "The decision is based on the fact that although you belonged neither to the NSDAP nor to any of its branches, your behavior during the National Socialist regime was regarded as that of a collaborator."[20] To add insult to injury, less than a month later the Austrian Commission extended the ban after its members realized that they had failed to include the performances of the Vienna Philharmonic that Krauss conducted after the Russian siege of the city. The American forces had stepped in to prevent him from conducting a New Year's Day concert in 1946.

The commission "sincerely hoped" that within the probationary period Krauss would take the opportunity "to prove his positive attitude towards the new democratic Austria by participating in the reconstruction of Austrian cultural life."[21]

Krauss, a proud Austrian, had been branded a traitor to his beloved country—a blow from which he would never recover.

CHAPTER 11

The Open Window

I f the end of the war ushered in a shining period of hope and joy for Ida and Louise, who could resume their busy social lives around opera, it brought new challenges and in some cases despair for their refugees as they attempted to rebuild shattered lives. Many tried to reclaim their businesses and properties that had been expropriated by the Nazi regime and to reconnect with family members and friends separated by the war, only to find that most of them had died in the Nazi gas chambers.

Such was the case with Maliniak's beloved mother in Poland, who had disappeared. "The deepest tragedy of his life was the news that his old mother was gassed by the Germans" following the liquidation of the Warsaw Ghetto in the spring of 1943, although it's not clear when he finally heard the news that she had been killed.[1] Without the means to return to Poland or Austria after the war, Maliniak was devastated. He was also besieged by debt, and, a decade after arriving in London, the trusted deputy of the great Clemens Krauss was still struggling to make his mark in the opera world, scrounging for sporadic work coaching singers and preparing them for the stage.

Maliniak, sickly and harried, continued to work for Pomeroy's Music Art and Drama Society. In 1947 he begged the impresario to allow him to conduct opera, even on a semi-regular basis. "I told him then quite frankly that whilst I thought him the greatest coach, I looked upon his conducting as of a very modest nature and not sufficiently good for our opera," wrote Pomeroy. "He left me, but only for a few days and then returned on the same terms as before and carried on in that capacity for another year, only now and again, whenever required by us, assuming the conductor's baton."[2]

On at least one occasion Maliniak came close to conducting a dress rehearsal of *Don Pasquale* when a foreign conductor was not able to perform, and the society's music director Alberto Erede was ill and could not fill in himself. "So as not to offend Maliniak and a younger coach…I drew lots as to which of them should conduct," recalled Pomeroy. The younger coach won, and went on to conduct the dress rehearsal.[3]

But in the summer of 1949, Maliniak seemed to have secured the chance of a lifetime. He had found another impresario who was ready to sign him to a major contract, "with a view to engaging him as the conductor for his opera company," wrote Pomeroy. The unnamed impresario wanted to see Maliniak in action, conducting Italian opera. He wanted to attend the Music Art and Drama Society's final performance of *Don Pasquale* for the spring season, under Maliniak's baton. Days before the performance, Maliniak asked Erede to plead his case with Pomeroy to allow him to conduct *Don Pasquale*. Pomeroy refused. "I immediately replied that I expected at that performance some important people and as that performance was the last of *Don Pasquale* during this season, I suggested that we give Maliniak to conduct an opera at Croydon during this fortnight," said Pomeroy,[4] who was himself facing grave financial problems and was on the verge of bankruptcy for unpaid taxes. The debt would eventually wipe out his theatrical empire.

It's not clear if Maliniak or any of the artists associated with Pomeroy's Music Art and Drama Society had any inkling that the company was in deep financial trouble. But in Maliniak's case, he appeared not to have been paid for months and was owed £206 in back wages. Maliniak and his wife, who continued to clean houses to earn a living, were scraping by, barely able to make the £7.70 monthly rent on their modest apartment. Gerda Maliniak, who suffered from a painful injury to her knee, was also having difficulty working in a job that required her to stand for most of the day.

On the morning of June 23, 1949, Maliniak woke up despondent in the family's Compayne Gardens flat. He did not go to work that day, "and [was] practically in tears," his wife later told a police officer. He waited until both his wife and daughter had left the apartment before preparing his formal conductor's outfit. He dressed in his tuxedo in anticipation of the opera he had recently spent countless hours rehearsing, coaching his singers at the French Renaissance–style Stoll Theater with its bas-reliefs of the world's most famous composers on fluted gold and white columns in the lobby.[5]

Fate has made a beggar of me.

The line belongs to the rebellious Ernesto in *Don Pasquale*, and Maliniak surely heard it sung dozens of times, coaching the baritone who took on the role in rehearsals. In Donizetti's comic opera, Ernesto is referring to the machinations of his uncle Don Pasquale who threatens to disinherit him after he refuses the woman his uncle has chosen for him to marry.

Sometime in the late afternoon of that summer Thursday, Maliniak cranked up the Ascot gas cooker and took a seat in a deckchair. Having escaped the gas chambers of the Third Reich and having lost his mother to them, Maliniak killed himself in his kitchen. On the dining table, investigators found an envelope marked "finance." Inside was the neatly penciled ledger that listed his worldly assets: a bank balance of £48 followed by a column stacked with debts and monies owed.

It was Gerda who discovered her husband slumped in the chair hours later. "I turned off the gas of the gas cooker, opened the windows and called the doctor," she told Hugh MacKay, the police constable who arrived at the flat soon after she found her husband.

An autopsy followed, and over the next few days the coroner conducted a formal inquiry, collecting statements from Gerda Maliniak and Jay Pomeroy, who could not appear at the coroner's court in person because he claimed in a letter that he was suffering from "an attack of glandular fever."

"There were two years in England during which time my husband was really happy, that was when he had the chance to conduct Italian opera," wrote Gerda Maliniak. "Unfortunately, this enterprise had to come to an end and there again there was no prospect of getting similar work."[6]

In the neatly typed Northern District County of London Coroner's Officer's Report Concerning Death, Maliniak's cause of death was listed as asphyxiation by "coal gas poisoning." The report noted that "he was a professional musician employed by the Jay Pomeroy Productions but for some time his engagements had been very few. Only the day before he was found dead he had had a great disappointment— he had been hoping for a chance to secure an engagement but it was a failure."

And Thomas Day, the coroner's officer, thought to add the following coda: "Deceased had never actually threatened his life. But in 1939, when things were not going very well, he did mention something to the effect that there was always the open window."[7]

Ten days after Maliniak's suicide, his friends Viorica Ursuleac and Clemens Krauss were the star attractions at a special, intimate concert at Wigmore Hall in London. Wigmore Hall was an ideal setting for such an event. It is a small concert venue with near-perfect acoustics usually reserved for chamber music or a selection of lieder, Romantic poems set to music. The Renaissance-inspired theater, with its marble and alabaster walls, features an unusual cupola above the small stage covered in an idealized painting depicting a young, nude man as the soul of music, gazing in a kind of rapture at the ball of fire that is meant to represent the "genius of harmony." Crowned by the cupola, the lone singer on stage seems transported into a sacred, holy space.

Built in 1901 by the C. Bechstein *Pianofortefabrik* next to its piano showroom on Wigmore Street, the hall was seized as enemy-alien property by the authorities during the First World War after the passage of the Trading with the Enemy Amendment Act of 1916 ended trade with Germany. The concert hall and the company's showroom were shuttered. In the same year, the buildings were bought at auction by a local department store for a fraction of their worth and re-opened in 1917 as Wigmore Hall. The concert hall saw the London premieres of works by some of the world's greatest artists, including Richard Strauss and Béla Bartók, and recitals by Enrico Caruso and the German-born soprano Elisabeth Schwarzkopf, one of the greatest singers of lieder.

Ursuleac also sang a series of lieder at the concert, most of them somber poetry about lost love and death, while Krauss accompanied her on a grand piano. She sang in the original German, with English translations given in the program. As they listened to the couple perform "Liebestreu," by Brahms, they—the Cooks and Gerda and Ingeborg Daisy Maliniak—must have surely felt the absence of Maliniak.

'O sink deep, O sink deep the grief, my child
in the sea, in the deep dark sea!'
A stone must bide on the dark sea-floor
and grief comes back to me.[8]

They had all seen each other for the first time since the war two years before at a restaurant in Soho in the autumn of 1947. Ida and Louise had organized a dinner for the Maliniaks, the Mayer-Lismanns, and Krauss and Ursuleac, who had traveled to London with the Vienna Philharmonic. "We were all in tremendous spirits, though inwardly deeply moved to meet like this after so many years, and we were determined to drink a triumphant toast to 'Reunion outside Vienna.'"[9]

It was the first time that the sisters had seen the conductor and his wife following the war, and they had rushed to Victoria Station for what Ida called "the rapture of reunion."

"Once more, the exclamations, the questions, the half-answers, more questions and the endless exchange of news. It seemed that we would never be able to say or hear enough of what had happened in the years in between."[10] The sisters took the couple to their flat and soon learned that their own home in Munich had been completely wrecked by a phosphorous bomb that destroyed everything they owned. "We started to say something sympathetic but Krauss dismissed our exclamations with a gesture of his hand," said Ida. The sisters were so moved that at the end of their visit they presented the couple with a key to the Dolphin Square flat and told them to consider it their home when they found themselves in London. "There was a certain unspoken poetic justice about their being able to regard as home the place that sheltered so many people we might never have known or helped, if they had not first committed Mitia to our care."[11]

Of course, it was a different reunion at Wigmore Hall. Not only did Maliniak's death weigh heavily, but Krauss and Ursuleac were still deeply wounded over the ban imposed on Krauss's career in Austria. Although he was now able to perform, the conductor remained unable to take on any leadership role in Austrian musical institutions. However, he remained a living legend. On May 10, 1947, the Allies had agreed, after a great deal of political obstruction from the Soviets who were against any performances by Krauss, to allow him to conduct the Vienna Philharmonic. It was his first appearance since the end of the war and the audience showed its wild appreciation even before Krauss started conducting. "His return today was a triumph," said the *New York Times.* "He refused to recognize the heavy applause when he appeared on the stage, launching immediately into the program with no more than a quick bow to the audience. The applause continued and the first portion of his first number was drowned out." Observers at the concert told the *Times* reporter that the round on round of applause "was not a political demonstration, but that the audience was made up of typical Vienna music enthusiasts."[12]

Krauss had gradually eased back into the limelight, but he mostly took on jobs conducting orchestras outside Austria. Still deeply humiliated by his treatment after the war, Krauss and Ursuleac retreated to a traditional Alpine home in Ehrwald, a Tyrolean village under the shadow of the majestic Zugspitze Mountain, more than three thousand feet above sea level. Their two-story wood-and-stucco cottage was painted yellow, with dark-green shutters, and was a short drive from Richard Strauss's estate in Garmisch, a market town on the German side of the Alps where the 1936 Winter Olympic Games had been held.

But just as Krauss and Ursuleac settled into their Austrian mountain retreat, Strauss—Krauss's beloved mentor and collaborator—died of kidney failure, only a few months after his eighty-fifth birthday. More than two thousand mourners attended his funeral in war-ravaged Munich on September 12, 1949. In his will, Strauss had requested that music from Beethoven and his own opera *Rosenkavalier* be featured at the somber event, where his elderly wife, Pauline Maria de Ahna, a former soprano, appeared distraught in a black-lace mantilla. The couple had been married for fifty-five years, and although she had once been described by her husband as "very complex" and "a little perverse," the union was a happy one. Strauss often credited his wife with providing him with a great deal of inspiration. Pauline Strauss never recovered after her husband's death. She died eight months later.[13]

The death of one of Germany's most important composers was a cause for national mourning, even though Strauss had been associated with the Nazis just a few years before. At the funeral, all seemed forgotten. The sopranos who sang the final trio from *Der Rosenkavalier*—Marianne Schech, Maud Cunitz, and Gerda Sommerschuh—broke down at different times during their performance. And the composer was praised by a Munich city official as "one of the last few creative composers of this century."[14] Following the service, Strauss was cremated, and the ashes were spread in the garden at Garmisch.

In a tribute to Strauss, the directors of the Salzburg Festival decided to include his final opera, *Capriccio*, as part of its summer lineup in 1950. Krauss had worked on the libretto for the opera after the composer's original partner Stefan Zweig had gone into exile and then committed suicide. But Krauss was not appointed to conduct the opera, much to Ida and Louise's annoyance. His name appeared nowhere on the advance prospectus, which had been mailed to patrons, including the Cook sisters, in February 1950. "I am astonished and dismayed to see that Clemens Krauss's name does not appear in the list of conductors," wrote Ida Cook in February 1950. "We find it hard to believe. In fact, had the composer been alive, he would certainly not have entrusted the Salzburg performance to anyone but Clemens Krauss."[15] Whether she wrote the angry letter at Krauss's urging or whether it stemmed from her own initiative is unknown, although by then Ida had become an impassioned opera critic. She was also a fierce defender of Krauss and Ursuleac.

The letter, which was sent to Josef Klaus, the governor of Salzburg, was oddly signed by Mary Burchell, Ida's pen name, and sent from the Dolphin Square flat at Howard House. Ida always sent her letters from Morella Road, where she still worked in the attic and never signed them with her pseudonym. Perhaps in this case she sought to throw her weight around as one of the country's best-selling novelists. A year earlier, Mills & Boon published ads in newspapers and magazines heralding Mary Burchell as one of their most important authors. She had already written forty-one books, and sold 406,473 copies, mostly to libraries, according to Mills & Boon. The company's principals calculated that on average each book was lent a hundred times. From overall sales, her royalties topped £500,000.[16]

"*Capriccio* is as far as I know, actually the only case today where a current masterpiece could have the inestimable advantage of being presented by one, at least, of the men responsible for its existence," she wrote, adding that "there is an unpleasant feeling abroad that something as mean and unsavory as operatic intrigue is keeping us from hearing the really great performances that we were used to hearing in the old days."[17]

The sternly worded letter did nothing to help Krauss in Salzburg. It did, however, elicit a response from the governor of Salzburg who sent a polite reply a month later, saying that Austrian conductor Karl Böhm, who had also suffered a denazification ban after the war, would conduct *Capriccio*. "The decision was...made in favor of Böhm because he had conducted the premiere in Vienna at the time. I believe I have every right to say that no opera intrigues played a role in this election."[18]

Clemens Krauss would continue to be labeled a Nazi by protesters who clamored outside concert halls wherever he went. "So much lying propaganda was put out about her [Ursuleac] and Krauss, partly by disgruntled professional rivals and partly by people who judged," wrote Ida in a letter to her friend and fellow opera enthusiast Alfred Frankenstein. "I don't claim that they were superbly better than anyone else, but they did the best they could—and sometimes took risks that were very hard to take. One hopes one would have done as much in like circumstances."[19]

But the "lying propaganda" was difficult to take. As the important conducting jobs increasingly went to Krauss's rivals, he grew embittered, and his health began to suffer. He continued to perform everywhere he could, taking jobs at Covent Garden in the 1950s. Krauss finally regained some of his old respect when he was asked to conduct at the Bayreuth Festival in 1953. He also made a handful of well-regarded recordings.

Following his Covent Garden appearances, Krauss and Ursuleac prepared for a long journey in the spring of 1954. They were off to Mexico City where Krauss was scheduled to appear as a guest conductor of the Orquestra Sinfónica Nacional in a kind of cultural exchange organized by the embassy of the Federal Republic of Germany in Mexico. Krauss was once again the subject of heated protests in the city where critics accused him of being a Nazi collaborator. However, the conductor, now sixty-one, tried not to let them interfere with preparations for performances of works by Franz Josef Haydn and Johannes Brahms at the opulent, neoclassical Palacio de Bellas Artes. Completed in 1934, the theater was the showplace of Mexican cultural life, featuring giant murals by Diego Rivera and Rufino Tamayo.

On the night of May 16, Krauss appeared at the conductor's podium, glamorous and rather aloof in a smart tuxedo and wearing dark glasses to cut the glare from the giant television lights that had distracted him during the first few performances. Among the highlights of the evening was Mexican pianist Angelica Morales performing Brahms's Second Concerto for Piano and Orchestra and

Austrian composer and conductor Haydn's Symphony Number 88. Following rousing applause at the end of the performance, the conductor abruptly took his leave. He told his Mexican hosts that he wasn't feeling well and needed to lie down. He would see them at rehearsals the next day, he said. Krauss returned to the Hotel Monte Cassino accompanied by Ursuleac.

"Then while he was undressing she just went to get him a drink of water, and when she came back he was unconscious," continued Ida in her letter to Frankenstein. Krauss had suffered a cardiac arrest. "He never regained consciousness and died in less than an hour. One couldn't ask a better end for anyone one loves—but for her it must have been terrible."[20]

When they heard the details surrounding his death, Ida and Louise seized upon one of their favorite operas. They remembered how they had first encountered Krauss at his performance of *Arabella* at Covent Garden in 1934. In the opera, Mandryka tells Arabella shortly after he meets her that it is a village custom for a woman to offer a glass of water to the man she loves. Ursuleac had unwittingly repeated her famous role as Arabella on the couple's last night together in Mexico City when she walked into the bedroom with that final glass of water.

The sisters were beyond grief. As Ida noted in her letter to Frankenstein: "After our immediate family, he and Viorica were much the closest people to us, and we feel it badly."[21]

It took more than a month for Viorica Ursuleac to clear the bureaucratic hurdles of transporting her husband's body back to Austria, even though she had a great deal of help from the Austrian Legation in Mexico City, where Ida and Louise sent her a telegram as soon as they heard the sad news: "Thinking of you both my darling with all our love and sympathy your heartbroken Louise and Ida."[22] Ida followed up with a letter to Ursuleac on May 19, 1954, three days after Krauss's death, noting that it was the first time in the sisters' lives that they had "lost anyone inexpressibly dear to us."

> I will try not to write a sad letter, because you already have enough sadness.
>
> We want you to know how touching and wonderful we find it that, after all, you two—our beautiful darlings—were alone together at the end. Perhaps it was sad to be far from home. But it was right that you, who were all his world, should be there, without friends or enemies to suggest or decide anything. Whatever you want to arrange for him will be right.[23]

Ida described how lucky she and Louise were to live "within the radiance of the love between you two," calling it "the greatest inspiration of our lives. Because it was—indeed is—so beautiful, so complete and eternal, it is to us the strongest and simplest proof of something after this life."

Telegrams and letters poured in from all over the world from fellow musicians and opera singers Krauss had worked with during the war. There were heartfelt letters from Strauss's son in Germany, Adele Kern, and even rivals such as Karl Böhm. Mitia Mayer-Lismann, who had returned to live at the Dolphin Square flat after losing her job at the finishing school, was among the last to send her condolences, so overwhelmed was she by the death of the conductor who had helped to save her life. "What we feel is deeply rooted in the heartfelt connection we have had with him—with you," wrote Mayer-Lismann to Ursuleac. "As in happier days, we are full of admiration for the wonderful romantic love between you two."[24]

Before Ursuleac could return to Austria with the body, the Mexicans insisted upon paying tribute to the conductor in their own way. "Mexico has the privilege of being the first to pay homage," said Andrés Iduarte, the director of the National Institute of Fine Arts, who offered the theater's stage so that the conductor could lie in state. "The physical and spiritual place where Clemens Krauss's passing occurred is not so alien nor distant from his artistic greatness. After all, this artist died in a country dedicated to art."[25] The Orquestra Sinfónica Nacional played the Haydn symphony that they had performed the night Krauss died—a symbolic tribute from one of Austria's greatest composers to one of its greatest conductors.

At Ursuleac's request, Ida and Louise traveled to meet her and Krauss's remains for the trip to Ehrwald, where Ursuleac decided he would be buried. They were joined on that final journey by Else Mayer-Lismann; her mother Mitia was too ill and heartbroken to make the sad trip. "In Vienna they want to give him a great state funeral and bury him beside Schubert and Beethoven," wrote Ida to Ponselle. "But as the way they treated him contributed to his death, I think Viorica will refuse, and have him buried in Ehrwald, the little village in the Tyrol where they were so happy together. The Viennese are extraordinary towards their great men. They break their hearts, but they bury them splendidly."[26]

■   ■   ■

Months after their "sad summer," the sisters made plans to travel back to the United States and introduce their new friend, a certain American-born Greek soprano named Maria Callas, to Ponselle: "I think she's a great overall artist and much the most exciting thing since the War—but people do really forget the standards we had other days sometimes! It would be ungenerous of me to start listing faults at the moment of her triumph." But Ida couldn't help herself, and she went on to tell Ponselle—"just for the sake of artistic truth"—that in the months before Krauss died he would not allow the sisters to play a Callas record on their new record player when they were all at the Dolphin Square flat.

On that night—which would be their last together—Krauss and Ursuleac demanded to hear the singers of opera's glory days. They wanted Rethberg first, and Ida complied, fishing out one of her records from their large collection. "And now, I should like to hear Ponselle," said Ursuleac, who surprisingly had never heard the American soprano sing. Krauss himself had only heard Ponselle once, many years before. Ida carefully unsheathed her precious recording of *La Vestale* from its wax-paper sleeve and slowly placed it on the turntable. It was a rarely performed opera by Gaspare Spontini that Ponselle revived for the Metropolitan Opera's 1925–26 season and sang again at that unforgettable performance in Florence in 1933.

"I can't tell you how touching and exciting it was playing what we considered the greatest singer of all for the man we considered the greatest judge of all," continued Ida. At the end of the recording, Krauss turned to everyone and said, "She's engaged! She's the best of the lot!" It was a typical Krauss joke, explained Ida, "but contained the highest praise he could give—measuring you against…artists they thought supreme."

And then as Ida prepared to put on another Ponselle recording, Krauss stood up quite suddenly and took charge. Gripping an invisible baton, he began to "conduct" tenor Giovanni Martinelli and Ponselle in the Nile duet from *Aida*. "And as though you were standing there following him, you did everything to perfection," Ida told Ponselle. "They nearly went mad with joy. Then we played the 'Bois épais' and Viorica cried."

"We shall never, never hear anything like that again," Krauss pronounced, putting down his make-believe baton. "Such a voice and such an art doesn't come more than once."

"Don't you think it was lovely that our dear Krauss, whose opinion we valued above all others, confirmed our own views on the last evening we ever spent with him?" wrote Ida to Ponselle. "It also, I think, gave him the great pleasure to find that, entirely independent of him our judgment was all he could have wished. It was a very happy last evening to remember."[27]

Finally, on that distant February evening in the Dolphin Square flat, Krauss left the sisters with a gift—a recording of all the tone poems by Richard Strauss that he had conducted. He signed the album cover, "To my best friends, Ida and Louise, with love—Clemens Krauss."

My best friends? With love? "We were astounded at the time, for it was most unlike him ever to use such terms," Ida told Frankenstein. "It was as though he had some sort of premonition and wanted to put the seal on 20 years of loving friendship. You can imagine how much we treasure this now."[28]

The following morning, Krauss and Ursuleac left London, and the sisters never saw him again.

"I hope you won't think us crazy if I tell you, Rosa, that he actually came back to us—to reassure us and comfort us," wrote Ida. "Do you believe that occasionally this does happen? I have always believed it, but never imagined it happening to us."[29]

CHAPTER 12

The Ghosts

Ida and Louise had been fascinated with ghosts their entire lives. From the time their mother told them the story of meeting a troubled phantom at their home in Barnes when they were still young children, they maintained a strong belief in life after death. "They always said that they had their angels who followed them everywhere," noted one of their friends.[1]

The Cooks lived with friendly spirits all around them and sought their counsel and even eavesdropped on their busy lives in what they referred to as "the other side." They were devotees of British medium Leslie Flint, who purported to communicate with famous historical figures, including Frédéric Chopin and Oscar Wilde, during seances at his London home. It was not unusual for them to sit in a circle in the dark for hours, holding hands until they were able to communicate with the dead. "We always say it's just like trying to get the first telephone across the Atlantic," said Ida in a letter to a friend. "No good sending out signals from Newfoundland (or wherever it was) unless someone sits patiently in Ireland ready to register the first 'hello!' It will come!"[2]

At different sessions, they were able to communicate with their friend Pinza, who died of a stroke in 1957, and Amelita Galli-Curci, who died in 1963. They even managed to speak to their beloved Krauss and once claimed to have overheard the conductor and Richard Strauss in an argument with another composer. The subject was, of course, opera. "Strauss was indignant and Krauss, though he didn't speak, was backing him up," the medium said.[3]

So the sisters were perhaps only mildly surprised when Ida began to receive random reports that Krauss had been present during Ida's appearance on *This is Your Life*, which was broadcast in March 1956, nearly two years after his death. According to Ida, four people in different parts of England told her that they saw a man standing next to Ursuleac, who had been flown to London by the show's producers to appear on the program. The producers had also found some of the Cooks' refugees who were still living in Britain to appear on the show. The announcer promised the audience "a story more romantic than fiction—a story that might have come straight from the casebook of a modern Scarlet Pimpernel," likening the Cooks' adventures in the Reich to those of the fictional aristocrat who went undercover to save his French counterparts from the guillotine in eighteenth-century France.[4]

Ida first heard about the apparition months after the broadcast when an elderly woman approached her after a lecture she gave at the Women's Institute in Surrey. The woman told Ida that she had loved the program, especially the couple "with the refugee work." Ida assured her there were no couples on the program and left it at that. But later, on a trip to Northumberland to visit friends, another woman asked, "Who was the tall, very good-looking foreigner who absolutely dominated the program?" When Ida returned armed with photos of Krauss, the woman positively identified the conductor although she pointed out that his hair was dark not grey. "He was young again, you see," said the wistful Ida, who believed that Krauss was never far away from her and Louise.[5]

The year following the *This Is Your Life* broadcast was a difficult one for Ida and Louise. Not only did they lose their friend Pinza in 1957, but Mitia Mayer-Lismann—the first Jew they'd ever met who was among their first successful cases—died in London after battling a long illness and poverty.

For years before her death, Mayer-Lismann had hired a lawyer to seek restitution from the West German government, largely because she was unable to find steady work after losing her job teaching music at a private school. Not only had she demanded the return of her property in Frankfurt, but she also sought compensation for the suffering the Nazis had inflicted on her and her entire family. Although her lawyer managed to obtain a small pension for her, she was largely unsuccessful; and when she died in early 1957 at the age of seventy-two, she was broke and still fighting for restitution.

The Cook sisters helped Mayer-Lismann, who "earned very, very little" in London. "Their interest and active help when needed never stopped during all the years," said Else Mayer-Lismann. "The Cook sisters have been and are always there."[6]

In addition to their own refugees, many others wanted to thank Ida and Louise for their active help. Still, Ida was rather taken aback when Ella Mahler, a researcher at Yad Vashem, the Holocaust memorial in Jerusalem, wrote to her in London in 1963. She wanted to know more about the sisters' work in the Third Reich. Mahler had been contacted by May Sayers, a Jewish philanthropist who knew the Cook sisters and thought they deserved widespread recognition for their bravery. "Ida and Louise Cook established a kind of 'private' rescue committee in which they had been the sole promotors, executors and financial supporters," read the "Proceeding on Collecting Data on Sisters Cooks' Rescue Work" for the Israeli organization.[7]

In an introductory letter to Ida, Mahler wrote: "Yad Vashem looks upon your and your sister's activities as an important chapter in the history of pre-war help extended to the Jews by non-Jews and would like to preserve a detailed account of it." She added that if the committee voted to name the Cooks "Righteous Among the Nations," a tree would be planted in their honor along the Avenue of the Righteous, a park at Yad Vashem inaugurated in 1962.[8]

'We are fascinated by the possibility of having a tree planted in our name," wrote Ida in a letter to Mahler dated September 8, 1963. "The idea makes me feel quite tearful....But meanwhile, thank you so much my dear, for starting this. Even if nothing comes of it, the thought was darling."[9]

After Ida provided a partial list of the refugees she and Louise had helped escape the Nazis, Mahler requested more information about their flight from Germany and Austria. Several former refugees paid tribute to the Cooks and told their stories in long, often rambling letters to Mahler, thrilled that both Louise and Ida were being considered for the distinction. In Jerusalem, letters arrived from Lisa Basch, Else Mayer-Lismann, Friedl Bamberger Orlando, Ilse Bauer, Gerda Maliniak, and others. Newspaper clippings and excerpts from Ida's memoir were all translated into Hebrew and collected in a thick dossier labeled "File #223—Cook Unit." The file was sent to Israeli jurist Moshe Landau, who had presided over the trial of Nazi war criminal Adolf Eichmann in a Jerusalem courtroom two years before.

Landau had studied law in London before the outbreak of the war, and he had no need for the Hebrew-language translations. A refugee from Nazi Germany who had made his way to Palestine in 1933, Landau focused on the halting English of the letters from German, Polish, and Austrian Jews who wrote from England, the United States, and as far away as Brazil to pay tribute to Ida and Louise Cook, who had used opera to cloak their dangerous relief work.

In his capacity as chair, Israel's Supreme Court President was just beginning to read a great deal about the diplomats, soldiers, and ordinary people who worked in the resistance and risked their own lives to save Jews during the Holocaust. But at his first meeting of the Committee for the Righteous at the Holocaust Memorial Yad Vashem in 1963, nothing could have prepared Landau for the extraordinary story of how two plucky British music fans saved dozens of Jews from the gas chambers in real-life dramas that resembled the elaborate plots of some of their favorite operas.

"It was curiously enough the love of opera, shared by Louise and Ida from their girlhood on, which started the sisters on their refugee activities," read the slightly bemused introduction to the Cook Unit dossier. "What originally started as a gesture of goodwill extended by Ida and Louise to their operatic friends, developed into a regular, exciting, but heart-breaking task." According to the notes in the Cook file, the sisters were "guided by their compassion for the persecuted, and their revulsion against the injustice and brutality of Nazi insanity" to plunge "body and soul into the refugee work."[10]

"With infinite patience and humility in the face of so much human misery, they interviewed as many as 10 to 15 people at a time," wrote Sayers. "This personal contact with the unfortunates helped the sisters to view the problems of the refugees in terms of human beings, not just names and photographs."[11]

Landau and his committee of experts needed little time to make a decision on the Cook sisters' good works, and on July 28, 1964, he signed the Certificate of Recognition of the Yad Vashem Martyrs and Heroes Remembrance Authority honoring "Miss Ida Cook and Miss Louise Cook for their many noble and courageous acts of humanity in rescuing Jews from Germany and from Austria during the dark days of the Nazi regime and in helping them to rebuild their lives in freedom."[12]

The sisters were thrilled with the honor, but Ida wanted to make sure that Yad Vashem somehow recognized Krauss as well. In a letter to Mahler, dated March 22, 1964, she pleaded to have Krauss's nationality corrected to Austrian from German. "He was so very much a Viennese that I think he would want it that way," said Ida. "Otherwise, I can't tell you how delighted we are that there should be a record of the fact that he and his wife were the mainspring of our work. So many spiteful and completely untrue things were said of them largely by professional rivals in later years and the issue became rather fogged. It gives us real joy to see tribute paid to them."[13]

Although Krauss's nationality was duly corrected, the conductor was never officially recognized by Yad Vashem or his own country for his role in helping the Cooks save Jews.

Arthur Lourie, the Israeli ambassador to London, presented the awards to the sisters on March 23, 1965, at a special ceremony at the Israeli Embassy. Honoring the Cooks was his last official act as ambassador in London, where he was joined for the ceremony by Britain's foremost Jewish leaders, including solicitor and Labour Member of Parliament Victor Mishcon. Ida, then sixty and Louise, sixty-three, each wore silky day dresses, pillbox hats, and gloves for the occasion. "Two unobtrusive non-Jewish English spinsters traveled from their quiet suburban home today to receive Israel's thanks for smuggling 29 Jews out of pre-war Germany," noted *New York Times* reporter James Feron on the newspaper's front page. "They seemed to think it was all unnecessary."[14]

But around the world those who had helped them in their relief work rejoiced. "It made me happy for the two of them," said the soprano Adele Kern, who remained in Germany after the war. "They really deserved it.... They did a lot for the emigrants."[15]

Their refugees were also thrilled with the distinction. "When we were given our award at the Israeli Embassy in London, Ilse gave a party in our honor to all her friends in Brazil, on the other side of the world," said Ida.[16] Ilse Bauer, now Ilse Bauer Winter, who had fled to Frankfurt with her mother Irma after Kristallnacht in Vienna, was now happily living in Curitiba, a city in southern Brazil. "We found it immensely touching," said Ida.[17]

There was some scattered media attention in England following the ceremony, but the Cooks' tendency to play down any accomplishments meant that their work was quickly forgotten, relegated to the occasional fundraising luncheon for Israel Bonds in New York City and the Westchester suburbs. Shortly after the Israeli distinction, a woman approached the sisters at one of these events at Manhattan's Waldorf Astoria and asked how many Jews the sisters had saved.

"Twenty-nine, directly," said Louise.

"Oh, how many!" replied the woman, clearly impressed.

"How very few," said Ida.[18]

■   ■   ■

"Dear Friends," wrote Ida in a letter on July 16, 1968, to her new Hollywood acquaintances. "Several times during the last two months we have had to resist the temptation to write to you about this or that aspect of 'our' film."[19] Although they were clearly excited about Hollywood's interest in their wartime adventures, Ida and Louise were also worried. In mostly one-sided correspondence stretching over four years with filmmaker Joshua Logan and producer Fred Kolhmar about a potential biopic, the letter belies an undertone of contretemps, a profound difference of opinion between the demands of Hollywood and the sisters' desire to protect what to them was surely a sacred story. Ida had already presented her own treatment to Logan and Kolhmar that was passed on to a professional screenwriter and heavily rewritten.

"Our chief criticism would be that the whole thing is a fictional exercise on a true theme. But in the process the real stature of the whole has somehow been reduced." Ironically, Ida, the romance writer, bristled at "the completely fictitious love story" that anchored the plot. The proposed script involved an opera producer character who "is not a sufficiently olympian (or indeed complex) figure" and his fiancée, who "should be a beastly but attractive girl of the Prussian nobility."[20]

A friend had introduced Ida to Joshua Logan, at the time he met the Cooks in the late 1960s one of Hollywood's greatest producers and directors. He won the Pulitzer Prize for drama in 1950, sharing the honor with Richard Rodgers and Oscar Hammerstein with whom he had collaborated on the musical *South Pacific*, which starred the Cooks' friend Pinza in the leading role of French planter Emile de Becque. In addition to Pinza, Logan had worked with some of the biggest stars of the day, including Marilyn Monroe, Marlon Brando, Bette Davis, and Burt Lancaster. The successful filmmaker behind some of world's most celebrated musicals had been taken with the odd British sisters and was at first fascinated by the prospect of using their 1930s exploits as material for a melodrama. "We still remember our thrilling day with you and your sister," Logan wrote to Ida while on location in Oregon where he was filming *Paint Your Wagon* with Clint Eastwood and Jean Seberg in the summer of 1968. "I still long to have a chance to work on your thrilling story."[21]

Ida and Louise felt their own real-life narrative with its tense checks at the borders, improbable cover story, and triumphant rescue of artists and their families and friends—in some cases, mere hours before their arrest by the Gestapo—would make a great film, and Ida labored for weeks on her Hollywood-style treatment.

But while their rescue efforts were indeed daring, who would pay to see a movie about two women who were the antithesis of glamor?

The question had undoubtedly occurred to Logan and fellow producer Fred Kolhmar, whose last movie before meeting Ida and Louise was *How to Steal a Million*, a 1966 comedy about an art heist in which its gamine star Audrey Hepburn looked exceptionally chic in Givenchy couture. It's not clear why Logan and Kohlmar ultimately passed on the Cooks' story. Perhaps Hollywood studios just weren't ready to finance a film focused entirely on the heroism of two modest-looking, middle-aged women who faced down evil and won.

Evidently Ida had difficulty trusting someone else to tell the tale, and negotiations with Logan resulted in an impasse. "Ida was very strong willed and very upset that they had assigned someone else to tell her story," said a friend of the sisters. "She often said it was their story, not someone else's story to tell."[22] Ida tried various tactics to insert her views into the script. At one point, she even offered to send a tape-recording of her telling the tale. "This sounds dreadfully egotistical, but I do know one can't possibly retain every detail of a story for months," she wrote on December 1, 1968, to Joshua Logan and his wife Nedda.[23] Ida's offer to tape the story met with no reply, nor did a letter sent to the Logans four years later on March 5, 1972.

Logan's secretary filed Ida's letters and treatment away, where they were forgotten among dozens of film budgets and legal papers. Years after Logan's death in 1988, the papers were packed up, along with Logan's other correspondence, and donated to the Library of Congress. For years, Ida Cook's film dreams languished there. And for decades afterwards, the Cooks' story was simply forgotten.

Reading Ida's film treatment, I was struck once again by the sisters' genuine innocence and humility, as in their "magnificent dazzlement" when Clemens Krauss kissed their hands for the first time. "We were tremendously in awe of him even when we knew and loved him well," writes Ida in the film treatment. "And it was typical that at no time in the twenty years of our friendship would we have dreamed of addressing him as Clemens. He was always Herr Direktor or Mr Krauss...a fascinating mixture of the grand seigneur and a great man of the theater...the greatest opera director of the century."[24]

The treatment went on to describe how the sisters continued to queue for cheap opera tickets outside Covent Garden even after Ida had started to make sizable advances as a writer. Coming from what Ida called "cloud-cuckoo land," they could never quite get their civil service heads around the Nuremberg Laws, that Jews were being arrested and sent to concentration camps simply because they were Jews. "Surely one can complain?" asked the Ida character in the film script. But as she quickly found out in real life, "There is no one to whom one *can* complain if one is a Jew."[25]

In many ways, the very rigid principles of those "two squares" who, according to Ida's treatment, were "brought up on a great deal of affection, very little money, and some sound maxims" simply collided with the glitzy, glamorizing demands of Hollywood.[26]

"Finally, I much prefer my own ending," wrote Ida at the end of a densely typed two-page letter to Logan. "This is the story which invariably reduced people to tears."[27]

In Ida's version, the final scene, which was drawn from real life, had a London taxi driver striking up a conversation with the sisters while they were in the back seat of his cab. He said he had just seen them on television telling their story about saving Jews from the Holocaust.

"Know what I think?" offered the cabbie. "I think you could make a movie out of that story."

The sisters exchanged knowing looks and explained that they almost had, but that Hollywood rejected them because the story lacked any love interest.

"No *love* in it?" He leaned his arm on the window ledge, grinning but sincere. "Why, bless your heart, you loved 'em all! Else why did you do it?"

For a moment they considered this profound truth. Then Louise smiled and Ida looked halfway to tears, and Louise said, "Well, yes, in that sense, of course, you're right."[28]

EPILOGUE

The Record Player

The late 1960s and 1970s were busy times for the sisters. In addition to her romantic novels and keeping up a voluminous correspondence with friends around the world, Ida became a ghostwriter. She completed two biographies of Tito Gobbi, a celebrated Italian baritone, who became a close friend. Although well into their sixties, the sisters still seemed to have unlimited energy and maintained their good health. Into old age, they had "the fine white skin and ruddy cheeks of English country dwellers," as one observer put it.[1]

After the successful publication of Ida's memoir about the sisters' opera-world adventures and relief efforts in 1950, an editor at *Woman's Illustrated* asked her to write two romantic serials set during the Cold War. At the editor's request, Ida set two love stories in Budapest, a place she confessed she was at a loss to describe because she had never been there, but "at least I knew the awfulness of the police knocking on the door at five in the morning...and your father or your husband dragged away in front of you."[2]

In fact, soon after the war ended, Ida and Louise learned firsthand about life in Hungary after they had "adopted" two Hungarian refugee families in a Displaced Persons Camp in Bavaria, where the sisters spent a great deal of their time helping many who were still homeless more than a decade after the end of the Second World War. Ida wrote to Rosa Ponselle shortly after that visit:

> Louise and I are just back from Munich where we visited a camp for Displaced Persons in which we are interested. It was the most moving and incredible experience. All these people, with no country and no home to go to. Either Poles who were brought to Germany for slave labour and didn't want to go back under the Russians after the War, or people who escaped from the Baltic States or the Ukraine when the Russians came in, or a few who got over the border from Hungary—and on and on. We were afraid there wouldn't be much we could do—but we've got quite a few plans in our heads now and are most cheered and enthusiastic.[3]

Those "few" Hungarians soon grew exponentially, fleeing Soviet tyranny. Tensions in the country reached a fever pitch and erupted in a nationwide revolution with thousands of protesters taking to the streets to demand a more democratic political system in the autumn of 1956. On November 4 the Soviets under Nikita Khrushchev shocked the world when they sent tanks and troops into Budapest, brutally crushing the pro-democracy activists as fierce fighting broke out in the streets. Thousands of Hungarians were rounded up, with Soviet forces searching for opposition activists for months after the uprising. Many of those arrested ended up in Soviet labor camps, and more than two thousand people died in the conflict.

To none of their friends' surprise, Ida and Louise somehow found themselves enmeshed in world events yet again. Their relief work at the camp in the Bavarian Alps also brought them close to Ehrwald and their dear friend Ursuleac. "We have been having a thrilling time working out possible schemes to help," wrote Ida in another letter to Ponselle, describing how she and Louise were volunteering in a program to end a tuberculosis epidemic at the camp. "A few months ago it seemed almost impossible to do anything. But now at least we have a plan to help the unfortunate post-TB cases which are a tragic feature of the camp."[4]

If she had strong views about opera before the war, Ida became a positively fierce critic after the conflict. She continued to heap faint praise on the opera world's latest sensation, Maria Callas, who was nevertheless turning into an icon. "She's such an interesting creature on the stage. With all her faults (and she has them) she somehow lights the authentic flame. But if I may venture the opinion of the non-professional, I don't think she's ever equalized her scale."[5] Ida also lamented the state of the opera world in general, "full of confident amateurs, drunk with their own mediocre gifts."[6]

When Ida's foray into making a Hollywood film met with failure, she focused again on her fiction, crafting a thirteen-part series of romance novels to honor Clemens Krauss. She was determined to keep Krauss's memory alive, even if it meant turning him into a dashing protagonist in a series of pulp novels. Like Krauss, the fictional Oscar Warrender was handsome and domineering.

"Fear of the musical director is the beginning of wisdom, so far as the operatic student is concerned," says the imperious conductor in the first book of the series. "That is my theory and I act on it."

In *A Song Begins*, Warrender falls in love with his student, the soprano ingénue Anthea Benton, who quickly realizes just how passionate her new teacher's relationship to music really is.

"How he loves it all!' mused Anthea. "That's why he can do it with that great romantic sweep. For all his arrogance, he serves the work with everything he has, like a dominating but adoring lover."[7]

Although the book describes a growing attraction between Anthea and Warrender, it was the author's description of the music itself that perhaps made the reader blush. Years after his death, Ida was still deeply infatuated with Krauss. "She had heard this a hundred times before, of course," wrote Ida as Mary Burchell. "But it unfolded that night like the petals of a flower, so that she thought she must be hearing it for the first time. And she realized that the talented but slightly brash tenor was being held superbly in check by the conductor, so that everything which was beautiful in his voice was plain to hear, and everything slightly foolish in his approach was disciplined and moulded with infinitely stylish care."[8]

While Ida continued to write fiction into the 1980s, completing her Warrender series in 1985, her work was seen by a new crop of romance novelists as outdated. As the president of the Romantic Novelists' Association since 1966, an organization she helped to found, Ida—or Mary, as she was known by her fellow writers—railed against the "modern" trend towards "soft porn."

Ida recounted a difficult exchange with a young novelist at a *Romantic Times* convention in New York. "The rather dreadful young woman who ran it, came over first and interviewed me," recalled Ida. "She asked the most idiotic questions, like, 'Do you believe in sustained sensuality?' So I said, 'Well, my dear, if by that you mean soft porn with overtones of vulgarity, no.'" And she went on, "The sad thing about prose today is that people are under the impression that if you call something by a different name, it's no longer unpleasant. You know, when you all write about pre-marital sex, what you mean is fornication."[9] As a result, Ida's star began to fade in the Mills & Boon universe, and her output dwindled as she grew older.

If writing wasn't filling her days, Ida came up with other ways for her and Louise to enjoy their semiretirement. By the 1970s, Louise

Mani Mekler, Tilde Gobbi, Ida Cook, and Louise Cook. The Cooks financed Mekler's operatic studies and traveled throughout the world to attend her performances. *Courtesy of Mani Mekler Baker*

had long left her civil-service job and had more freedom to travel. Through their friendship with Tito Gobbi and his wife, the sisters agreed to finance the education of a handful of worthy opera hopefuls, and they even sponsored an annual scholarship in their name for talented young singers at an opera academy in Florence. Among those whose careers they helped to develop was Mani Mekler, an Israeli-born singer, whose parents had escaped to Palestine from Poland and Germany before the beginning of the war. The rest of her family perished in the Holocaust.

"And now I want to say how truly delighted we are with dear Mani," Ida wrote to the Gobbis. "It was wonderful to have the opportunity of hearing her, and to be able to judge for ourselves what real progress had been made since we last heard her. The friends who were hearing her for the first time were immensely impressed by the great potential."[10] Ida and Louise sent Mekler regular cash infusions when she was studying in Rome and Florence and found her lodging among their opera-world friends in Manhattan when she needed to be in New York for classes or performances. When Mekler made her professional debut in Stockholm, the Cooks attended with a group of friends.

Ever the prude, Ida worried about her new young charge. "My dear, you are not going to be taking your clothes off?" asked Ida before one of Mekler's performances in *Salome*.

"They had very rigid rules about what one does, and there was a certain way you needed to comport yourself with them," said Mekler, who recalled chiding them for their penchant for flowered Marks & Spencer dresses that they both wore into old age, though they thought Marks & Spencer absolutely the best place in the world to shop.[11]

While Ida was very critical, for her part Louise was quiet and contemplative. Whenever she listened to a record of Ponselle's or a piece of music that Krauss conducted, she would close her eyes and tears would roll down her cheeks, said Mekler. They were traditionalists, and both sisters were outraged when Mekler starred in a student production of *Porgy and Bess*.

"They just didn't consider it to be opera," she said. They also cautioned Mekler about not living a profligate diva lifestyle like so many of their own opera stars who carried on affairs with fellow performers and conductors.

Nevertheless, they embraced Mekler and her entire family, who had all come to settle in Los Angeles. The Cooks even invited Mekler to their seances in London after her brother Gabriel, an accomplished pianist and record producer who worked on albums for Janis Joplin and Steppenwolf, died in a motorcycle accident in California in 1977.

"They were very hesitant in asking me to come," said Mekler. "They told me, 'We would like to offer this to you.'" Mekler said her brother came through in "direct voice" at the seance and complimented her on wearing the ring that he had given her before he died. She was stunned because she hadn't told the sisters that the ring she wore was a present from Gabriel. "I couldn't explain it," recalled Mekler many years later.[12]

Despite Ida's earnings from her fiction, the sisters continued to live very frugally. They still frequented Covent Garden, and still queued up for cheap seats. They eschewed modern conveniences such as a color or even a black-and-white television set or a renovation of their flat at Dolphin Square, which Mekler described as "untouched since the war." The small apartment was filled with "bibelots and an impressive collection of pictures of their opera stars."

"We ate sitting in the living room with trays on our laps," said Mekler, adding that the sisters would indulge in an occasional glass of sherry but were not drinkers. "They always said that they were constantly on a diet—white bread, double cream, and double butter on the tea sandwiches they made without crusts."[13]

In addition to supporting Mekler's operatic career, one of the highlights of the Cooks' later years was the Queen's Silver Jubilee celebrations in 1977. After her wild excitement over the coronation in the 1950s, Ida and Louise watched the celebrations on their neighbor's color television set, pronouncing it "UNBELIEVABLE," in capital letters in a letter to the Gobbis in Rome. "What a demonstration of love and confidence and good will. And what a wonderful darling she is. To see her wandering about among the people and chatting, after the great service at St Paul's—and hardly a policeman in sight—made one feel proud and happy and reassured."[14]

Two years later, after Margaret Thatcher came to power as Britain's new Prime Minister, Ida excitedly wrote to a friend:

Don't you like Mrs Thatcher? We do. And although it will
take years to get out of the mess it is so refreshing to have
someone acting from principle and commonsense. She
seems quite unflappable too, and must have the strongest
nerves of anyone who has been in power since Churchill.[15]

■   ■   ■

As they approached their seventies, the sisters showed no signs of
slowing down, even as more of their friends began to fade away.
Ponselle, who had become a recluse, died on May 25, 1981, three days
shy of the fifty-fourth anniversary of her unforgettable Covent Garden
debut. Viorica Ursuleac died on October 22, 1985.

In one of the letters she wrote to Ponselle, in December 1973, Ida
elucidated what they had all meant to the sisters: "We may have had
two world wars in our time, but I reckon we had the best of it. Why,
people like you and…Pinza and Martinelli and Galli-Curci and others
just irradiated our world for us.…You were like gods and goddesses
to us, and we expected to go without meals to pay for a gallery seat
just to be transported to another world by you."[16]

And, with the help of Leslie Flint, they were determined to continue being transported to that other world. The sisters simply refused
to let go of their beloved friends and opera stars—even after their
deaths.

Ida and Louise persisted with their Dolphin Square gramophone
parties, inviting old friends and new to listen to their gods and goddesses. Else Mayer-Lismann, who had followed in her mother's footsteps training opera singers and had established her own opera
institute in London, brought one of her students. Jeanne Henny
described the get-togethers at Dolphin Square as "quasi-religious
experiences," in which Ida would crank up the record player and

regale the gathering with tales of the sisters' adventures in both care-free and dangerous times. Louise sat quietly, occasionally interrupting her brash younger sister to correct her recollection of an event.[17]

But on some level, Louise, at least, wanted to forget the past—at any rate the past that involved Nazis and refugees. As she grew older, Louise retreated even further behind the shadow of her garrulous younger sister, who seemed ever ready to entertain listeners with the stories of their heroics. Perhaps she was simply too talkative and revealed too many intimate details about their refugees and their own underground sources, such as the mysterious Pauline Jack who loaned them her family home in Frankfurt as a secret meeting place.

At one point, it must have been too much for Louise, the discreet civil servant. In a never-explained incident, Louise unilaterally decided to burn all the documents that the sisters had collected from their refugee work. Ida had kept all the letters from "those terrible years" although she admitted that she never got around to filing them away neatly. She had packed them into a cardboard box pushed into a corner of the Morella Road attic because, "tragic though they are, I cannot bring myself to destroy those pages out of history."[18]

But Louise did it for her.

"Ida came home one day and found a grate full of charred letters," said Henny, who had been told the story by her teacher Else Mayer-Lismann. "Louise had burned a pile of wartime letters, and Ida was furious and could not understand it and was fuming when she told Else."[19]

There was never any reason given, and it seemed a rather uncharacteristically rash act for someone as quiet and retiring as Louise. Could she have been a spy? "Louise was the most absolute staunchest believer in integrity and serving her country, and if she were sworn to secrecy, she would not tell even Ida," said Henny. "It may also explain [why] Louise hardly ever gave her opinion on anything that was not singers."[20]

Or maybe, like her sister, she found it simply too difficult to look at the letters and the photographs "and see face after face of the people for whom we could do nothing." For among that correspondence that Ida could never get around to organizing were letters from "two little boys, eight and ten, who insisted on writing out their own records in round, painstaking handwriting."[21] Their letters arrived too late for the sisters to save them.

As Ida wrote in her memoir, the sound of the telegraph boy's motorcycle screeching to a halt in front of 24 Morella Road during those dramatic years before the war filled them both with terror.

Louise preferred not to dwell on the painful past. When she wasn't attending opera with Ida or listening to records at their gramophone soirées, she retreated to a world of romance and fantasy. Friends remember that she kept up with all the television soap operas, even though she never watched them on television. "She read the plots in the newspaper and knew everything," said Henny. But she depended still on Ida's outgoing confidence. "I remember thinking how interesting she was and what a shame Ida had always done all the talking, but then she was a mesmerizing speaker."[22]

Ida was also in charge of their daily lives. She shopped, cooked, and paid all the bills. Not surprisingly, when Ida was diagnosed with cancer, her main concern was for her sister. She drew up a will, leaving Louise the Morella Road house and created a trust that would allow Louise to collect the royalties from her romance novels, which numbered a staggering one hundred and twelve books. Ida died at a hospital in Wimbledon a few days before Christmas in 1986. She was eighty-two.

Louise was helpless. She had no idea how to do even the most mundane of household tasks. She didn't know how to use the stove "because Ida had always done everything," said Henny, who offered to show Louise how to turn on the cooker. "She said it wasn't necessary because she didn't care much about what she ate." After Ida's death, the opera-listening parties ended abruptly at Dolphin Square, and friends worried that without Ida, Louise wouldn't be able to carry on.[23]

Louise missed her beloved sister so much that less than six months after her death, she sought to communicate with her in "the other world." According to Leslie Flint's diary, Louise made an appointment to visit the medium on May 26, 1987.

"I love you, I'm very close, I shall never be far." Ida's voice came through clearly on the tape that Flint made during their emotional session. He gave the tape to Louise to take home. "I am just waiting for the time eventually when you join us, but you have got a little longer to go yet…"

"Oh, darling!" wailed Louise. "Oh, darling, is that you? Oh, darling…"

"I love you. I want you to be happy. I want you to be patient with yourself. You have to take things as they come. I'll come again! I'll come again," said the Ida voice as it began to fade.[24]

Following the seance, Louise retreated to the flat, becoming a virtual recluse until her own death from septicemia at Westminster Hospital on March 27, 1991.

Louise was so bereft without her younger sister that she never played their opera records again. Without Ida, Louise had no idea how to use the record player.

But it didn't matter, Louise told a friend. She said she had all the music in her head.

Acknowledgments

In the nearly four years that it took to research and write about the Cooks, I was fortunate to meet so many people around the world who shared my enthusiasm and excitement about these incredible sisters.

When I told Holocaust historians Jonathan Petropoulos and Wendy Lower that I was working on a book about opera and the Nazis, these august professors at Claremont McKenna College both seemed to drop everything to help me. Jonathan Petropoulos pointed me in the direction of the scholarship on classical music and opera in the Third Reich, providing important introductions to scholars such as Michael Kater in Toronto, who was also generous with his time.

Wendy Lower made introductions for me at the United States Holocaust Memorial Museum in Washington, D.C., and at Yad Vashem in Jerusalem. I am certain that without her guidance, I never would have been able to access the Cooks' file at Yad Vashem. Many writers had tried in the past—I know because I saw their letters in the file asking for the Cooks' archive to be opened to them. For more than half a century those incredibly important documents that contain the missing personal stories of the refugees the sisters brought to safety in Britain had been closed to researchers. Without the Yad Vashem documents, there would be no *Overture of Hope*.

Unfortunately, Yad Vashem does not have a complete list of the twenty-nine refugees that Ida and Louise brought to safety.

The Holocaust memorial's files only include letters from a handful of refugees that Ida provided to them. Still, these made all the difference in being able to tell their harrowing stories of escape from the Third Reich.

Although I used Ida Cook's *We Followed Our Stars* and *Safe Passage* as guides to the lives of the refugees, there were few clues as to what happened to them after they reached London. The career setbacks and hardships faced by Clemens Krauss and Viorica Ursuleac are only briefly mentioned in Ida's book, but they came into harsh reality in the mounds of official documents scattered throughout archives in Germany and Austria. Using archives and public documents, I was also able to flesh out what were heart-wrenching stories of the trials faced by the refugees in adapting to a new country.

Berlin-based researcher Orsolya Thorday conducted invaluable research at archives throughout Germany and Austria, translating epic stacks of documents related to Clemens Krauss's career and his denazification after the war. She found long-forgotten letters from Ida Cook that had eluded other researchers and helped me piece together many of the lives of the Jewish refugees the sisters saved, extracting a great deal of their personal histories from public records in Austria and Germany. I am also grateful to her for the brilliant work she did helping to resurrect Georg Maliniak, Krauss's deputy conductor and a tragic figure in this story.

In Northumberland, I owe a great deal of thanks to Michael Grant, a volunteer archivist at the Bailiffgate Museum in Alnwick, where the Cook sisters spent many of their childhood years before and during the First World War. Grant not only searched out school records for Ida and Louise at the all-girl Duchess's School, but he also volunteered to walk from their old family residence at Lovaine House in the market town to the site of their old school when I asked him how long the walk to the school might have taken the girls every morning. His answer? "Twelve minutes at a steady pace" on a straight walk mostly downhill. "I guess if the girls were late they could have run it in much less," he said. Grant sent me photographs chronicling some of the landmarks the sisters would have seen along the way, and even dug up a YouTube video showing the interior of the nineteenth-century stone structure where they lived with their family. He provided me with some of Ida's earliest stories, including important chronicles of the sisters' first trips to America and Ida's first stab at romantic fiction.

In London, Joe Zigmond at John Murray has been a tough and exacting editor. I am grateful to him and his colleagues, including the brilliant Caroline Westmore and Morag Lyall, for their professionalism and uncompromising devotion to the narrative. Zigmond was the first publisher to be excited about the project, even as some of the research seemed daunting, knowing that Louise had burned much of the sisters' correspondence regarding their refugees.

Thank you to my agent Frank Weimann for his professionalism and unwavering enthusiasm in this project.

I am grateful to the entire staff at Regnery Publishing in Washington for their support and passion for this book, particularly Tom Spence, Tony Daniel, Joshua Monnington, and the marketing team.

The staff at the Victoria & Albert Theatre and Performance Collections at Blythe House were extremely helpful and kind, never flinching even as I asked to see multiple envelopes in the Ida and Louise Cook Collection that needed to be weighed and recorded over and over again.

In England, John Harris and his family were very generous with their family stories about the sisters, as was Jeanne Henny, who also shared her stories about the Mayer-Lismann family. In Rome, Cecilia Gobbi was incredibly generous with her time, and allowed me unfettered access to her father Tito Gobbi's private correspondence with the Cook sisters at the Associazione Musicale Tito Gobbi. I will never forget her wonderful hospitality at the Associazione, which is located at the beautiful Gobbi family home on the outskirts of the city where Ida and Louise would spend part of every summer in their later years.

Thank you to the staff at the New York Public Library for the Performing Arts, Dorothy and Lewis B. Cullman Center at Lincoln Center for the Performing Arts. It was here that I found an important trove of letters Ida had written to her idol Rosa Ponselle that chronicled a great deal of the sisters' post-war history.

Research staff at the NYPL's main branch and the Center for Research in the Humanities were incredible. I was really privileged to be able to occupy a research study room during the work on this book, even if access to the library was cut off during the worst of the coronavirus pandemic. Still, I had the luxury of being able to ask a team of NYPL archivists for assistance even while the library was closed. A special thank you to Melanie Locay at the Center for Research in the Humanities and Lyudmila Sholokhova, the curator of the Dorot Jewish Collection, as well as to my colleagues in the program who offered so many good suggestions during a works-in-progress discussion.

Linda Zagaria was among the early readers of the manuscript, and I am grateful for her piercing and exacting study.

In Washington, I am extremely grateful to the staff at the United States Holocaust Memorial Museum for their efforts on behalf of this project, and also to archivists at the Library of Congress for their help with the Joshua Logan Papers.

In Los Angeles, thank you to Paul Baker and Mani Mekler Baker for sharing letters and stories from Ida and Louise, and for opening up their home to me when I visited. I would also like to thank Jonathan Marc Feldman, a tremendous screenwriter, who first suggested I pick up Berta Geissmar's *The Baton and the Jackboot*, and who has adapted the Cooks' incredible story for the screen.

Staff at the Self-Realization Fellowship in Los Angeles also combed their archives for correspondence between Amelita Galli-Curci and her friend and guru Paramahansa Yogananda.

On Long Island, I want to thank the staff at Geek Hampton in Sag Harbor, especially Tristin Theret who somehow managed to restore the manuscript when it seemed to vanish from my computer. It took him less than twenty minutes to find it, and he then dramatically restored it seconds before power went out during a summer tornado.

Thank you also to the staff at the University of Manitoba that houses an archive devoted to British medium Leslie Flint. I also want to thank Karl Jackson-Barnes at the Leslie Flint Educational Trust in the United Kingdom, who provided insights into how the celebrated medium conducted seances in London that were attended by the Cooks.

Hannah Milic excitedly transcribed most of those seances from tapes made by Flint and helped research the book's complicated endnotes and sourced photographs. I am incredibly grateful for her support and proud to be her mother.

Thank you to my family and friends in Canada and the United States, including Franklynne and George Vincent. Melissa Klein and Serena French, as well as Sasha Josipovicz, Isabel Madden, Milosh Pavlovicz, Tom Anderson, and Caroline Bongrand have been faithful supporters of my work and good friends. Also, a big thank you to my incredible colleagues at the *New York Post*, among the most intrepid reporters and editors I know.

In Westhampton Beach, I want to thank the Burner family, especially Nancy and Mike Burner who so generously gave me the keys to an office when I had nowhere else to work. Thank you to Kerry Dowd for putting up with the insanity.

A very special thank you to Ray Dowd who provided a wonderful place to work during the worst of the pandemic and a great deal of love and support during the challenges involved in writing this book. His equanimity and compassion kept me sane and grounded.

Film producers Andreas Roald and Donald Rosenfeld have never wavered in their enthusiasm for this project. The discovery of the Cook sisters began with Donald's old and dear friend Bryan Bantry encountering them at Yad Vashem and telling Donald: "Wow, do I have a Merchant Ivory movie that we just have to make!" Donald, especially, loves the Cooks as much as I do. He delighted in every new archival discovery I made about the sisters and their opera-world friends, and faithfully read every draft—sometimes several times.

Selected Bibliography

Archives

Austria

Archiv der Isrealitischen Kultusgemeinde Wien / Archive of the Jewish Community of Vienna

Archiv des Musikvereins Graz / Music Association Archive, Graz

Archiv des Theatermuseums Wien / Archives of the Vienna Theater Museum

Archiv der Universität für Musik und darstellende Kunst Wien / Archive of the University of Music and Performing Arts, Vienna

Österreichische Nationalbibliothek Musiksammlung—Clemens Krauss Archiv Wien / Austrian National Library Music Collection—Clemens Krauss Archive, Vienna

Österreichisches Staatsarchiv / Austrian State Archives, Vienna

Stadt- und Landesarchiv Wien / Municipal Archives, Vienna

Canada

The Jim Ellis Collection (Leslie Flint Recordings), Psychical Research and Spiritualism Collection, University of Manitoba

Germany

Archiv der Akademie der Künste Berlin / Archive of the Academy of Arts, Berlin

Bayerische Staatsbibliothek München Bildersammlung / Bavarian State Photo Archives, Munich

Bayerische Hauptstaatsarchiv München / Bavarian State Archives, Munich

Bibliothek des Staatlichen Instituts für Musikforschung des
    Preußischen Kulturbesitz in Berlin / State Institute for Music
    Research of the Prussian Cultural Heritage Foundation, Berlin
Bundesarchiv Berlin Lichterfelde / German State Archive, Berlin
Hessisches Hauptstaatsarchiv Wiesbaden / Hessian State Archives,
    Wiesbaden
Hessisches Staatsarchiv Darmstadt / Hessian State Archives,
    Darmstadt
Institut für Stadtgeschichte Frankfurt am Main / City History
    Institute, Frankfurt
Musikwissenschaftliche Bibliothek der Humboldt Universität zu
    Berlin / Humboldt University Library of Musicology, Berlin
Staatsbibliothek zu Berlin—Musikabteilung / State Library—
    Musicology, Berlin

Israel
Yad Vashem Archives: Files of the Department of the Righteous
    Among the Nations, File #60, Jerusalem

Italy
Associazione Musicale Tito Gobbi, Archivo Storico, Rome

United Kingdom
Duchess's School Archives, Bailiffgate Museum, Alnwick
Ida and Louise Cook Collection, Victoria & Albert Theatre &
    Performance Collections, London
Leslie Flint Educational Trust, London
London Metropolitan Archives, City of London
The Wiener Holocaust Archives, London
The Opera Archive, Glyndebourne, East Sussex
Wigmore Hall Archives, London

United States

Center for Jewish History, New York

Joshua Logan Papers, Library of Congress, Washington, D.C.

Leo Baeck Institute, New York

National Institute for Holocaust Documentation, United States Holocaust Memorial Museum, Washington, D.C.

Rosa Ponselle Papers, Music Division, New York Public Library for the Performing Arts, New York

United States Holocaust Memorial Museum, Washington, D.C.

Books

Bartrop, Paul R. *The Evian Conference of 1938 and the Jewish Refugee Crisis.* Cham, Switzerland: Palgrave Macmillan, 2018.

Burchell, Mary. *Wife to Christopher.* London: Mills & Boon, 1936.

———. *A Song Begins.* London: Mills & Boon, 1965.

———. *We Followed Our Stars.* London: Mills & Boon, 1950.

Cook, Ida. *Safe Passage: The Remarkable True Story of Two Sisters Who Rescued Jews from the Nazis.* Toronto: Harlequin, 2008.

Geissmar, Berta. *The Baton and the Jackboot: Recollections of Musical Life.* London: Hamish Hamilton, 1944.

Gourvish, Terry. *Dolphin Square: The History of a Unique Building.* London: Bloomsbury, 2014.

Grenville, Anthony. *Jewish Refugees from Germany and Austria in Britain, 1933–1970.* Edgware: Vallentine Mitchell, 2009.

Haddon, Jenny, and Diane Pearson. *Fabulous at Fifty: Recollections of the Romantic Novelists' Association, 1960–2010.* Great Britain: Romantic Novelist's Association, 2010.

Harris, Mark Jonathan, and Deborah Oppenheimer. *Into the Arms of Strangers: Stories of the Kindertransport.* New York: St. Martin's Press, 2000.

Kater, Michael H. *The Twisted Muse: Musicians and Their Music in the Third Reich.* New York: Oxford University Press, 1997.

Kende, Götz K., and Singe Scanzoni. *Der Prinzipal, Clemens Krauss: Fakten, Vergleiche, Rückschlüsse.* Tutzing: Hans Schneider, 1988.

Lebrecht, Norman. *Covent Garden: The Untold Story: Dispatches from the English Culture War, 1945–2000.* Boston: Northeastern University Press, 2001.

McAleer, Joseph. *Passion's Fortune: The Story of Mills & Boon.* Oxford: Oxford University Press, 1999.

Monod, David. *Settling Scores: German Music, Denazification, and the Americans, 1945–1953.* Chapel Hill: University of North Carolina Press, 2005.

Nicholson, Virginia. *Singled Out: How Two Million British Women Survived Without Men After the First World War.* New York: Oxford University Press, 2008.

Páramo, José Alfredo. *Allegro Molto: 60 Anõs de Anécdotas Musicales.* Cuernavaca, Morelos: Luzam, 2010.

Rose, Alexander. *Kings in the North: The House of Percy in British History.* London: Weidenfeld & Nicolson, 2002.

Sharples, Caroline, and Olaf Jensen. *Britain and the Holocaust: Remembering and Representing War and Genocide.* New York: Palgrave Macmillan, 2013.

Shirer, William L. *The Rise and Fall of the Third Reich: A History of Nazi Germany.* New York: Simon & Schuster, 1960.

Wilson, Alexandra. *Opera in the Jazz Age: Cultural Politics in 1920s Britain.* New York: Oxford University Press, 2019.

Notes

Preface: The Leaves

1. Jhan Robbins and June Robbins, "We Are Scarcely James Bond Ladies," *McCall's* 93 (September 1966).
2. Ida Cook, *Safe Passage: The Remarkable True Story of Two Sisters Who Rescued Jews from the Nazis* (Toronto: Harlequin, 2008), 133–34.
3. Robbins and Robbins, "We Are Scarcely James Bond Ladies."
4. Ibid.
5. Ida Cook to Rosa Ponselle, March 19, 1956, Rosa Ponselle Papers, Music Division, NYPL, New York.

Chapter 1: The Albert Memorial

1. Ida Cook, *Safe Passage: The Remarkable True Story of Two Sisters Who Rescued Jews from the Nazis* (Toronto: Harlequin, 2008), 23.
2. Ibid., 21.
3. Ibid., dedication page.
4. Ibid., 21.
5. Jenny Haddon and Diane Pearson, eds., *Fabulous at Fifty: Recollections of the Romantic Novelists' Association, 1960–2010* (Great Britain: Romantic Novelists' Association, 2010), 8.
6. Cook, *Safe Passage*, 24.
7. Jhan Robbins and June Robbins, "We Are Scarcely James Bond Ladies," *McCall's* 93 (September 1966).
8. Ibid.
9. Ibid.
10. Alexander Rose, *Kings in the North: The House of Percy in British History* (London: Weidenfeld & Nicolson, 2002), 2.
11. Anne Littlejohn, *The Duchess's School, 1808–1958* (Alnwick: The Duchess's School, 1958), 6.
12. Duchess's School Archives, Bailiffgate Museum, Alnwick.
13. Cook, *Safe Passage*, 24.
14. Duchess's School Archives.
15. Ibid.
16. *Duchess's School Magazine*, 1919, Duchess's School Archives, Bailiffgate Museum, Alnwick.
17. *Duchess's School Magazine*, 1920, Duchess's School Archives, Bailiffgate Museum, Alnwick.
18. Cook, *Safe Passage*, 25.

19. Virginia Nicholson, *Singled Out: How Two Million British Women Survived Without Men After the First World War* (New York: Oxford University Press, 2008), xi.
20. Ibid., 182–83.
21. Jeanne Henny, interview with the author, March 3, 2020.
22. Robbins and Robbins, "We Are Scarcely James Bond Ladies."
23. Cook, *Safe Passage*, 26.
24. Ibid., 26–27.
25. Robbins and Robbins, "We Are Scarcely James Bond Ladies."
26. Ibid.
27. "The Vocal Sensation of the World," *Dundee Courier*, May 20, 1924.
28. Robbins and Robbins, "We Are Scarcely James Bond Ladies."
29. "Royal Albert Hall Opened by Queen Victoria," *The Guardian*, March 30, 1871.
30. Cook, *Safe Passage*, 28.
31. "Queen of Song Wins All Hearts," *Courier and Argus*, October 13, 1924.
32. Cook, *Safe Passage*, 29.
33. Robbins and Robbins, "We Are Scarcely James Bond Ladies."
34. Galli-Curci to Ida Cook, November 26, 1924, V&A Archives, London.
35. Robbins and Robbins, "We Are Scarcely James Bond Ladies."
36. "English Girls Arrive to Hear Galli-Curci," *New York Times*, January 5, 1927.
37. Cook, *Safe Passage*, 32.
38. Ibid., 33.
39. Ibid., 34.
40. Ida Cook, "Across the Atlantic to Hear Opera," *Duchess's School Magazine*, 1927, Bailiffgate Museum, Alnwick.

Chapter 2: The Photograph

1. "English Girls Arrive to Hear Galli-Curci," *New York Times*, January 5, 1927.
2. Ida Cook, "Across the Atlantic to Hear Opera," *Duchess's School Magazine*, 1927, Bailiffgate Museum, Alnwick.
3. Ida Cook, *Safe Passage: The Remarkable True Story of Two Sisters Who Rescued Jews from the Nazis* (Toronto: Harlequin, 2008), 37.
4. Cook, "Across the Atlantic to Hear Opera."
5. "English Girls Arrive to Hear Galli-Curci."
6. Cook, *Safe Passage*, 37.
7. "English Girls Arrive to Hear Galli-Curci."
8. Cook, "Across the Atlantic to Hear Opera."
9. Cook, *Safe Passage*, 38.
10. Cook, "Across the Atlantic to Hear Opera."
11. Ibid.
12. "To Fame by Song," *Daily Mail*, October 8, 1924.
13. "Galli-Curci Tells of Her Simple Life," *New York Times*, November 8, 1921.
14. "English Girls Arrive to Hear Galli-Curci."
15. Cook, "Across the Atlantic to Hear Opera."

16. Ida Cook letter, cited in Louise Carpenter, "Ida and Louise," *Granta* 98, July 2, 2007.
17. Cook, "Across the Atlantic to Hear Opera."
18. Ibid.
19. Ibid.
20. Cook, *Safe Passage*, 45.
21. *Duchess's School Magazine*, 1927.
22. Cook, *Safe Passage*, 46–47.
23. Ibid., 49.
24. Ibid.
25. Galli-Curci to Ida Cook, June 13, 1927, V&A Archives, London.
26. Galli-Curci to Ida Cook, June 26, 1928, V&A Archives, London.
27. Galli-Curci to Ida Cook, July 21, 1929, V&A Archives, London.
28. Cook, *Safe Passage*, 58.
29. "Rosa Ponselle has a London Triumph," *New York Times*, May 29, 1929.
30. "Irrepressible Applause," in "Men and Women of Today" column, *Courier and Advertiser* (Dundee), May 31, 1929.
31. Cook, *Safe Passage*, 59.
32. Ibid., 57.
33. Ibid., 61; Cook, "Across the Atlantic to Hear Opera."
34. Ida Cook, "It's Fun in Fleet Street," *Duchess's School Magazine*, Bailiffgate Museum, Alnwick.
35. Galli-Curci to Ida Cook, March 6, 1930, V&A Archives, London.
36. Ibid.
37. "Ovation for Galli-Curci," *New York Times*, November 16, 1930.
38. Galli-Curci to Ida and Louise Cook, October 16, 1931, V&A Archives, London.
39. Galli-Curci to Ida and Louise Cook, undated letter, V&A Archives, London.
40. Cook, *Safe Passage*, 69–70.
41. Ibid., 77.
42. Ibid., 64–65.
43. "Pinza: 'Met' and Stage Star Dies, Won New Fame in 'South Pacific,'" *New York Times*, May 9, 1957.
44. Ibid.
45. Cook, *Safe Passage*, 81.
46. Ibid., 84.
47. Olin Downes, "Clemens Krauss Conducts Again," *New York Times*, April 5, 1929.
48. Cook, *Safe Passage*, 85.
49. Ibid.
50. Ibid., 85–86.
51. Ibid.
52. Ida Cook, photograph of Clemens Krauss and Viorica Ursuleac, V&A Archives, London.

Chapter 3: The Romance Writer

1. Ida Cook, *Safe Passage: The Remarkable True Story of Two Sisters Who Rescued Jews from the Nazis* (Toronto: Harlequin, 2008), 94–95.
2. Associated Press, "War Fear Needless, Asserts Hailsham," *New York Times*, July 30, 1934.
3. Cook, *Safe Passage*, 95.
4. Ida Cook, film treatment, undated, Joshua Logan Papers, Library of Congress, Washington, D.C., 26–27.
5. Ibid.
6. Cook, *Safe Passage*, 96.
7. Cook, film treatment, 27.
8. Ibid.
9. Clemency Burton-Hill, "Richard Strauss: A Reluctant Nazi," BBC, June 10, 2014.
10. Götz K. Kende and Signe Scanzoni, *Der Prinzipal, Clemens Krauss: Fakten, Verleiche, Rückschlüsse* (Tutzing: Hans Schneider, 1988), 183.
11. "Strauss Hissed and Applauded at Salzburg: Composer's Presence Held to Defy Hitler," *New York Times*, August 17, 1934.
12. Frederick T. Birchall, "Nazis Fail to Harm Salzburg Festival," *New York Times*, August 1, 1934.
13. Ida Cook letter cited in Louise Carpenter, "Ida and Louise," *Granta* 98, July 2, 2007.
14. Ibid.
15. Cook, film treatment, 27.
16. Ibid., 25.
17. Cook, *Safe Passage*, 99.
18. Ibid., 98.
19. Viorica Ursuleac to the Cooks, June 2, 1934, V&A Archives, London.
20. Cook, *Safe Passage*, 101.
21. Ibid., 102.
22. Ibid.
23. Ibid., 103.
24. British Pathé, "King George V—Jubilee Speech Aka George 5th (1935)," YouTube, April 13, 2014, https://www.youtube.com/watch?v=Lx4p523wLdU.
25. Joseph McAleer, *Passion's Fortune: The Story of Mills & Boon* (Oxford: Oxford University Press, 1999), 4.
26. Ibid., 71.
27. John Harris, interview with the author, March 20, 2019.
28. McAleer, *Passion's Fortune*, 72.
29. Ibid., 154.
30. Ibid., 156.
31. Ibid., 3.
32. Cook, film treatment, 29.

Chapter 4: The Flat

1. Margaret Aitken, interview with the author, October 3, 2019.
2. Terry Gourvish, *Dolphin Square: The History of a Unique Building* (London: Bloomsbury, 2014), 56, 75–77. *The Times* notice referenced by Gourvish was from the "Flats and Chambers" page, *The Times*, June 19, 1936.
3. Elisabeth Rethberg to Ida Cook, December 20, 1936, V&A Archives, London.
4. Elisabeth Rethberg to Ida Cook, September 15, [year missing], V&A Archives, London.
5. The dialogue with Mayer-Lismann is taken from Ida Cook, film treatment, undated, Joshua Logan Papers, Library of Congress, Washington, D.C., 30–31.
6. Ibid., 31.
7. Ida Cook, *Safe Passage: The Remarkable True Story of Two Sisters Who Rescued Jews from the Nazis* (Toronto: Harlequin, 2008), 136.
8. Ibid., 109.
9. Ibid.
10. Ibid., 113.
11. Ibid., 104.
12. Ida Cook, film treatment, 33.
13. Ibid., 34.
14. Ibid., 28.
15. Herbert F. Peyser, "The Future of Vienna's Opera," *New York Times*, September 22, 1934.
16. Ibid.
17. Götz K. Kende and Signe Scanzoni, *Der Prinzipal, Clemens Krauss: Fakten, Verleiche, Rückschlüsse* (Tutzing: Hans Schneider, 1988), 316.
18. Ibid., 183.
19. The machinations around the firing of Fritz Busch are detailed in Michael H. Kater, *The Twisted Muse: Musicians and Their Music in the Third Reich* (New York: Oxford University Press, 1997), 121–22.
20. Ibid., 198.
21. Berta Geissmar, *The Baton and the Jackboot: Recollections off Musical Life* (London: Hamish Hamilton, 1944), 129–30.
22. "Hitler and Wagner," *The Telegraph*, July 25, 2011, https://www.telegraph. co.uk/culture/music/classicalmusic/8659814/Hitler-and-Wagner.html.
23. English translation of the final lines of Richard Wagner's *Die Meistersinger von Nürnberg*, 1868.
24. Philippe Jacquard, "L'atelier du Maître," Société Wilhelm Furtwängler, https:// furtwangler.fr/wp-content/uploads/2017/04/Atelier-Jacquard-.pdf; Geissmar, *Baton and the Jackboot*, 129–30.
25. Kende and Scanzoni, *Der Prinzipal*, 179.
26. Geissmar, *The Baton and the Jackboot*, 144.
27. Kater, *The Twisted Muse*, 48.
28. Furtwängler to unknown addressee, May 9, 1936, in Kende and Scanzoni, *Der Prinzipal*.
29. Herbert F. Peyser, "Berlin and Vienna: Shake-Up of Conductors Causes Uncertainty in Plans of Both Capitals," *New York Times*, February 3, 1935.

30. Kater, *The Twisted Muse*, 53.
31. Herbert F. Peyser, "A Tale of Two Conductors: Positions of Directors of Berlin and Vienna Operas Undergo Changes," *New York Times*, September 27, 1936.
32. Kater, *The Twisted Muse*, 18.
33. Richard Strauss to Clemens Krauss, October 8, 1935, in Kende and Scanzoni, *Der Prinzipal*, 206–7.
34. Furtwängler to unknown addressee, May 9, 1936, in Kende and Scanzoni, *Der Prinzipal*.
35. Peyser, "Berlin and Vienna."
36. Kater, *The Twisted Muse*, 40.
37. Kende and Scanzoni, *Der Prinzipal*, 10.
38. Bronislaw Huberman's letter to the *Manchester Guardian* is quoted in full in Geissmar, *The Baton and the Jackboot*, 95–97.
39. Ibid.
40. Cook, *Safe Passage*, 124.

Chapter 5: The Operas

1. Viorica Ursuleac to Ida and Louise Cook, May 23, 1937, V&A Archives, London.
2. Ibid.
3. Ida Cook, *Safe Passage: The Remarkable True Story of Two Sisters Who Rescued Jews from the Nazis* (Toronto: Harlequin, 2008), 128.
4. Ibid., 126.
5. Ibid., 127.
6. Jhan Robbins and June Robbins, "We Are Scarcely James Bond Ladies," *McCall's* 93 (September 1966).
7. Ida Cook, film treatment, undated, Joshua Logan Papers, Library of Congress, Washington, D.C., 44.
8. Ibid.
9. Robbins and Robbins, "We Are Scarcely James Bond Ladies."
10. Else Mayer-Lismann to Ella Mahler, January 10, 1964, Yad Vashem Archives, Jerusalem.
11. Cook, film treatment, 54.
12. Ibid., 38.
13. Robbins and Robbins, "We Are Scarcely James Bond Ladies."
14. Ibid.
15. Friedl Bamberger to Ella Mahler, undated, Yad Vashem Archives, Jerusalem.
16. Ibid.
17. Ibid.
18. Ibid.
19. Cook, *Safe Passage*, 149.
20. Friedl Bamberger to Ella Mahler, undated.
21. Ibid.
22. Financial information is contained in Friedl Bamberger Orlando's restitution file at the Hessian State Archives, Darmstadt.

23. Friedl Bamberger to Ella Mahler, undated.
24. Cook, *Safe Passage*, 150.
25. "Hitler Strikes Again," *New York Times*, March 12, 1938.
26. "German Methods Scored in Britain," *New York Times*, March 13, 1938.
27. William L. Shirer, *The Rise and Fall of the Third Reich: A History of Nazi Germany* (New York: Simon and Schuster, 1960), 351.
28. Ibid.
29. Anthony Grenville, *Jewish Refugees from Germany and Austria in Britain, 1933–1970* (Edgware: Vallentine Mitchell, 2009), 6.
30. Cook, *Safe Passage*, 143.
31. "Miss I. Cook Talks on a Visit to Germany," *Alnwick and County Gazette*, May 1938.
32. Cook, film treatment, 41–42.
33. The Hyde Park Corner speech is detailed in Robbins and Robbins, "We Are Scarcely James Bond Ladies."
34. Clemens Krauss to Adolf Hitler, April 25, 1938, in Kende and Scanzoni, *Der Prinzipal*, 7.
35. WNYC radio interview with Ida and Louise Cook, April 25, 1950.
36. Robbins and Robbins, "We Are Scarcely James Bond Ladies."
37. Ibid.
38. Cook, *Safe Passage*, 165–66.
39. WNYC radio interview with Ida and Louise Cook, April 25, 1950.
40. Ibid.
41. Cook, film treatment, 45–46.
42. Robbins and Robbins, "We Are Scarcely James Bond Ladies."
43. Cook, film treatment, 46.
44. Robbins and Robbins, "We Are Scarcely James Bond Ladies."
45. Ida Cook to Erik Maschat, June 9, 1938, BayHStA Intendanz Bayer, Staatsoper 1727, Bayerisches Hauptstaatsarchiv, Munich.
46. Cook, *Safe Passage*, 122–23.
47. Cook to Maschat, June 9, 1938.
48. Cook, *Safe Passage*, 122–23.
49. Ida Cook to Erik Maschat, July 13, 1938, BayHStA Intendanz Bayer, Staatsoper 1727, Bayerisches Hauptstaatsarchiv, Munich.
50. Paul R. Bartrop, *The Evian Conference of 1938 and the Jewish Refugee Crisis* (Cham, Switzerland: Palgrave Macmillan, 2018), 47.
51. Ibid., 49.
52. "Winterton Appointment Stirs Comment," *Jewish Telegraph Agency* 4, no. 72, June 24, 1938.
53. Bartrop, *The Evian Conference*, 49.
54. Ibid., 48.
55. Edwin L. James, "Refugee Task Looming as Enormous Problem," *New York Times*, July 10, 1938.
56. Ibid.
57. Robbins and Robbins, "We Are Scarcely James Bond Ladies."

Chapter 6: The List

1. Ida Cook, film treatment, undated, Joshua Logan Papers, Library of Congress, Washington, D.C., 61.
2. Ida Cook, *Safe Passage: The Remarkable True Story of Two Sisters Who Rescued Jews from the Nazis* (Toronto: Harlequin, 2008), 164.
3. Ilse Bauer Winter to Ella Mahler, undated, Yad Vashem Archives, Jerusalem.
4. Cook, *Safe Passage*, 164; Jhan Robbins and June Robbins, "We Are Scarcely James Bond Ladies," *McCall's* 93 (September 1966).
5. Cook, *Safe Passage*, 164.
6. Ibid., 165.
7. Ibid.
8. Robbins and June Robbins, "We Are Scarcely James Bond Ladies."
9. Ida Cook, "Letter to the Editor," *Daily Telegraph*, October 31, 1939.
10. Cook, *Safe Passage*, 166.
11. Ida Cook, "Letter to the Editor."
12. Ibid.
13. Ibid.
14. Ibid.
15. Cook, *Safe Passage*, 166.
16. "Diplomatic Responses: The Smallbones Scheme," in *Holocaust and Human Behavior*, Facing History and Ourselves, https://www.facinghistory.org/holocaust-and-human-behavior/chapter-7/diplomatic-responses-smallbones-scheme; "Robert Smallbones (1884–1976)," Jewsih Virtual Library: A Project of AICE, https://www.jewishvirtuallibrary.org/robert-smallbones.
17. "Robert Smallbones (1884–1976)"; Klaus Wiegrefe, "How the World Shrugged Off Kristallnacht," *Spiegel International*, May 11, 2013.
18. Wiegrefe, "How the World."
19. Simon Rocker, "Diplomat Who Faced Down the Gestapo," *Jewish Chronicle*, October 24, 2013.
20. Ida Cook, "Letter to the Editor."
21. Cook, *Safe Passage*, 169.
22. Ida Cook, "Letter to the Editor."
23. Cook, *Safe Passage*, 169.
24. Ibid., 170.
25. Cook, film treatment, 42.
26. Biographical information about Pauline Jack and her sister Gertrud Roesler-Ehrhardt comes from their files in the Institute for City History, State Archives, Frankfurt.
27. Cook, *Safe Passage*, 128.
28. Ibid., 171.
29. Lisa Basch to Ella Mahler, February 22, 1964, Yad Vashem Archives, Jerusalem.
30. Elisabeth Bamberger, *History of Heinrich Bamberger's Family of Frankfurt, Germany During the Time of Hitler*, Center for Jewish History, New York, 41.
31. Lisa Basch to Ella Mahler, February 22, 1964.
32. Cook, *Safe* Passage, 173.

33. Mark Jonathan Harris and Deborah Oppenheimer, *Into the Arms of Strangers: Stories of the Kindertransport* (New York: St. Martin's Press, 2000), 52.

34. Ida Cook, "Letter to the Editor," *Daily Telegraph*, October 31, 1939.

35. Ida Cook, "Kindness und Nazi Terrorism" (letter to the editor), *Daily Telegraph*, November 4, 1939.

36. Cook, *Safe Passage*, 173–74.

37. Ilse Bauer Winter to Ella Mahler, undated, Yad Vashem Archives, Jerusalem.

38. Cook, *Safe Passage*, 166.

39. Otto D. Tolischus, "Reich Ousts Jews from Colleges; Forbids Them to Sell Their Stocks," *New York Times*, November 15, 1938.

40. Otto D. Tolischus, "Nazis in Final Phase of Their War on Jews," *New York Times*, November 27, 1938.

41. Mark Jonathan Harris and Deborah Oppenheimer, *Into the Arms of Strangers: Stories of the Kindertransport* (New York: St. Martin's Press, 2000), 125.

42. Friedl Bamberger to Ella Mahler, undated, Yad Vashem Archives, Jerusalem.

43. Anne Symonds, "Obituary: Ruggero Orlando," *Independent*, May 4, 1994.

44. Cook, film treatment, 42.

45. Friedl Bamberger to Ella Mahler, undated.

46. Bamberger, *History of Heinrich Bamberger's Family*, 62.

47. Friedl Bamberger to Ella Mahler, undated.

48. Cook, *Safe Passage*, 117–18.

49. Friedl Marburg to Ella Mahler, January 29, 1964, Yad Vashem Archives, Jerusalem.

50. Cook, film treatment, 67.

51. Cook, *Safe Passage*, 145.

52. Cook, film treatment, 67.

53. Cook, *Safe Passage*, 145–47.

54. Ibid., 147.

55. Friedl Marburg to Ella Mahler, January 29, 1964.

56. Cook, *Safe Passage*, 174–76.

57. Cook, film treatment, 7.

58. Friedl Marburg to Ella Mahler, January 29, 1964.

59. Robbins and Robbins, "We Are Scarcely James Bond Ladies."

60. Ibid.

Chapter 7: A Friend in Downing Street

1. Jhan Robbins and June Robbins, "We Are Scarcely James Bond Ladies," *McCall's* 93 (September 1966).

2. Ida Cook, *Safe Passage: The Remarkable True Story of Two Sisters Who Rescued Jews from the Nazis* (Toronto: Harlequin, 2008), 154.

3. Ibid., 155.

4. Sir Benjamin Drage, "Letter to the Editor," *The Times*, July 4, 1939.

5. Cook, *Safe Passage*, 155.

6. Ibid.

7. John Harris, interview with the author, November 10, 2017.

8. Cook, *Safe Passage*, 155–56.
9. Ida Cook, film treatment, undated, Joshua Logan Papers, Library of Congress, Washington, D.C., 53.
10. Cook, *Safe Passage*, 157.
11. Ibid., 158.
12. Ibid., 153.
13. *Neues Grazer Tageblatt*, March 2, 1922, 12.
14. Otto Konig, "Kritik der Kritik: Gesprach mit Alban Berg und Clemens Krauss," *Neues Wiener Journal*, April 2, 1930.
15. Otto Stieglitz, *Das Forum: Abrechning*, Eigenvig, Vienna, 1932.
16. Gerda Maliniak to Ella Mahler, January 10, 1964, Yad Vashem Archives, Jerusalem.
17. Ibid.
18. Cook, film treatment, 50.
19. Ibid., 52.
20. Gerda Maliniak to Ella Mahler, January 10, 1964.
21. Robbins and Robbins, "We Are Scarcely James Bond Ladies."
22. Ibid.
23. Gerda Maliniak to Ella Mahler, January 10, 1964.
24. Cook, film treatment, 57.
25. Robbins and Robbins, "We Are Scarcely James Bond Ladies."
26. Cook, film treatment, 58.
27. Ibid.
28. Cook, *Safe Passage*, 160.
29. Cook, film treatment, 60.
30. Gerda Maliniak to Ella Mahler, January 10, 1964.
31. Ibid.
32. Cook, *Safe Passage*, 181.
33. Ibid., 181–82.
34. Ibid., 182–84.
35. Robbins and Robbins, "We Are Scarcely James Bond Ladies."
36. Cook, *Safe Passage*, 189–90.
37. Robbins and Robbins, "We Are Scarcely James Bond Ladies."
38. Cook, *Safe Passage*, 193–96.
39. Robbins and Robbins, "We Are Scarcely James Bond Ladies."
40. "Neville Chamberlain's Declaration of War," *The Guardian*, September 6, 2009, https://www.theguardian.com/world/2009/sep/06/second-world-war-declaration-chamberlain.

Chapter 8: The Bombs

1. Ida Cook, *Safe Passage: The Remarkable True Story of Two Sisters Who Rescued Jews from the Nazis* (Toronto: Harlequin, 2008), 201.
2. John Ezard, "MI5 Wary of Mosley's 'Dangerous Wife,'" *The Guardian*, November 23, 2002.
3. Friedl Bamberger to Ella Mahler, undated, Yad Vashem Archives, Jerusalem.

4. Cook, *Safe Passage*, 202.
5. Ibid., 203.
6. Ibid., 203–4.
7. Ibid., 229–31.
8. Ibid., 300.
9. Ibid., 208.
10. David Anderson, "London Is Pounded," *New York Times*, April 17, 1944.
11. Cook, *Safe Passage*, 225–26.
12. Ibid., 57.
13. Ibid., 123.
14. Anderson, "London Is Pounded."
15. Cook, *Safe Passage*, 224.
16. Myra Hess to Ida Cook, December 8, 1940, V&A Archives, London.
17. Gerda Maliniak to Ella Mahler, January 10, 1964, Yad Vashem Archives, Jerusalem.
18. Anthony Grenville, *Jewish Refugees from Germany and Austria in Britain, 1933–1970* (Edgware: Vallentine Mitchell, 2009), 19.
19. Lore Segal's story is retold in Mark Jonathan Harris and Deborah Oppenheimer, *Into the Arms of Strangers: Stories of the Kindertransport* (New York: St. Martin's Press, 2000), 145.
20. The suffering of Alfred Kerr is detailed in the obituary of his son Sir Michael Kerr, *Daily Telegraph*, April 23, 2002.
21. Grenville, *Jewish Refugees from Germany*, 19.
22. Ian Wallace, *Nothing Quite Like It* (London: Elm Tree, 1982), 17; "Jay Pomeroy: An Introduction," Lightly Peated, September 14, 2017, http://lightlypeated.org.uk/history/jay-pomeroy-and-introduction/.
23. Grenville, *Jewish Refugees from Germany*, 19.
24. Jay Pomeroy letter, June 27, 1949, "Notes of Evidence," Coroner's Inquest, Northern District County of London.
25. Ibid.
26. "Stefan Zweig, Wife End Lives in Brazil," *New York Times*, February 24, 1942.
27. Clemens Krauss to Martin Bormann, March 24, 1942, BayHStA Intendanz Bayer, Staatsoper 1726, Bayerisches Hauptstaatsarchiv, Munich.
28. Ibid.
29. Clemens Krauss to Adolf Hitler, July 6, 1944, BayHStA Intendanz Bayer, Staatsoper 1726, Bayerisches Hauptstaatsarchiv, Munich.
30. Clemens Krauss to Martin Bormann, December 16, 1944, BayHStA Intendanz Bayer, Staatsoper 1726, Bayerisches Hauptstaatsarchiv, Munich.
31. Michael H. Kater, *The Twisted Muse: Musicians and Their Music in the Third Reich* (New York: Oxford University Press, 1997), 52.

Chapter 9: The Aria
1. Ida Cook, *Safe Passage: The Remarkable True Story of Two Sisters Who Rescued Jews from the Nazis* (Toronto: Harlequin, 2008), 232–33.

2. Associated Press, "Galli-Curci Returns to Opera in Chicago," *New York Times*, November 25, 1936.
3. Cook, *Safe Passage*, 233.
4. Sarah Goodyear, "When Being Italian Was a Crime," *Village Voice*, April 11, 2000.
5. Margaret Aitken, interview with researcher, October 3, 2019.
6. Cook, *Safe Passage*, 240, 242.
7. Ibid., 242
8. Elisabeth Bamberger, *History of Heinrich Bamberger's Family of Frankfurt, Germany during the Time of Hitler*, Center for Jewish History, New York, 66.
9. Cook, *Safe Passage*, 244.
10. Harold Schonberg, "There Was Nothing like the Ponselle Sound, Ever," *New York Times*, January 23, 1972.
11. Cook, *Safe Passage*, 244.
12. Giuseppe Verdi, *La Forza del destino*, libretto by Francesco Maria Piave (1861).
13. Cook, *Safe Passage*, 252–53.
14. Ibid., 254–55.
15. Friedl Bamberger to Ella Mahler, undated, Yad Vashem Archives, Jerusalem.
16. Cook, *Safe Passage*, 253–55.
17. Ibid., 257–58.
18. Ibid., 258.

Chapter 10: The Trial

1. Anonymous letter to Salzburg Police, November 6, 1945, Clemens Krauss Folder, Special Denazification Series, Austrian State Archives, Vienna, Ka 23, 26.
2. United States Forces in Austria Information Services Branch communiqué, 1945, included as exhibit in Austrian Commission evaluating Clemens Krauss, Clemens Krauss Folder, Special Denazification Series, Austrian State Archives, Vienna.
3. Ibid.
4. Ibid.
5. *Völkischer Beobachter*, January 19, 1935, quoted at the meeting of the evaluation commission, November 6, 1946, Clemens Krauss Folder, Special Denazification Series, Austrian State Archives, Vienna, 8.
6. Joseph Goebbels, Die Tagebücher von Joseph Goebbels Online, De Gruyter, 2012, https://www.degruyter.com/database/tjgo/html?lang=en.
7. Erik Maschat, interview with Otto de Pasetti, described in United States Forces in Austria communiqué, December 21, 1945, Clemens Krauss Folder, Special Denazification Series, Austrian State Archives, Vienna, 5.
8. Memo from Otto de Pasetti to General McChrystal et al, "Clemens Krauss Investigation Munich," December 21, 1945, 3–4, F59, Clemens Krauss Archive, Vienna, 65/15.
9. Ibid.
10. Ibid.

11. Lothar Wallerstein to General Robert McClure, October 26, 1946, Clemens Krauss Folder, Special Denazification Series, Austrian State Archives, Vienna, 54.
12. Ibid.
13. Ida Cook, *Safe Passage: The Remarkable True Story of Two Sisters Who Rescued Jews from the Nazis* (Toronto: Harlequin, 2008), 262.
14. United States Forces in Austria Information Services Branch communiqué, January 2, 1946, included as an exhibit in Austrian Commission transcripts on Clemens Krauss, Clemens Krauss Folder, Special Denazification Series, Austrian State Archives, Vienna, 2.
15. Memo of the vote by the Austrian Commission evaluating Clemens Krauss, December 20, 1946, Clemens Krauss Folder, Special Denazification Series, Austrian State Archives, Vienna, 84–90.
16. Clemens Krauss to Egon Hilbert, December 8, 1946, Clemens Krauss Folder, Special Denazification Series, Austrian State Archives, Vienna, 80.
17. Clemens Krauss to Ministerial Councilor Egon Hilbert, Federal Theater Administration, December 10, 1946, Clemens Krauss Folder, Special Denazification Series, Austrian State Archives, Vienna, 82.
18. Memo of the vote by the Austrian Commission evaluating Clemens Krauss.
19. Vote of the Federal Commissioner Freelance Artists, State Office for Popular Enlightenment, Education and Cultural Affairs, December 20, 1946, Clemens Krauss Folder, Special Denazification Series, Austrian State Archives, Vienna, 88.
20. Memo of the vote by the Austrian Commission evaluating Clemens Krauss.
21. Ibid.

Chapter 11: The Open Window

1. Jay Pomeroy letter, June 27, 1949, "Notes of Evidence," Coroner's Inquest, Northern District County of London.
2. Ibid.
3. Ibid.
4. Ibid.
5. Gerda Maliniak to Ella Mahler, January 10, 1964, Yad Vashem Archives, Jerusalem.
6. Ibid.
7. Details of what was in the Maliniak apartment described in an autopsy report, Northern District of London Coroner's Officer's Report Concerning Death.
8. Johannes Brahms, "Liebestreu," lyrics by Robert Reinick.
9. Ida Cook, *Safe Passage: The Remarkable True Story of Two Sisters Who Rescued Jews from the Nazis* (Toronto: Harlequin, 2008), 263.
10. Ibid., 261.
11. Ibid., 261, 265.
12. "Krauss Triumphs on Vienna Podium," *New York Times*, May 11, 1947.

13. Elizabeth Forbes, "De Ahna (-Strauss), Pauline," Grove Music Online, December 1, 2002, https://doi.org/10.1093/gmo/9781561592630.article. O901200.

14. Associated Press, "2,000 at Strauss Rites: Bavarian Leader in Eulogy at Rites for Composer," *New York Times*, September 13, 1949.

15. Mary Burchell to Josef Klaus, February 12, 1950, Clemens Krauss Folder, Special Denazification Series, 73/2, Austrian State Archives, Vienna, 73/2.

16. Joseph McAleer, *Passion's Fortune: The Story of Mills & Boon* (Oxford: Oxford University Press, 1999), 94.

17. Burchell to Klaus, February 12, 1950, Clemens Krauss Folder.

18. Josef Klaus to Mary Burchell, March 7, 1950, Clemens Krauss Folder, Special Denazification Series, 73/2, Austrian State Archives, Vienna, 73/2.

19. Ida Cook to Alfred Frankenstein, December 6, 1951, Alfred Frankenstein Archive, Archiv der Akademie der Künste, Berlin.

20. Ibid.

21. Ibid.

22. Ida and Louise Cook, undated telegram to Viorica Krauss in Mexico, Clemens Krauss Folder, Austrian State Archives, Vienna, 47/2.

23. Ida Cook to Viorica Ursuleac, May 19, 1954, Clemens Krauss Folder, Austrian State Archives, Vienna, 47/2.

24. Mitia Mayer-Lismann to Viorica Ursuleac, June 29, 1954, Clemens Krauss Folder, Austrian State Archives, Vienna, 47/2.

25. "A 61 años de la muerte de Clemens Krauss," Vericuentos musicales y literarios blogspot, May 23, 2015, translated by the author, http://vericuetosmusicalesylite rarios.blogspot.com/2015/05/a-61-anos-de-la-muertede-klemens-krauss.html.

26. Ida Cook to Rosa Ponselle, June 9, 1954, Rosa Ponselle Papers, Music Division, NYPL, New York.

27. Ida Cook to Rosa Ponselle, September 27, 1954, Music Division, NYPL, New York.

28. Ida Cook to Alfred Frankenstein, June 12, 1954, Alfred Frankenstein Archive, Archiv der Akademie der Künste, Berlin.

29. Ida Cook to Rosa Ponselle, November 28, [no year], Music Division, NYPL, New York.

Chapter 12: The Ghosts

1. Mani Mekler Baker, interview with the author, November 1, 2018.

2. Ida Cook to Elayne Duke, October 8, 1979, Rosa Ponselle Papers, NYPL, New York.

3. "The Cook Sisters Collection," Leslie Flint Trust, March 23, 1969, https://leslieflint.com/the-cook-sisters-collection.

4. Ibid.

5. Ida Cook, "Viewers Watch Spirit Form on Their TV Screens," *Two Worlds*, November 29, 1958.

6. Else Mayer-Lismann to Ella Mahler, January 10, 1964, Yad Vashem Archives, Jerusalem.

7. "Proceeding on Collecting Data on Sisters Cooks' Rescue Work," Yad Vashem Archives, Jerusalem.
8. "Cook Unit" file, Yad Vashem Archives, Jerusalem, 033172.
9. Ida Cook to May Sayers, September 8, 1963, Yad Vashem Archives, Jerusalem.
10. "Cook Unit" file at Yad Vashem Archives, Jerusalem, 033172.
11. Ibid.
12. "Certificate of Recognition" of the Yad Vashem Martyrs' and Heroes' Remembrance Authority, Har Hazikaron, Jerusalem, in the "Cook Unit" file, Yad Vashem Archives, Jerusalem, 033172.
13. Ida Cook to May Sayers, March 22, 1964, Yad Vashem Archives, Jerusalem.
14. James Feron, "Sisters Hailed for Rescuing Jews," *New York Times*, March 23, 1965.
15. Adele Kern to Alfred Frankenstein, December 2, 1965, Alfred Frankenstein Archive, folder 5, Academy of Arts in Berlin.
16. Ida Cook, film treatment, undated, Joshua Logan Papers, Library of Congress, Washington, D.C., 66.
17. Ibid.
18. Jhan Robbins and June Robbins, "We Are Scarcely James Bond Ladies," *McCall's* 93 (September 1966).
19. Ida Cook to "Dear Friends," July 16, 1968, General Correspondence: Cook, Ida and Louise, 1968–1972, box 20, folder 5, Joshua Logan Papers, Library of Congress, Washington, D.C.
20. Ibid.
21. Joshua Logan to Ida Cook, August 5, 1968, Joshua Logan Papers, Library of Congress, Washington, D.C.
22. Mani Mekler Baker, interview with the author, October 27, 2018.
23. Ida Cook to Joshua Logan, December 1, 1968, Joshua Logan Papers, Library of Congress, Washington, D.C.
24. Cook, film treatment, 21.
25. Ibid.
26. Ibid., 1.
27. Ida Cook to Joshua Logan, July 16, 1968, Library of Congress.
28. Cook, film treatment, 76.

Epilogue: The Record Player

1. Jhan Robbins and June Robbins, "We Are Scarcely James Bond Ladies," *McCall's* 93 (September 1966).
2. Joseph McAleer, *Passion's Fortune: The Story of Mill & Boon* (Oxford: Oxford University Press, 1999), 246.
3. Ida Cook to Rosa Ponselle, April 29, 1956, Rosa Ponselle Papers, Music Division, NYPL, New York.
4. Ida Cook to Rosa Ponselle, October 11, 1956, Rosa Ponselle Papers, Music Division, NYPL, New York.
5. Ida Cook to Rosa Ponselle, May 15, 1953, Rosa Ponselle Papers, Music Division, NYPL, New York.
6. Ida Cook to Rosa Ponselle, May 18, 1955, Rosa Ponselle Papers, Music Division, NYPL, New York.

7.   Mary Burchell, *A Song Begins* (London: Mills & Boon, 1965), 101.
8.   Ibid.
9.   McAleer, *Passion's Fortune*, 289.
10. Ida Cook to Tito and Tilde Gobbi, March 3, 1973, Associazione Musicale Tito Gobbi, Archivo Storico.
11. Mani Mekler Baker, interview with the author, October 27, 2018.
12. Ibid.
13. Ibid.
14. Ida Cook to Tilde and Tito Gobbi, June 8, 1977, Associazione Musicale Tito Gobbi, Archivo Storico.
15. Ida Cook to Elayne Duke, October 8, 1979, Rosa Ponselle Papers, Music Division, NYPL, New York.
16. Ida Cook to Rosa Ponselle, December 1973, Rosa Ponselle Papers, Music Division, NYPL, New York.
17. Descriptions of Louise Cook's final years are from an interview with Jeanne Henny, March 3, 2020.
18. Ida Cook, *Safe Passage: The Remarkable True Story of Two Sisters Who Rescued Jews from the Nazis* (Toronto: Harlequin, 2008), 148.
19. Jeanne Henny, interview with the author, June 18, 2018.
20. Jeanne Henny, interview with the author, March 3, 2020.
21. Cook, *Safe Passage*, 148.
22. Jeanne Henny, interview with the author, March 3, 2020.
23. Ibid.
24. Louise Cook made an appointment to see Leslie Flint on May 26, 1987, according to the Leslie Flint Educational Trust. The tape of that seance is referenced in Louise Carpenter, "Ida and Louise," *Granta* 98, July 2, 2007.

Index